The End of the Russian Empire

MICHAEL T. FLORINSKY

Professor of Economics, Columbia University

THE END OF

THE RUSSIAN
EMPIRE

COLLIER BOOKS
NEW YORK, N.Y.

Preface

THE PRESENT BOOK was written as the twelfth and final volume of the Russian Series of the Social and Economic History of the (First) World War published by the Carnegie Endowment for International Peace. James T. Shotwell, Professor of History at Columbia University, was the General Editor and Sir Paul Vinogradoff, F.B.A., Corpus Professor of Historical Jurisprudence, University of Oxford, was the Editor of the Russian Series. As Associate Editor it was my good fortune to work in close collaboration with these two eminent historians; my responsibilities were greatly increased after the death of Sir Paul which occurred before any of the Russian volumes were published.

The Russian Series, as planned by Vinogradoff, remains a unique contribution to Russian historiography—not only in the English language. Few students of Russia would question the significance of the first World War as a major turning point in the history of the former tsarist empire. Yet the rapid sequence of dramatic events that followed the fall of the monarchy tended to overshadow the importance of the historical period where are to be found—to use a mixed metaphor—the immediate roots of the revolution of 1917. Soviet historians, prisoners of an inflexible doctrinaire concept of human development, had at first ignored the recent past as trivial and inconsequential and later, when the study of imperial history again gained acceptance, have mercilessly distorted the picture by forcing events into the rigid pattern prescribed by Marxism-Leninism. In the West, except perhaps in Germany, Russian studies prior to World War II made little progress and were largely centered on the Soviet period. The uniqueness of the Russian Series of the Carnegie Endowment History of the World War consists in enlisting the services of men—all of them Russians—who were participants or close observers of the developments that proved to be forerunners of the revolution. The volumes of the Series, whatever their shortcomings, reflect an intimate knowledge of Russian conditions at the time and, taken together, present a picture of Russia during the war which has not been, and probably never will be, duplicated.

The End of the Russian Empire, as the final volume of the

Russian Series, depended partly on the other studies of that Series but it also used extensively other sources. It endeavored to explain why and how the monarchy came to its doom and was replaced by a Communist dictatorship. The place of the Soviet Union in world affairs being what it is, the subject of this book is perhaps even more timely today than it was when the volume was written. Nothing that appeared in print in the intervening years calls for revision or amendment of my study which is reprinted without any changes. Although written three decades ago and long out of print, *The End of the Russian Empire* is still widely consulted and used. I take particular pleasure in expressing my gratitude to the Crowell-Collier Publishing Company for making it available to a wide circle of readers.

Michael T. Florinsky

Columbia University
New York City
May 1, 1961

Contents

Military Reverses of 1915. The War Industries Committees. The Zemgor. The Awakening of Public Opinion. The Attitude of the Sovereign and the Government. The Trend of Public Opinion at the End of 1916. The Parties of the Extreme Right. The Middle Class and the Revolution.

The End of the Russian Empire

Chapter 1

Russia on the Eve of the War

A Current Misunderstanding

AMONG the dramatic changes which took place in Europe at the close of the Great War none has the same appeal to popular imagination and is likely to exercise the same influence upon the political and economic ideas of our own and probably of future generations as the spectacular and tragic fall of the Empire of the Tsars. Little is known abroad about the Russian Empire, with its vast territory, its inexhaustible resources, its government which appeared to the western world as a survival of a bygone age, its refinement of culture at the top and the illiterate masses of its people living under almost primitive conditions, its cosmopolitan aristocracy speaking every language and equally at home in St. Petersburg, Berlin, Paris, London, and New York, and its no less cosmopolitan revolutionaries who kept and still keep busy the secret police of the world. The number of foreigners who ventured across the Russian frontier was relatively small. The difficulties of the language and the immensity of the country greatly complicated the task of making detailed study of actual conditions. Some of the more flagrant abuses—and we shall see that there was no lack of them—attracted a great deal of attention abroad, and led to the creation of a strong body of public opinion decidedly unfavorable to the Imperial *régime*. On the other hand the less spectacular, but perhaps no less fundamental developments in the field of education, public health, and economic progress, having little news value, passed almost unnoticed. The Russians themselves greatly contributed to these one-sided impressions as to conditions in their country, which became firmly established outside the frontiers of the Empire. With that disarming capacity for self-criticism which has so often surprised the foreign observer, they missed no opportunity to emphasize the grave and numerous faults of the Imperial *régime*, and little if anything was ever said of the more favorable aspects of the situation. We are speaking here not of professional revolutionaries, but of those liberal-minded representatives of the middle classes who used to be frequent visitors to the capitals and health resorts of Europe. The newly-born patriotism of this group, which constitutes the bulk of the "White" emigration of recent years, does not belie this statement. It is a patriotism which may be traced to the same roots: a refusal to accept the existing order coupled with a sincere, if belated, regret for a past which, with all its imperfections, had a place for them now entirely denied them by the Union of Soviet Socialist Republics.

In approaching the Russian problem it is particularly important to keep in mind that Russia, as a modern State, is of very recent origin. In spite of the epoch-making reforms of Peter the Great and Catherine, in spite of the rebuilding of the State machinery by the able hands of Speransky under Alexander I, Russia, until the emancipation of the serfs in 1861 and the Great Reforms of Alexander II, was still living in an age different from that of the rest of Europe. One can hardly speak of modern development in a country where the immense majority of the population were almost chattels and could be sold and bought at will. The fifty-three years which separate the emancipation of the serfs from the outbreak of the War are, undoubtedly, a very short time in the life of a nation, particularly short when the entire social, political, and economic framework has to be rebuilt from top to bottom, when experience in statesmanship, and the tradition of self-organization and initiative are completely lacking, and when general educational and cultural standards are unbelievably low.

No attempt will here be made to whitewash the Imperial Government and to represent its work in an unduly favorable light. Indeed, the general impression which will be given by the following pages will be anything but flattering. We believe that the breakdown of Imperial Russia was the inevitable result of its own internal weakness; but this does not necessarily mean that the Government and its many official and semiofficial agencies, such, for instance, as its institutions of local government, intentionally barred the advance of the country along the path of progress. The policy of the Government of the Tsar may frequently appear to us unsound and reactionary; much of it deserves the severest criticism. In spite of that the fact remains that in the fifty years preceding the War Russia had gone far on the road followed several decades before by other European countries. Her financial position was immensely improved. Her economic development was undeniable. An agrarian reform of the utmost importance had been introduced and was being carried out with a surprising degree of success. It did seem indeed as if the "peasant question" with its innumerable complications was nearing a favorable solution. The number of schools, still grievously inadequate, was nevertheless rapidly increasing, and plans were made for the introduction of universal education by 1922. The organization of the public health service was also making progress. The form of government itself was evolving, slowly, it is true, but in the same direction as the great democracies of the world. Russia in 1914 was decidedly a very different country from what it was in 1861. To realize the importance of these changes is essential not only as a matter of justice toward a *régime* which has ceased to exist, but also in order to be able to understand the developments of today and to provide them with a historical background. The ignoring of the past is a frequent source of grave errors.[1]

The Tradition of Absolutism

To the outside world the Russian Empire was personified until recently by the Tsar, ruler of All the Russias, by the grace of God. In the course of a thousand years of Russia's history the Tsars and their predecessors performed the important function of unifying the country and organizing the vast territory, which partook of the character of both Europe and Asia, into a fairly coherent whole. The nature of the autocratic rule of the Tsars may be traced to the influence of the Mongols, on the one hand, and to that of Byzantium, on the other. The Byzantine ideas of the sanction of the State by the Church, and of the close union between the two, found its external expression in the coronation of Ivan IV in the middle of the sixteenth century.[2]

[1] As an illustration of the danger of disregarding the historical background we may quote the following example taken at random. The authoritative and useful volume, *Soviet Russia in the Second Decade* (A Joint Survey of the Technical Staff of the First American Trade Union Delegation, edited by Stuart Chase, Robert Dunn, and Rexford Guy Tugwell, New York, 1928), contains an interesting article by Professor Tugwell on Soviet agriculture. The author puts considerable emphasis upon land surveying, the creation of enclosed holdings, the organization of experimental farms, and the advancement of general education among the peasants. These developments, it seems, are among the chief reasons which led Professor Tugwell to form his very optimistic conclusions as to the outlook of Russian farming. No indication is given in the article that all these measures are not new. Professor Tugwell is undoubtedly perfectly familiar with the land reforms of Stolypin which revolutionized land tenure, and were directed against communal ownership. He must also know of the immense work carried on by the zemstvos in the field of education, public health, and the spread of agricultural knowledge among the farmers; and also that before the War an ever increasing number of experimental stations and model farms were opened every year by the Department of Agriculture, especially in connection with the Stolypin land settlement plan. None of these facts, however, is mentioned by Professor Tugwell, probably for lack of space; and those of his readers who have little knowledge of pre-revolutionary Russia will get the impression that all these important measures originated with the Soviet Government when, as a matter of fact, they are merely a revival, and not infrequently a very inadequate one, of a policy pursued by Imperial Russia for a great many years. The optimistic forecast by Professor Tugwell, we venture to suggest, will lose some of its point if the developments he describes are connected with their historical setting.

[2] George Vernadsky, *A History of Russia* (New Haven, 1929), pp. 56–57.

Then followed a period of struggle between Church and State which ended with the complete defeat of the former. In 1721 Peter the Great reduced the Church to the position of a mere government department; and in 1797 the Emperor Paul proclaimed the doctrine "the Tsar is the head of the Church," which found its way into the Statute Books under Nicholas I.[3] Clothed with the unlimited powers of autocracy, and enjoying the added glamor of ecclesiastical rulers, the Russian Tsars of the nineteenth century dominated eastern Europe and their own realm from their snow-clad capital, created by the indomitable will of Peter the Great, on the marches of the northern outskirts of the Empire. The several attempts made in the nineteenth century to bring Russia into the current of constitutional reforms proved abortive. None of them had any serious chance of success until the abolition of serfdom which, it will be remembered, took place in 1861. But even after the Emancipation the tradition of absolutism was very strong in high places, and many were they who sincerely believed that autocracy was essential to the welfare of the Empire. One of the best-known advocates of this view was Constantine Pobedonostsev who as late as 1901, writing to the Tsar, spoke of the spread of "the foolish desire for a constitutional government which would be the ruin of Russia."[4] It was also generally believed that the masses of the illiterate peasantry had a real and deep affection for their God-anointed ruler. There is little doubt that tsardom, as an expression of absolutism, was the only form of government within the grasp of the masses. The extraordinary ease, however, with which the Empire was overthrown in 1917 seems to indicate that the traditional devotion of the peasants to the throne had been greatly overrated. The peasants merely accepted the rule of the Tsars in that spirit of passive submission which seems to constitute so important a part of the Russian national character. They did nothing to defend the throne when it crumbled under the strain of the War.

The Bureaucracy

Until the manifesto of October 17, 1905,[5] Russia was *de jure* an autocratic empire. But the unlimited powers of the sovereign were in practice greatly curtailed by the executive machinery which was created to carry out his orders. Its origins may be

[3] *Ibid.*, p. 116.
[4] *Pisma Pobedonostseva k Alexandru III s Prilozheniem Pisem k Velikomu Knyazu Sergeyu Alexandrovichu i Nikolayu II (Letters of Pobedonostsev to Alexander III together with His Letters to the Grand Duke Sergius Alexandrovich and Nicholas II)*, published by *Tsentroarkhiv* (Moscow, 1926), II, 332.
[5] All dates in this monograph are given in accordance with the Russian calendar.

traced back to the reforms introduced in 1809–1811 by Speransky, the liberal-minded minister of Alexander I. Speransky was a staunch supporter of the theory of the division of power; and while he did not succeed in putting into effect the whole of his plan, he achieved the very important result of creating a State Council, appointed by the Emperor, it is true, but nevertheless enjoying wide legislative powers, including that of examining the budget.

The second most important part of his plan consisted in the reorganization of the administrative services on a new basis which included their subordination to a minister responsible for his department. The modern Russian bureaucracy was thus brought into being, and as time went on its influence upon the conduct of public affairs became more and more pronounced. Baron Nolde affirms that Nicholas I was the last Russian monarch whose personal will directed the course of the ship of State. After his death in 1856 the sovereign, it is said, was gradually reduced to the position of a mere cog in the complex machinery of State. He became the chief of the State employees, the head of a huge bureaucratic machine which produced the measures to which he affixed his signature. One should not, however, push this idea too far. While under normal conditions the Tsar was merely the head of the bureaucratic hierarchy, from time to time he also exercised his powers as a sovereign. The most important instance of the application of these powers was the selection of the ministers of the Crown. Then, again, they were called into play on those relatively rare occasions when the personal views of the Tsar happened to be in direct opposition to those of his official advisers. Such occurrences were extremely infrequent under Alexander II, Alexander III, and Nicholas II (with the notable exception of the period 1915–1916). On the other hand, it would be a mistake to minimize the influence of the fact that the tenure of office of the ministers depended on the pleasure of the sovereign. This necessarily forced them to exercise extreme caution whenever they had reason to suspect that their views and policies might not meet with the approval of their Imperial master.[6] In spite of these highly important limitations the Russian bureaucracy achieved a place of primary importance among State institutions.

We are not prepared to accept the rather extreme and paradoxical view advanced recently by the distinguished Russian historian and statesman, Baron Meyendorff, that the bureauc-

[6] Baron Boris E. Nolde, *L'ancien régime et la révolution russes,* collection Armand Collin, Paris, 1928, pp. 96–97.

racy was the only bearer of the ideas of European civilization in the Russian State.[7] We see no reason why the relatively small but highly cultured group of liberal-minded intelligentsia who remained outside government service but were engaged in an important civilizing mission through the press, the universities, the Duma, the zemstvo, and the municipalities should be excluded from the list. But it is undoubtedly true that the bureaucracy succeeded in drawing into its ranks a very large number of educated men from all stations in life and in creating a strong and honorable tradition of public service. We shall see later that at a moment of national emergency the majority of the ministers of the Russian Crown did not shrink from their responsibility, had the courage of their opinions, and were prepared to sacrifice their personal well-being to what they understood to be the interest of the country. The list of Russian bureaucrats since the days of Speransky contains the names of many men whose intelligence, vision, and public zeal compare not unfavorably with those of the statesmen of democratic countries. The reign of Nicholas II has to its credit two Prime Ministers who displayed real statesmanship and unusual ability, although of a very different kind: Count Witte and Stolypin. Among the members of the Government of the last Tsar we find a number of men who commanded the highest respect, and whose culture, honesty, and keen sense of duty were above reproach.[8]

The Russian bureaucracy while, in a way, a civilizing force in the life of the nation, strong in its traditions and its relatively high cultural level, also suffered from the weaknesses common to all the bureaucracies of the world. To begin with, not all even of its most prominent representatives were using their high positions to further the progress of the country. Some of the outstanding figures of the bureaucratic Olympus were notorious reactionaries, for instance, Pobedonostsev, Maklakov, Shcheglovitov, Goremykin (about whom more will be said below); or, still worse, they were men, for instance Sturmer,[9] of so doubtful a character that it reflected on the whole system. The very wide powers enjoyed by holders of important offices and the impunity attached to them, were apt to create abuses. Most striking examples of this were the Ministry of the Interior and the State Police Department, of which we shall speak a little more in detail before the end of this chapter. And then, of

[7] See Baron Alexander F. Meyendorff's stimulating little volume *The Background of the Russian Revolution* (New York, 1929).
[8] *See below,* pp. 84–86.
[9] *See below,* pp. 88–89.

course, the whole system was lacking in elasticity, it was rigid and unadaptable, and it developed that *esprit de corps* which made the State employee treat with hostile condescension all those who were not fortunate enough to belong to his privileged caste. This hostility manifested itself with particular force in the relations between the officers of the central administration and the institutions of local government. The whole history of the zemstvos and the municipalities is a long struggle against repression and outright persecution by the autocracy and the bureaucrats, who looked upon local representatives as mere intruders in a field which was rightly reserved for the central authorities. Concessions, no doubt, were finally made, but they were slow in coming.[10] This unfortunate lack of collaboration proved fatal during the War.

The Duma

The disastrous outcome of the Russo-Japanese War and the tide of labor and agrarian disturbances which swept the country in 1905–1906 were rightly taken to be an indication of the necessity of making concessions to the spirit of the age. These were embodied in the Imperial manifesto of October 17, 1905, which brought into existence the Duma, a legislative assembly elected by the representatives of various social groups. It became the lower chamber of the Russian parliament, while the State Council was reorganized and became the upper chamber. The powers of the Duma were limited. The ministers continued to be responsible to the Emperor alone. We shall see below[11] that the Duma suffered from serious constitutional disabilities, on the one hand, and, on the other, that the Emperor was never completely reconciled to the limitations it imposed upon his powers.[12] A number of influential bureaucrats of the old school took the same view and made no secret of their dislike of the new institution. The First and Second Dumas,[13] it will be remembered, were dissolved before the expiration of their term. The election law was altered, in violation of the Fundamental Laws, by the Act of June 3, 1907, which introduced a new and

[10] See T. J. Polner, Prince V. A. Obolensky, and S. P. Turin, *Russian Local Government during the War and the Union of Zemstvos* (Yale University Press, 1930); and N. J. Astrov, "Municipal Government and the All-Russian Union of Towns" in the volume *The War and the Russian Government* (Yale University Press, 1929) in this series of the "Economic and Social History of the World War."

[11] See below, pp. 95 sqq.

[12] See below, pp. 55–56.

[13] The First Duma was convoked and dissolved in 1906; the Second Duma was convoked and dissolved in 1907. Then the electoral law was changed (the Act of June 3, 1907), the Third Duma was elected and served its full term of five years. In 1912 the Fourth Duma was convoked and continued its work until the Revolution of February–March, 1917.

greatly restricted franchise; and only after it had been enacted was the new parliament allowed to function. In spite of these important handicaps one must admit that the introduction of an elective legislative chamber presented a striking and extremely important departure in the political and social life of the country. The first and most difficult step toward the establishment of a constitutional system of government had been made. Not only were the autocratic powers of the Tsar limited by the legislative control of the two chambers, the Duma and the State Council, but, what seems far more important, the country at large in the person of its chosen representatives was at last called to take a direct part in the conduct of public affairs. It is not denied that the franchise was limited and that the law secured the election of a majority representing the landed gentry. The really significant fact seems to be that the admission of the country to a participation—however slight it was at first—in the work of government offered an extraordinary and novel opportunity for the political education of the masses. Progress along these lines naturally was slow, but it was a forward movement and ended the political stagnation in which the country had been kept for centuries. There was no immediate prospect of an expansion of the franchise; but years or even decades are very short periods in the life of a nation, and it was perhaps not unreasonable to expect that in due course democratic institutions in Russia would develop along the same lines as in other countries. The door for these changes was now open.

Local Government

While the Duma, in 1914, was still a very new body with merely a few years' experience in handling public affairs, the institutions of local government, the zemstvos in rural districts and the municipal councils in the cities and towns, had already had time to gain a firm footing and develop their activities on a large scale. The organization of municipal government dates back to the days of Catherine II, who in 1758 issued a very liberal charter "for the defense of the rights and interests of towns." Its provisions, however, were entirely out of keeping with the whole social structure of the State, and especially with the institution of serfdom. They necessarily remained a dead letter until after emancipation of the serfs in 1861. This fundamental reform was naturally followed by the Zemstvo Act[14] of 1864, which gave self-government to rural localities, and by

[14] The zemstvos were institutions of local government outside the urban areas. The term zemstvo is derived from the Russian word *zemlya*, land, and is traditionally associated with social groups connected with land, the landed gentry, and the farmers.

he Municipal Act of 1870, which brought municipal organiza-
ions into line with the new conditions. It goes without saying
hat the institutions of local government were to be fitted into
he framework of the autocratic and bureaucratic State, and
hat the whole reform bore the inevitable marks of a compro-
nise between the principles of centralization and local autonomy
vith a decided leaning toward the former. Both the franchise
.nd resources of the local institutions were extremely limited
.nd were restricted still further by the reactionary legislation
.nacted in the 'nineties.[15] But in spite of these restrictions and
he unceasing, irritating, and vexatious interference with the
vork of the zemstvos and municipalities by the central govern-
nent, they succeeded in maintaining their work on a surpris-
ngly high level. This is especially true of the zemstvos. With
.ntiring energy and remarkable sense of duty they proceeded
o build schools, hospitals, dispensaries, and orphanages. They
.rganized experimental farms and instructed the peasants in
he best methods of handling their crops and live stock. They
.mported agricultural machinery and erected fireproof build-
ngs. They introduced fire insurance and established banks
vhich advanced credit to farmers on reasonable terms. In carry-
ng out this immense work, which contributed more than any-
hing else to helping the Russian peasant to get rid of his
gnorance and prejudices and to begin at last to make real
.rogress, the zemstvos were fortunate enough to secure the
vhole-hearted cooperation of men and women drawn from all
.ocial strata and, in their ideals, sincerely devoted to the enlight-
.nment of the masses and the betterment of their economic
.tandards. That they had to overcome immense difficulties goes
vithout saying. The stubborn opposition of the bureaucracy,
vhich was inclined to see in the zemstvo leaders a mere gang
.f revolutionaries trying to undermine the very foundations of
he Russian State, an opposition to which we have already re-
.erred, was only one obstacle.

First and foremost among the many obstacles they had to contend
vith [writes M. Polner[16]] were the inertia and indifference of the
.eople themselves. These looked askance upon the enterprises started
.y the zemstvos. Unable as yet to realize the need of education, they
.efused to let their children go to school; in case of sickness they
.ontinued to appeal to quacks and charlatans for help; and, adhering
.o traditional agricultural policy, they had only ridicule and distrust
.or the expert advice of trained agronomists placed at their service.
More than two decades of persistent and untiring effort were re-

[15] The Zemstvo Act of 1890 and the Municipal Act of 1892.
[16] Op. cit., p. 22.

quired before the people became at last impressed with the advantages of education and progress.

The enthusiasm and energy of the zemstvos triumphed over all obstacles, those created by the bureaucracy and those resulting from the ignorance and inertia of the masses. The work of the zemstvos was so obviously necessary, and it so clearly met the fundamental requirements of a sound national development that it grew in scope and importance notwithstanding the legal and technical shortcomings in the organization of the local institutions themselves. To give just one example of the scale of their work, we may quote M. Polner's estimate of the development of the zemstvo schools, which were from the very beginning one of their principal concerns. M. Polner puts the number of zemstvo schools in 1914 at fifty thousand, with some eighty thousand teachers and no less than three million pupils.[17] This was much even for a country as vast as Russia; but the achievement of the zemstvos in promoting education will appear still more striking if one remembers that only fifteen years before practically none of these schools was in existence. If the organization of schools, hospitals, experimental farms, etc., was still grievously inadequate, the real source of this inadequacy should be sought in the shortage of funds rather than anywhere else. In this connection it is worth remembering that the zemstvos were managed by the landed gentry, the much-needed reform in the zemstvo franchise having not yet materialized.

Making full allowance for the legal disabilities of the zemstvos, the inadequacy of their franchise, the limitation of their resources, and the unfortunate opposition which they continually encountered in the central government, we are nevertheless driven to the conclusion that by 1914 they had grown into an immense and most important factor in the life of the nation. The necessity of a zemstvo reform was discussed in the Duma, and an extension of franchise and a general liberalization of zemstvo institutions were merely matters of time. The remarkable tradition of public work which the zemstvos succeeded in building up in so short a period was put to severe tests on many occasions. National calamities, such as famine and war, always found them ready to do their utmost to alleviate the sufferings of the people. The popularity enjoyed by Prince George E. Lvov, president of the inter-zemstvo organization and of the Union of Zemstvos, which brought him to the head of the Provisional Government in March, 1917, is in itself eloquent testimony to

[17] *Ibid.*, p. 38.

he prestige possessed by the zemstvos in the esteem of the masses.[18]

Universal Education

A question closely connected with that of local government was the question of universal education. The idea itself was forcibly advanced as early as in the 'sixties and the 'seventies by the zemstvo leaders, who naturally realized that no real progress in self-government was possible so long as the country remained illiterate. It was not until the revolutionary outburst of 1905–1906 that the question was seriously taken up by the Government with the whole-hearted support of the Duma. The issue was complicated by rivalry between the various authorities who claimed jurisdiction over the elementary schools. The institutions of local government had little confidence in the methods of the Ministry of Education and still less in the church schools which enjoyed the support of the Tsar and of influential members of the bureaucracy. The urgent counsels of Pobedonostsev were still remembered. "All the strength of a State is in its people," he wrote on March 21, 1901,[19] "and the salvation of the people from ignorance, from barbarous customs, from corruption, from fatal contamination by foolish and revolting ideas can be achieved only through the Church and through schools connected with it." Many conservative statesmen still clung to this belief, although the church schools had little to commend them. They were looked upon as a safeguard against the revolutionary ideas which, it was believed, would spread through the zemstvo schools. This was one of the reasons why the important bill for the unification of the entire school system under the leadership of the institutions of local government prepared by the Duma was finally rejected by the State Council in 1911. In spite of these hindrances important and real progress was made toward the introduction of universal education. The first decisive step in this direction was embodied in the Law of May 3, 1908, which provided that all children between the ages of eight and eleven were to receive primary education for four years. We cannot here go into the details of this project which was moreover amended by later legislation. In accordance with the final estimates of the School Committee of the Duma, by 1922, when the introduction of universal education was to be completed, the number of children of school age would be about

* See, however, below, pp. 225–226.
  Pisma Pobedonostseva k Alexandru III s Prilozheniem Pisem k Velikomu Knyazu ergeyu Alexandrovichu i Nikolayu II, II, 335.

15,852,000. The number of schools needed for them was pu
at 317,000, of which fewer than 100,000 existed in 1908. B
1914 the number had increased only to some 149,000; so th
task that confronted the country, if it was to carry out this tas
by the proposed date, was certainly not an easy one. The num
ber of schools to be opened in the course of the next nine year
would be about 168,000, or more than the existing numbe
The whole plan was to be financed by the Treasury, the zemst
vos' demands for an extension of their power to tax having bee
rejected. This, of course, was inspired by the Government'
intention to retain a more complete control over the schools
The grants for the putting into effect of the plan were large
From 10,000,000 rubles for the first year they were to increas
to 100,000,000 rubles by the tenth. It seems difficult to main
tain, in view of this evidence, that the Imperial Governmen
was intentionally keeping the people in darkness and was pre
venting the spread of education. It is unfortunately only to
true that at the outbreak of the War the number of schools wa
still grossly inadequate, and the quality of education obtaine
in the existing schools might well be questioned. But it is als
true that a decidedly heroic effort was being made to bring t
an end the disgraceful illiteracy of the Russian peasant.[20]

It will be readily understood that the immense expansion o
the school system which called for more than a threefold in
crease in the number of existing schools within twelve years wa
in itself a huge undertaking. It demanded, in addition to th
erection of a large number of school buildings, the training o
a whole army of teachers, which, again, made necessary th
opening of numerous teachers' colleges. Provisions for all thes
activities were included in the project. Whether the Governmen
would have succeeded in carrying it through by 1922 is ope
to doubt. The rate of progress between 1908 and 1914 offers n
ground for too optimistic a view. The normal course of th
reform was interrupted by the War. But even if a delay di
occur, as seems reasonable to expect, the immense significanc
of the plan itself as a definite step toward the abolition o
illiteracy can hardly be denied.[21]

[20] D. M. Odinetz, "Primary and Secondary Schools" in the volume *Russian School
and Universities in the World War* (Yale University Press, 1929), pp. 8–14, i
this series of the "Economic and Social History of the World War."
[21] In this connection we may venture the suggestion that the real obstacle to th
promotion of education in Russia was not so much the reactionary policy of th
Government, although we have not attempted to minimize its evil effects, as tha
lack of funds which also crippled the work of the zemstvos. Poverty, unfortunatel
is something more difficult to get rid of than even an autocratic government. Thi
is one of the problems that the present rulers of Russia have to face. "There is stil
a great disparity between the comparative poverty of Russia and the great task o

The Peasants and the Reforms of Stolypin

That in a country with a rural population of some 85 per cent the welfare of the farmers should be the primary concern of the government seems a foregone conclusion. Unfortunately this is just what was not true of Russia. With unjustifiable levity the government postponed the solution of a problem on which depended not only the welfare of the immense majority of the people, but also the very existence of the Russian State in its historic form, shaped by centuries of aggrandizement and expansion. It is impossible to explain in a short paragraph the complexity of the Russian "agrarian problem." A more detailed treatment of this all-important question will be found in Chapter 8. The roots of the agrarian problem in its modern aspect, like those of most of the fundamental economic problems of pre-war Russia, may be traced to the Great Reforms of Alexander II. The Emancipation Acts of 1861, granting personal freedom to the former serfs, created at the same time a highly complicated system of economic and legal relationships which amounted, in the last resort, to the establishment of a new bondage for the now "free" tiller of the soil, his bondage to the land commune. Established primarily for fiscal reasons—in order to secure the collection of redemption payments imposed on the liberated serfs in exchange for the parcels of land transferred to them on their emancipation—the land commune became one of the chief obstacles to the economic development of the country. Not only did it prevent any improvement in agriculture, but it also greatly hindered the formation of a permanent class of hired labor, of a town proletariat, which is one of the indispensable conditions of industrial progress.

Although the necessity of a reform was generally conceded and various half measures for the alleviation of the position of the peasants were taken from time to time, it was not until the shock of the Russo-Japanese War and the terrible agrarian disturbances which followed it that the Government undertook a radical agrarian reform. It was devised by Stolypin, then President of the Council of Ministers, and was carried through by an Imperial ukase of November 9, 1906, over the opposition of the Duma which favored a still more radical plan, one aimed at the abolition of large agricultural estates. It was eventually ratified by the Third Duma and became the Law of June 14, 1910. The reform of Stolypin had for its purpose the elimination of the land commune, the enclosure of scattered strips, and the abolition of the legal anarchy which prevailed in the sphere of peasant ownership of land.[22] The ultimate goal of the reform was twofold: on the one hand, it was aimed at the raising of the standard of farming through the abolition of antiquated methods of husbandry inseparable, it was maintained, from communal tenure; on the other, it was expected to produce a conservative and stable class of peasant farmers upon whom the Government could rely and whose absence was particularly felt after the Duma had been instituted. The reception given to the reform was a mixed one. It was both immensely admired and greatly criticized. In spite of the short time this legislation was in force—it was repealed in 1917 and, of course, the rate of progress was greatly reduced during the War—it involved the immense area of some 30,000,000 acres, while applications for the delimitation of holdings were received from 8,700,000 peasant households or more than one-half of all the peasant farms.[23] The experiment was much too short-lived to allow one to reach a definite conclusion as to its ultimate effects. It has been maintained, however, by economists and agricultural experts, both Russian and foreign, that it was an immense and unqualified success. Like the attempt to introduce universal education it came too late. The peasantry, emerging from the three-year struggle against Germany and inspired by the new revolutionary slogans which embodied its own secular claims, found a different solution for the agrarian problem. It may be plausibly argued nevertheless that, if the reforms of Stolypin had been given a few more years to grow in strength and take real roots, the fate of Russia would have been very different from what it is now.

The State Police Department

An attempt has been made in the preceding pages to bring out some of the factors which may be placed, with due reserva-

[22] A detailed analysis of the reforms will be found in a monograph by A. D. Bilimovich, "The Land Settlement in Russia and the War," in the volume *Russian Agriculture during the War* (Yale University Press, 1930) in this series of the "Economic and Social History of the World War."
[23] *Ibid.*, pp. 358, 367.

tions in every case, on the credit side of the balance sheet of the Imperial Government. We may now consider the less favorable aspects of the *régime*. The reports of the proceedings of the Committee of Inquiry of the Provisional Government[24] contain extraordinarily valuable information of this kind. This, of course, is perfectly natural as the Committee was appointed for the special purpose of investigating the abuses of the Imperial Government. It may be said at once that the endeavor to discover grave breaches of the law in the Department of Justice did not succeed. In spite of certain pressure on the part of the Minister of Justice and discrimination against Judges who did not accept suggestions which reached them from above as well as against men of liberal views, and non-Russians in general, nothing of any importance could be discovered to show that the work of the courts was gravely impaired even under the rule of the notorious Shcheglovitov.[25]

Very different, however, is the story of the State Police Department. Like a gigantic spider this institution spread its web all over the country and had under its supervision and control not only those revolutionary organizations and individuals suspected of conspiring against the Government, but also anyone

[24] The Committee of Inquiry of the Provisional Government was appointed immediately after the Revolution of February–March, 1917, to investigate the crimes of which the higher officials of the fallen *régime* were suspected. It was vested with wide powers and examined fifty-nine persons, including not only the former ministers and heads of departments, but also a number of men prominent in public life or in revolutionary circles whose evidence, it was held, was material for any broad picture of the conditions prevailing under the Empire. While the Committee conspicuously failed in fulfilling its judicial task, it succeeded in accumulating a vast amount of historical material of inestimable value in the shape of evidence given by the men who played a leading part in the direction of public affairs. If it had not been for the Committee, most of this evidence would have been lost to the historian. The verbatim reports of the evidence given before the Committee were published in seven volumes edited by P. E. Shchegolev under the title *Padenie Tsarskago Rezhima (The Downfall of the Tsarist Régime)* (Leningrad, 1925–1927). An abbreviated French edition is also available: *La Chute du Régime Tsariste* (Paris, 1927). The evidence given before the Committee is, of course, not uniform in its value and reliability. In many cases, however, the unwillingness of the witnesses to answer questions was just as eloquent as the most outspoken confession. All things considered, the proceedings of the Committee present a picture of Russian conditions before the Revolution unique in its completeness and bewildering in its wealth of details. It is probably the only achievement of lasting value of the many well-intended, but invariably abortive, undertakings of the Provisional Government.

[25] Evidence of Shcheglovitov in *Padenie Tsarskago Rezhima*, II, 340 *sqq.;* evidence of Verevkin in *ibid.*, VI, 221 *sqq.* It may be observed in this connection that with the declaration of a "state of emergency," which was a prerogative of the Emperor, the normal powers of the law courts were greatly curtailed. During a "state of emergency" political cases were usually dealt with either by the military courts or, in case of minor offenses, by administrative officers. This put in the hands of the Government a most powerful weapon to dispose of its political opponents without exercising direct pressure on the law courts. These powers had been widely used since 1878, and especially in 1905–1914, when the "state of emergency" became the rule in a considerable portion of the territory of the Empire.

who might arouse the curiosity of the Police Director and his undercover agents. Members of the Cabinet were frequent objects of police supervision. Count Witte tells in his memoirs that the Dowager Empress Maria Feodorovna had her letters intercepted by the secret police. Witte himself had to write his memoirs abroad, because he knew they were not safe in St. Petersburg. The Department maintained its undercover agents everywhere, in the army,[26] in the schools,[27] in political organizations and clubs. The so-called *agents provocateurs* made their way into the secret revolutionary societies, sometimes organized them, and took an immediate part in the planning of political murders and other acts of violence. It would seem that a number of statesmen paid with their lives for the existence of this revolting *régime*, which smacks of the era of the Medicis. One of its victims was Stolypin himself, Prime Minister and Minister of the Interior, who was murdered in 1911 at a gala performance in the opera house in Kiev, in the presence of the Emperor, by an undercover agent employed by the Department of which he was officially the head. Plotting political murders was for the agents of the Russian secret police as natural and ordinary a business as it is for the officers of the prohibition enforcement squads to sip cocktails and highballs in a New York speakeasy. Allowing for due proportion, the legal and moral implications of the two cases are not perhaps entirely unlike.

One of the most shocking instances of the methods of the Department was the introduction of an agent, Malinovsky, into the Duma to which he was duly elected, with the effective support of the police, as a member of the Social Democratic Party. He performed his parliamentary duties not without distinction, and was elected leader of his group. Rodzianko describes him as an intelligent and able speaker.[28] It seems impossible to imagine how political cynicism and contempt for parliament could go any further. The tragic end of the Empire is in itself a most eloquent condemnation of the police *régime* which was supposed to protect it.

National and Religious Problems

Even less defensible, if possible, than the activities of the State Police Department was the attitude of the Imperial Government and official circles toward national and religious problems. The system of spies and *agents provocateurs*, after all,

---

[26] Evidence of Beletsky in *Padenie Tsarskago Rezhima*, III, 270, 289-290, 330-331; evidence of Dzhunkovsky in *ibid.*, V, 69-70.
[27] Evidence of Beletsky in *Padenie Tsarskago Rezhima*, III, 269.
[28] Evidence of Rodzianko in *Padenie Tsarskago Rezhima*, VII, 167.

26

affected merely individual members of the community and relatively small groups, while national and religious discrimination and prosecutions were directed against whole blocks of the subjects of the Russian Crown. The absurdity of this policy was fully realized by the more enlightened representatives of the bureaucracy.

Every school boy can easily discover for himself [wrote Count Witte[29]] that the great Russian Empire has been formed in the thousand years of its history by the fact that the Slavonic race gradually swallowed, by force and by other methods, an immense number of other nations, and therefore, strictly speaking, there is no Russia, but only the Russian Empire. And now, after we have swallowed a mass of foreign nations and have seized their territory, a new and rather absurd national party has made its appearance in the Duma and *Novoe Vremya*, and declared that Russia must be for the Russians, that is, for those who belong to the Greek Orthodox Church, whose name ends in "ov," and who read *Russkoe Znamya* and *Golos Moskwi*.[30]

Unfortunately the simple truths accessible to every schoolboy were completely ignored by venerable statesmen. Stolypin, who displayed real statesmanship on more than one occasion, associated himself with a policy of ruthless "Russification" of the border provinces of the Empire. This policy went to such absurdities as the prohibition of the Polish language in Polish schools and in municipal councils of Polish towns where the population could not speak any Russian. Still worse was the position of the Jews who were systematically submitted to a treatment as humiliating, vexatious, unjustifiable, and cruel to them, as it was pernicious and destructive from the national point of view.

The same must be said of the policy of the Government toward religious denominations other than the official Greek Orthodox Church. The history of the Russian Church, especially after the reforms of Peter the Great in 1721 and Catherine II in 1764, had been merely the history of another government department. The absorption of the Church by the State was complete. The general effect of this situation upon the cultural standards of the clergy was deplorable. The Church can hardly be reckoned among the constructive factors in Russian history. In spite of, or perhaps because of this inferiority, it developed an aggressive and intolerant attitude toward other religious denominations, especially toward the Roman Catholic Church,

---

[29] Count S. J. Witte, *Vospominanya (Memoirs)*, Reign of Nicholas II (Berlin, 1922), I, 116.
[30] Two notoriously reactionary papers.

the Reformed Churches, and the Jews. By creating innumerable vexatious and futile conflicts with other denominations, the Russian Church undoubtedly made its contribution to those forces which worked on the disintegration of the Empire.[31]

A peculiar aspect of the problem of national minorities in Russia was the fact that the policy of "Russification" was frequently directed against national groups whose cultural and political standards were, broadly speaking, superior to those of Russia herself. This is particularly true in the case of Finland and, in a lesser degree, Poland. The same may be said about the aggressive actions of the Russian Church, with its often half-educated clergy, against the more enlightened representatives of the Roman Catholic and of the Reformed Churches. Tolerance and humility are the two Christian virtues which the Greek Orthodox Church never learned.

Lack of National Unity

In spite of the very real efforts made by the zemstvos and even by the Government for the promotion of education, it must be admitted that the percentage of illiteracy on the eve of the War was still extraordinarily high. We know that only a small percentage of Russian children went to school. A still smaller portion had received any scholastic training in the past, with the result that it seems doubtful whether the general average of literacy was more than 20 or 25 per cent. One should remember that even among those children who went to school many never saw a newspaper or a book in later years, and their knowledge of even the rudiments of reading and writing therefore was purely nominal.

Just as low were the economic standards of the peasants. In spite of the remarkable progress in the general economic condition of the country since the days of the Emancipation, the overwhelming majority of the farmers, as a result of the imperfections of the Emancipation Acts, lived in a state of most sordid poverty. The reform of Stolypin was too short-lived to bring any considerable change. No wonder therefore that their aspirations and ambitions seldom went further than the bare necessities of life, which they hoped to obtain through the only method they could understand—the expansion of their area under crops.[32]

The natural and unavoidable result of this situation was the

---

[31] "The Church with us has degenerated into a dead bureaucratic institution," writes Count Witte, whom it is difficult to suspect of anticlerical views, "the church ministry—into the ministry not of Our Lord, but of earthly gods, orthodoxy—into orthodox paganism." *Vospominanya*, I, 329.

[32] *See below,* Chapter VIII.

complete divorce between the lower and the upper classes of society. We have already had an opportunity to speak of the traditional antagonism between the bureaucracy and the liberal-minded groups that gathered around the institutions of local government. This antagonism, to which we shall have frequent opportunities to refer, had an important part in the war history of Russia. More fundamental and far-reaching, however, were the effects of a complete cleavage between the educated classes and the masses of the people. The Russian intelligentsia has had a long and honorable tradition, one that has secured for it a very high place in the intellect of the world. To whatever branch of art or science we may turn, we find Russian names among those at the head of the list. The scholastic standards of Russian universities were themselves very high. The general attitude of the educated classes toward progress and learning was one of deep respect, even of veneration. The many-sided interest in, and enthusiasm for, literature, art, and science among educated Russians, frequently coupled with a surprising knowledge of the most abstruse subjects, has often been recorded by foreign observers. But it is true that the enthusiasm was sometimes superficial and the knowledge academic and futile. Nevertheless, the refined intellectual atmosphere of certain Russian circles, as well as the generally high cultural level, was some indication of what had been attained.

Unfortunately it had also its drawbacks and, instead of adding to the strength, rather contributed to the weakness of the nation as a whole. A Russian intellectual or bureaucrat was as remote from a Russian peasant, often living next door to him, as a Washington politician is from a native of Fiji Islands. The complex and dazzling structure of that Russian culture, of which the educated classes were so justly proud, meant nothing to the peasant. The names of Tolstoi and Dostoevsky, of Tschaikovsky and Rimsky-Korsakov, were an empty sound to them. They had never heard of the Moscow Art Theater and the Imperial Ballet, which won the applause of the world; nor would they have been capable of enjoying or appreciating them if, by some extraordinary turn of fortune, they happened to be present at a performance.

This complete cleavage between the masses and the educated classes was the most fundamental aspect of the Russian situation. Its explanation lies in the general conditions of historical development, especially in the illiteracy of the masses. That great popularizer of general knowledge and the equalizing influence in the modern world—the press, especially the daily press—was entirely nonexistent. There was nothing in Russia like organized sports, such as football, cricket, or baseball which obliterate all class and social distinctions and are, perhaps, among the most powerful tools of modern democracy; there was nothing that could be compared to the big boxing match in America or England, which has a universal appeal and carries away in one stirring emotion the wealthy occupants of ringside seats and the men in the top gallery, who have deprived themselves of tobacco or their customary glass of beer in order to see something of the great event. Religion, which in certain communities has exercised a similar unifying influence, entrusted to the unskilful hands of the Russian clergy, themselves very nearly social outcasts, was entirely incapable of fulfilling its task. Living side by side the Russian peasant and the educated classes knew and understood little or nothing of each other.

The whole situation is not unlike the one that has so often struck the traveler in the Far East, in India, or China, where a luxurious palace, full of wonderful treasures of art, rises in the midst of the sordid surroundings of a native village. Its architecture, workmanship, and inspiration are purely national and nothing like it can be found anywhere else. Nevertheless it remains entirely outside the daily life of the natives. It is a highly national product, and at the same time it is foreign to the nation as a whole. The same may be said of those refinements of the intellectual and artistic life which produced such rich fruit from the Russian soil. While highly national in itself, it failed to become an integral part of the existence of the masses of the people and had just as little influence upon the doings of a Russian peasant as exquisite Chinese painting has upon the everyday work and preoccupation of a coolie. This lack of balance between classes is a sign of a dangerous weakness in the whole national structure. Sooner or later the upper classes are called to pay the price for it.

The Outlook on the Eve of the War

If we attempt to take a general view of the Russia of 1914 we discover a number of important evidences of the rapid and assured advance of the country toward modernization, especially since the Emancipation. The venerable structure of the autocratic State had gone through a very remarkable transformation. The Tsar of All the Russias was now limited in the exercise of his legislative powers by the Duma, where the sons of the serfs of yesterday were rubbing shoulders with their former masters. The bureaucracy succeeded in reaching a considerable degree of efficiency and in creating an honorable tradition of public service. Institutions of local government, especially the zemstvos, were working with remarkable devotion to raise the economic and educational standards of the masses. A real movement had been made, at last, to put an end to illiteracy by introducing the compulsory education of children. A no less drastic step had been taken in the direction of advancing the prosperity of the farmer by freeing him from the bondage of the land commune. The general economic progress of the country could not be seriously questioned. In spite of all the imperfections and drawbacks of the new departures, it seems safe to say that they contained the elements for the future progress of the nation along the road that had been followed by other countries.

On the other hand, the weaknesses of the Imperial *régime* were numerous and grave. The reactionary tendencies in high places were as strong as ever. Concessions to liberal ideas were made under duress and coöperation between the bureaucracy and the liberal elements was slow in coming. Fraught with danger was the harsh and aggressive policy toward national minorities, the contemptuous attitude toward the non-Russian subjects of the Crown. Still more ominous was the aloofness of the educated classes from the masses, the abyss between the sophisticated admirers of the most advanced social and political theories and the illiterate peasants.

It is idle to speculate on what might have been the fate of the Russian Empire if it had been allowed to follow its course of development without the interference of a new factor of overwhelming importance, the World War. Baron Nolde believes that for many years to come the Russian State would have been able to continue successfully to combat the forces which tended to its disintegration, provided that the democratization of its institutions could have been allowed to proceed without interruption.[33] Whether we agree or not, it will readily be admitted that the outbreak of the War put the whole political and social framework of the State to a severe test. This brought to the fore all its inherent weakness. None of its complex elements proved equal to the ordeal. Resting as it did on a shifting foundation, the imposing but fragile and unbalanced edifice of the Empire went down under the strain of the War.

[33] Nolde, *L'ancien régime et la révolution russes*, p. 101.

Chapter 2

The Immediate Effects of the War

The Supreme Test

THERE IS PROBABLY no more effective, if onerous, method of testing the solidity and soundness of the political, social, and economic structure of a nation than a great war. As the real character of a man reveals itself in a moment of trial and often surprises not only the outside world but even the actor himself by the manifestations of his unsuspected inner self, so a nation under the strain of an emergency discloses its power of resistance, its strength and weakness, in ways for which little occasion is given in time of peace. The history of the Great War offers a unique opportunity for the study of national character, that imponderable and undeterminable, but nevertheless all-important factor of national development.

However great may be the disappointments of the aftermath of the War and however wasteful and futile may appear the sacrifices and enthusiasm of the war period in the light of post-war experiences, it must be admitted that the courage, self-denial, and spirit of collaboration displayed by the more advanced belligerent nations command our admiration. The terrible test of blood and iron so successfully endured by the great Allied democracies as well as by Germany (until the complete exhaustion of her resources forced her to surrender to the Allies) was not merely a sordid squabble for colonies or the attempted destruction of a potential rival. The creative genius of the nations displayed its full power in these trying days. Great Britain may be cited as an example. None of the countries involved in the great conflict had to face more formidable problems and none overcame them with greater success than the British Empire. And it is with a fully justified pride that the Report of the British War Cabinet, summing up the achievements of the critical year 1917, a year which saw the launching and the defeat of the submarine campaign, remarks that "the whole community has received an education in the problems of practical democracy such as it has never had before."[1] The students who wonder at the secret of the expan-

[1] *The War Cabinet. Report for the Year 1917*, published by His Majesty's Stationery Office (London, 1918), p. xvi.

ion of British influence over all the world will find some useful ꞓints in its war history, and those who have doubts as to the Empire's future may derive no little comfort from the same source.

But if war can disclose one nation's greatness and strength with remarkable clarity, it can also bring to light another's weakness and backwardness, its lack of national unity and absence of common ideals. The spectacular defeat of the Russian colossus by the Japanese in 1905 gave the world the first serious warning that the imposing and majestic façade of the Russian Empire concealed little real strength or adaptability. The blow it inflicted upon Russia's national pride, aggravated by the recognition of the fact that she had nobody but herself to blame for the unfortunate Far Eastern venture, led to a long period of internal troubles and agrarian disturbances which constitute what is often called the first Russian revolution. It was not sufficient however to overthrow the monarchy. The timely concessions of Count Witte followed by the iron rule of Stolypin in dealing with the revolutionary and liberal elements succeeded in restoring order. But they could not eliminate the forces which worked for the disintegration of the Empire. We have seen that in the period after 1905 important steps were taken in what seemed to be the right direction. But they needed time to produce their effects. The Great War brought such progress to an end, and imposed upon the country a burden which proved beyond its powers.

The Effects of the Mobilization

One of the most obvious consequences of a declaration of war is the mobilization of a large number of men for military service and the creation of an army administration which exercises more or less dictatorial powers over a section of the national territory. With the retreat of the Russian army in the spring of 1915 the territory thus exempted from the jurisdiction of the civilian government was considerable and tended to increase still further. We shall see that the ignorance and arrogance of the military authorities led by General Headquarters and the Commander-in-Chief—during the first year of the War the Grand Duke Nicholas Nikolaevich—were in no small degree responsible for the mismanagement of public affairs and the breakdown of the bureaucratic system.[2]

Even more important was the withdrawal of millions of men from their habitual occupations. There is a divergence of opinion among the various sources and authorities as to the exact num-

See below, Chapter IV and Chapter IX.

ber of men mobilized.[8] The following figures, based on the data of the Mobilization Department and accepted with slight modifications by some of the leading Russian economists, are sufficiently reliable for our purposes.[4] The peace-time army at the outbreak of the War was estimated at 1,370,000 men. In 1914 5,115,000 were mobilized; 5,210,000 in 1915; 2,745,000 in 1916; and 630,000 in 1917, giving a total of 15,070,000. It would seem, however, that this figure is too small, that the actual number of men called to the colors was still larger. In relation to the total male population of working age these numbers were equal to 15 per cent in 1914, 25 per cent in 1915, 36 per cent in 1916, and 37 per cent in 1917. That the withdrawal of so large a number of men was bound to have far-reaching effects upon the economic life of the country hardly need be said. Its consequences for agriculture and industry were, however, by no means uniform.

Industry was by far the greatest sufferer. To begin with, Russian industry had always been inadequately provided with labor. Much of it was of seasonal character and with the depletion of the reserves of peasant labor many industries were faced with a very serious shortage. To a certain extent the situation was relieved by the employment of refugees, prisoners of war and oriental labor. But the relief obtained from these sources was slow in coming and never amounted to much, although by the middle of 1917 the number of prisoners of war employed under the Ministry of Commerce and Industry was 376,000. The mobilization of skilled workmen proved particularly harmful to industry as it was naturally extremely difficult to replace such workers by men drawn from the new categories of labor mentioned above. The military authorities were extremely slow in recognizing the simple fact that a skilled man was of much greater use at his machine tool than in a reserve battalion or even in the trenches; and the granting of exemption to such men was surrounded with much delay and red tape. On the

---

[8] See *Rossya v. Mirovoi Voine (Russia in the World War)*, published by the Central Statistical Board (Moscow, 1925), Table I, p. 17; N. N. Golovine, *The Russian Army in the World War* and S. S. Kohn, *Vital Statistics in Russia during the War* in this series of the "Economic and Social History of the World War" (in the press).

[4] S. N. Prokopovich, *Voina i Narodnoe Khozyaistvo (War and National Economy)* (Moscow, 1918), p. 151; N. D. Kondratev, *Rinok Khlebov i Ego Regulirovanie vo Vremya Voini i Revolutsii (The Grain Market and Its Regulation during the War and the Revolution)* (Moscow, 1922), pp. 41, 72; also A. N. Antsiferov, A. D. Bilimovich, M. O. Batshev, and D. I. Ivantsov, "Rural Economy," in the volume *Russian Agriculture during the War* (Yale University Press, 1930), p. 116; and S. S. Demosthenov, "Food Prices and the Market in Foodstuffs," in the volume *Food Supply in Russia during the World War* (Yale University Press, 1930), p. 297, in this series of the "Economic and Social History of the World War."

34

other hand, the appearance of a new and huge demand for munitions of war and supplies of many kinds put an immense pressure upon the already inadequate industrial resources of the country. The result was the growing employment of women and children. In some branches of industry the number of women employed increased twofold, threefold, and sevenfold, and by the end of 1916 less than half the number of workers were men. Before the War the ratio of men to women in the whole of Russia's industries was three to two. Another effect of the shortage of labor was the lengthening of the working day and the increase in the number of overtime hours, accompanied by a decline in the productivity of labor. For instance, the monthly output per worker in iron smelting works decreased from 181 puds[5] in 1914 to 163 puds in 1915, 143 puds in 1916, and 119 puds in 1917. Similar conditions could be observed in other industries.[6]

Very different were the effects of mobilization upon farming. But here we must distinguish between peasant farming and farming on large estates. In dealing with the former it is important to remember that the exceedingly primitive methods of peasant husbandry provided only partial employment for the members of the household. It has been estimated that something like 50 per cent or even as much as 80 per cent of their labor power was wasted. And then a large number of peasants devoted to agriculture only a portion of their time, being also employed in various trades and forms of business. The withdrawal, therefore, of even a very large proportion of the rural male population could not have any markedly adverse effect upon peasant farming. Indeed, the area under cereal crops sown by the peasants in European Russia (excluding the provinces occupied by the enemy) increased during the three years of the War by some 13,000,000 deciatines,[7] or from an annual average of 47,000,000 in 1909–1913 to 59,800,000 in 1916.[8]

The position of large estates was far less favorable. Every laborer who was called up, or who left an estate to do some other form of work which had lately been done by a man now serving with the army, meant so much loss in working power. To replace him was imperative, but at the same time extremely difficult not only because of the general depletion of the labor

---

One ton = 62 puds.

S. O. Zagorsky, *State Control of Industry in Russia during the War* (Yale University Press, 1928), pp. 51–58, in this series of the "Economic and Social History of the World War."

One deciatine = 2.7 acres.

Antsiferov and others, "Rural Economy," pp. 118–120, 144; Demosthenov, *op. cit.*, pp. 297–303.

reserve, but also because the peasants, whose monetary resources, as we shall see, greatly increased during the War, were reluctant to accept so unprofitable an employment as that of an agricultural laborer. It is believed that the owners of large estates never succeeded in replacing the 300,000 or 400,000 hired laborers they lost through the mobilization in spite of the fact that, on a much larger scale than industry, agriculture drew upon the new sources of labor we have mentioned, that is, refugees, prisoners of war, and oriental labor. Shortage of labor was partly responsible for the decrease in the area under cereals on the large estates, an area reduced in European Russia (excluding the provinces occupied by the enemy) from an annual average of 21,300,000 deciatines in 1909–1913 to 6,500,000 in 1916, that is, by some 15,000,000 deciatines.[9]

The creation of a huge army had another important consequence: it resulted in the appearance of a new demand upon the market which soon acquired a dominating position. This demand included not only munitions of war and articles of military equipment, textiles, and leather goods, but also new demands for foodstuffs. This would not be true in countries which have a high general standard of living and where the army ration of a soldier does not differ favorably from the diet to which he is used as a civilian. But Russia was a country of low economic standards. The food habitually consumed by the Russian peasant was conspicuous neither for its abundance nor for its variety

The rural population [writes M. Brutskus[10]] meets its requirements in proteins to the extent of only one-fifth from the product of the live stock industry, whereas the urban population derive almost two-fifths of its proteins supply from such products. In the supply of fats for the city, animal products hold a more important place than they do for the rural population. Again, sugar plays an important part in the supply of the necessary carbohydrates for the city diet, whereas it is used merely as a sweetener in the fare of the peasantry. Calculated on a per capita basis, the consumption of meat, fish, eggs, sugar, butter, and cheese is several times as high in the city as in the country, the latter consuming more bread, grits, vegetables, and milk.

When the peasant reached the army his diet was brought up to the standard of the city population and included meat, butter, sugar, and other foodstuffs which appeared on his dinner table under ordinary conditions on rare occasions. The army

[9] Antsiferov and others, "Rural Economy," pp. 126–127, 144; Demosthenov, *op. cit.* pp. 297–303.
[10] B. D. Brutskus, *Ekonomya Selskago Khozyaistva (Rural Economy)* (Berlin, 1923), p. 83, quoted in Demosthenov, *op. cit.*, p. 330.

tion was not only more varied, but also much more abundant
an what he was used to at home. The importance of the new
ge demand which grew with the increase in the number of
en called to the colors was further emphasized by the fact
at it was extremely inelastic and highly urgent. Its appearance
the market upset to a large extent the existing balance of
oduction and consumption, and called for a complex system
measures of control which finally resulted in the establish-
ent of a system of State monopolies.[11]

he Isolation of Russia

Another most important consequence of the declaration of
ar against the Central Powers was the almost complete isola-
on of Russia from the outside world and a fundamental change
her trade routes accompanied by a drastic alteration in the
olume and nature of both exports and imports. The closing of
e land frontier with Germany and Austria-Hungary was fol-
wed by the maritime blockade of European Russia which
fected her two principal sea routes—the Baltic and the Black
eas. The only sea routes open to her were the Pacific Ocean—
hich, as a method of communication with her Allies, involved
journey by rail across Siberia and a voyage around the globe—
d the White Sea, icebound for a part of the year and con-
ected with the industrial centers of the Empire by a hastily
uilt railroad of doubtful efficiency. The closing of the trade
ute *via* the Baltic Sea was a result of the blockade of Russia
y Germany and the blockade of Germany by Great Britain.
he British blockade, it will be recalled, soon extended to the
eutral States adjoining Germany and to the Scandinavian
ountries. This had a most unfavorable effect upon Russia's
ansit trade *via* Sweden, which was her shortest available way
f communication with the outside world. Sweden protested
ith the utmost energy against the limitation of her foreign trade
y the iron rule of the British blockade; and as a measure of
etaliation she imposed rigorous restrictions upon the above
ansit trade, controlled by her. In January, 1915, Sweden passed
law which put an absolute embargo on "arms, munitions, and
ther war materials," a formula subject to a very wide interpre-
tion. The negotiations for the repeal of this law failed. At
e same time the blockade which made Sweden a victim in-
uced her to build up a rigid system of export restrictions; and
oods were not permitted to leave the country without special
censes. This naturally hindered trade between Sweden and

Antsiferov and others, "Rural Economy," pp. 188–190; Demosthenov, *op. cit.*,
. 329–336.

Russia, trade in which the latter was particularly interested at the time.[12]

A no less drastic change took place in the south where the key to the Black Sea, the Dardanelles, was in the hands of the Ottoman Porte. Although Turkey did not enter the War until October, the Straits were practically closed to shipping from the first days of August. There is little doubt that the chief importance of Turkey's entering the War on the side of the Central Powers lay in the closing of the Straits. This was fully recognized by the Germans as well as by the Allies.

If the Straits between the Mediterranean and the Black Sea had not been permanently closed to Entente traffic [wrote General von Falkenhayn[13]], all hopes for the successful conduct of the War would have been very considerably diminished. Russia would have been freed from her marked isolation. It was just this isolation which offered a surer guarantee than military successes that sooner or later a crippling of the forces of this Titan must take place, and to a certain extent automatically. If such a strictly disciplined organism as Germany, accustomed as she had been for centuries to conscientious work, and having at her disposal an inexhaustible wealth of skilled organizing forces in her own people, was barely able to accomplish the mighty task imposed upon her by the War, it was certain that the Russian State, so much weaker internally, would not succeed. So far as it was humanly possible to foresee, Russia would not be able for long to meet the demands of such a struggle and at the same time to bring about the reconstruction of her whole economic life, made necessary by her sudden isolation from the outside world, with the closing of the western frontiers and the Dardanelles.

Russian statesmen wholly shared this point of view. "The economic isolation of our country," said M. Kharitonov, member of the Russian Government, in the Duma in January 1915, "is one of the most painful and dangerous aspects of the War."[14] Great Britain made a gallant but futile attempt to break the wall which separated Russia from her Allies by launching the ill-fated Dardanelles expedition. Commenting on its failure, Mr. Winston Churchill, its chief advocate, says:[15]

There ended with the Dardanelles all hope of forming a direct and continuous contact with Russia. A railway 1,200 miles long might be

[12] Baron B. E. Nolde, *Russia in the Economic War* (Yale University Press, 1928) pp. 22–38, in this series of the "Economic and Social History of the World War."
[13] Erich von Falkenhayn, *The German General Staff and Its Decisions, 1914–1916* (New York, 1920), pp. 20–21.
[14] Nolde, *Russia in the Economic War*, p. 41.
[15] Winston S. Churchill, *The World Crisis, 1915* (London, 1923), p. 510.

38

built to Murmansk; Vladivostok might continue to pass supplies across a distance of 4,000 miles; but the intimate coöperation in men and munitions, the vast exportation of South Russian wheat, the expansion of a vitalizing trade, which could alone spring from the opening of the Black Sea, was forever denied to us.

The failure of the expedition was naturally a bitter disappointment and a real blow to Russia's most cherished hopes.

Foreign Trade

That the isolation of Russia from the outside world was followed by revolutionary changes in her foreign trade will hardly come as a surprise. The nature of these changes, however, deserves some attention. In the last pre-war year, 1913, Russian exports across her European and Caucasus frontier amounted to 1,420,949,000 rubles. Foodstuffs, raw and semi-manufactured goods represented 95 per cent of her total exports. In the first year of the War, August, 1914, to July, 1915, exports declined to 190,171,000 rubles, or 13.3 per cent of the pre-war figure; in the second year, August, 1915, to July, 1916, they improved to 418,763,000 rubles, or 29.4 per cent. They remained practically stationary during the third year, August, 1916, to July, 1917, amounting to 446,079,000 rubles, or 31.3 per cent. The export trade from Vladivostok and Nikolaevsk was insignificant, from 2 to 5 per cent of the total exports, and will not be considered here. It must be remembered that the depreciation of the ruble during the War was great, reaching about 39 per cent in 1916, and therefore the value of exports in gold rubles was really much smaller than the figures given above. About 31.8 per cent of Russian exports in 1913 went to Germany, 4.4 per cent to Austria-Hungary, and 2.5 per cent to Turkey. During the War most Russian exports went to Finland and Great Britain. A change also took place in the relative position of various articles of export. Foodstuffs which once held the first place were superseded, beginning with the second year of the War, by semi-manufactured goods, such as those of hemp, lumber, and flax. The drastic reduction in the export of foodstuffs was partly due to the growing demand for them on the home market.[16]

The import trade presented a very different picture. In 1913 the total imports amounted to 1,374,033,000 rubles. In 1914–1915 the imports *via* European and Caucasus frontiers declined to 404,415,000 rubles; in 1915–1916 they rose to 1,076,938,000; and in 1916–1917 they reached 2,104,460,000 rubles. If we add

[16] Nolde, *Russia in the Economic War*, pp. 124–126, 132–137.

to these figures the value of imports received through the ports of Vladivostok and Nikolaevsk which rose from 150,000,000 in 1914–1915, to about 598,000,000 in each of the following two years, we shall discover that after a sharp decline of some 40 per cent during the first year of the War, the imports exceeded by 20 per cent their pre-war value in 1915–1916, and almost doubled it in 1916–1917. In 1913, 47.4 per cent of the total imports came from Germany, 12.5 from Great Britain, 5.8 from the United States, and 4.1 from France. During the War, Great Britain, the United States, France, and Japan were by far the largest importers. The nature of these changes is not difficult to explain: the immense majority of the imports which reached Russia during the War were consignments for the army, military equipment, and such things as the machinery needed for the reorganization of industry on a war footing. In spite of this gallant effort of Russia's Allies, her industries suffered considerably from the breaking up of the old-established ties with Germany.[17]

The unavoidable consequence of the decline of exports and increase in imports was the reversal of the trade balance. In 1913 Russian exports exceeded imports by 46,916,000 rubles. Beginning with the first year of the War the situation changed. Imports exceeded exports by 214,244,000 rubles in 1915–1916; by 658,175,000 rubles in 1915–1916; and by 1,658,381,000 rubles in 1916–1917. Thus the total deficit in foreign trade for the three years of the War was 2,530,800,000 rubles. This situation affected unfavorably the exchange value of the ruble.[18]

Extreme caution must be used in judging the condition of trade during the War from its declared value. In connection with the discussion of export trade attention has been drawn to the depreciation of the ruble. The same warning must be repeated in dealing with imports. Professor Zagorsky points out that while the value of imports in depreciated rubles greatly increased, the weight of goods imported was considerably less. Measured by this standard it appears that in the course of the last three years of Russia's participation in the War, her imports amounted to merely about two-fifths of her imports in the three years that preceded the War. A detailed examination of customs returns also shows a considerable decline in raw materials and machinery, except those used for the army, on which industry largely depended. This was bound to have a most detrimental effect upon national production.[19]

[17] Nolde, *Russia in the Economic War*, pp. 127–130, 141–143.
[18] *Ibid.*, pp. 131–132.
[19] Zagorsky, *op. cit.*, pp. 32–37.

Disorganization of Transport and Loss of Territory

The working of railways and other means of transport in time of war is obviously a factor of extreme importance. They are called on to perform a twofold function. On the one hand, the mobilization and concentration of the army depend on the successful organization of transport, which is also responsible for the conveyance of military supplies, etc. On the other, on the orderly functioning of the railways depends the normal commercial and industrial intercourse of the nation. Much has been written about the disorganization of transport in Russia during the War. As M. Demosthenov rightly points out, what was known as disorganization was really nothing but the inadequacy of the railroads, which made it impossible for them to deal successfully with the new and immense demands of the army and at the same time to carry on their peace-time functions. Russian railroads were suffering from fundamental evils—insufficient rolling stock, the low carrying capacity of their lines, and their uneven geographical distribution. The lines east of the Petrograd-Moscow—Kharkov-Sebastopol railway had a maximum capacity which amounted to merely one-third of that in the western parts of the country. This proved a serious drawback, especially in dealing with the supplies of foodstuffs which were to be moved from the eastern provinces.[20]

The length of the whole network of railways in 1914 was 42,400 miles, but it decreased, through the loss of territory, to 39,300 miles by the end of the same year. Some 5,500 miles of new lines were built in 1914–1916. The strain imposed upon the railways by purely military requirements was very great. The military traffic increased from 51,127,000,000 pud-versts[21] in peace time, to 326,478,000,000 in 1914, and to 741,076,000,-000 in 1917. The amount of ordinary goods conveyed by rail decreased from 1,864,000,000 puds in 1913, to 1,157,000,000 in 1917, while the military stores handled by the railways in these years increased from 152,000,000 to 2,625,000,000 puds. It seems clear from these figures that railways were largely monopolized by the requirements of the army. This made it extremely difficult to maintain supplies of foodstuffs for the cities and the important industrial centers, and impaired the work of the railways themselves by depriving them of fuel, metal, machinery, and tools which were essential for the maintenance of their efficiency. The building of new engines, passenger and freight cars, and the reconditioning of those in need

[20] Demosthenov, *op. cit.*, pp. 392–393.
[21] One verst = 0.66 mile.

of repair were slowed down. The number of engines in working order decreased from 20,071 at the end of 1914 to 16,837 in 1916, and 9,201 in 1917. The number of cars decreased from 539,549 in 1914, to 463,419 in 1916, and to 174,346 in 1917. The output of rails declined from 43,122,000 puds in 1914, to 11,881,000 puds in 1917.[22] The tragic meaning of these figures hardly needs comment.

The heavy military reverses suffered by the Russian army in 1915 resulted in the abandonment to the enemy of substantial portions of the national territory. This loss must not be overlooked in our examination of the economic effects of the War. Russian Poland was one of the important industrial regions of the Empire, and the hasty removal of industrial establishments to the interior of the country naturally could not be carried out without seriously reducing their productivity. Sugar refineries were among the establishments which suffered heavily from their nearness to the front. The region of Riga, although not occupied by the Germans until a much later date, was greatly affected in its industrial activities by the steady advance of the Germans toward the city. A vast quantity of rolling stock and various valuable supplies was left behind during the retreat. It also gave rise to the immense tide of refugees which moved eastward, blocked railroads and highways, and presented a baffling problem with which the authorities were incapable of dealing.[23]

Prohibition of the Sale of Alcoholic Liquor

The changes produced by the War in the economic and social structure of the country discussed so far may be considered as the unavoidable consequence of the outbreak of hostilities and of the general trend of the War on the Russian front. The mobilization of a large number of men was an obvious necessity although the time of the calling of the various classes was a matter of government policy. The isolation of Russia from the outside world and the ensuing changes in the volume of foreign trade and in the direction of trade routes were factors over which the Russian Government had little control. The inability of the railroads to handle the largely increased volume of traffic was also an unavoidable consequence of the general inadequacy of the organization of transport which could not be remedied at a moment's notice. And the losses resulting to national economy from the advance of the enemy troops clearly belong to the same class. There was, however, at least one extremely important change which, while brought

22 Zagorsky, *op. cit.*, pp. 46–51.
23 *See below*, pp. 197 *sqq.*

about as a war measure, was not a necessary or natural consequence of war. We are speaking now of the prohibition of the sale of intoxicating liquor which was enacted as a temporary measure for the duration of the mobilization at the end of July, 1914. By a ukase of August 22, 1914, it was extended to the whole duration of the War, thus giving Russia the doubtful honor of being the first country to try compulsory temperance on a large scale, a road in which she was followed six years later by the United States.

Prohibition meant a very considerable loss to the Treasury. It will be remembered that the State monopoly of spirits was introduced in four provinces in 1893 and was gradually extended to practically the whole territory of the Empire. In 1913 it embraced seventy-five provinces with a population of some 142,000,000, and sold in 25,733 shops some 282,000,000 gallons of vodka valued at 886,000,000 rubles. It was one of the largest State undertakings that existed before the War. During the period 1904–1913, when the monopoly was applied over the whole territory of the country, it had yielded the Treasury an aggregate revenue of 5,329,000,000 rubles, or an average annual revenue of 500,000,000 rubles toward a budget which was balanced at an average of 2,000,000,000 rubles per annum. The revenue from this source grew steadily, and in 1913 it was estimated at 678,000,000 rubles.[24] The abandonment of such substantial receipts at a moment when the Treasury was facing new and immense expenditures was obviously a decision of the utmost importance.

It is characteristic of Russian conditions that it came wholly as an improvisation. It is true that with the resignation of Count Kokovzov from the Government early in 1914 his successor at the Ministry of Finance, P. L. Bark, received an imperial rescript directing him to take drastic measures for the abolition of drunkenness. In the discussion that followed the abolition of the spirit monopoly was never seriously suggested. How far the Minister of Finance himself was from contemplating any such measure will be made clear by the fact that while he ordered the closure of all State liquor shops during the mobilization, he introduced, on July 26, 1914, a bill in the Duma asking for an increase in the price of liquor. M. Bark argued that an increase in the price of vodka, which could not be classed as a necessity, was an excellent method for advancing temperance. The bill was duly passed by the Duma and became law on

[24] A. M. Michelson, "Revenue and Expenditure," in the volume *Russian Public Finance during the War* (Yale University Press, 1928), pp. 34–40, in this series of the "Economic and Social History of the World War."

July 27, 1914. Nevertheless the ukase of August 22, 1914, extended the operation of prohibition to the whole period of the War, which meant for the Treasury an annual loss of revenue of some 700,000,000 rubles. Whatever one may think of the State monopoly of spirits, the moment for trying the experiment seems most unfortunately chosen. A. J. Shingarev, rapporteur of the Budget Committee of the Duma, stated in one of his speeches:

From time immemorial countries waging war have been in want of funds. Revenue has always been sought either by good or by bad measures, by voluntary contributions, by obligatory levies, or by the open confiscation of private property. But never since the dawn of human history has a single country, in time of war, renounced the principal source of its revenue.

No wonder that in spite of the drastic reduction in expenditure and new taxes the Treasury did not succeed in filling the gap caused by the abolition of the monopoly.[25]

While prohibition contributed in no small degree to the financial difficulties of the Government, it seems extremely doubtful whether it actually helped to achieve its direct purpose, the advancement of temperance. The following statement written by Professor Ozerov in 1916 may sound rather familiar to the American reader:[26]

Drunkenness continues, the illicit sale of liquor proceeds undisturbed in the private rooms of luxurious restaurants. The distilleries are unable to satisfy the demand for liquor. Dealers make incredible profits. Chemistry is resorted to in the home, to rectify methylated spirit, varnish, and *eau de cologne*. Consumption of alcoholic liquor flourishes especially among the wealthier classes. The State has merely renounced the taxation of alcohol and has not succeeded in suppressing its consumption.

But if prohibition failed as a measure for the advancement of temperance, it nevertheless succeeded in effecting considerable savings among the masses of the peasantry who now turned from the State-sold liquor to various forms of home brew. The exact amount of savings derived from this source is variously estimated, but it is generally agreed that it substantially contributed to the growth of the monetary wealth of the peasantry and the ensuing rise in their standard of consumption.[27] How-

[25] Michelson, *op. cit.*, pp. 80–89.
[26] J. Ozerov, *Osnovi Finansovoi Nauki, Dopolnenie za Vremya Voini (Principles of the Science of Finance, Supplement for the War Period)* (Moscow, 1916), p. 59, quoted in Michelson, *op. cit.*, p. 87.
[27] Antsiferov and others, "Rural Economy," pp. 132–135; Demosthenov, *op. cit.*, p. 342.

44

ever desirable the latter may appear in itself, it added greatly, as we shall see before the end of this chapter, to the disorganization of the foodstuffs market, with all its consequences. The much-needed improvement in the economic standards of the peasants was purchased at an excessive price and proved extremely short-lived.

Loss of Revenue

The loss of revenue due to the abolition of the liquor monopoly was only one of many blows suffered by the Treasury on the outbreak of the War. The drastic reduction of foreign trade resulted in the cutting down of customs receipts. The revenue from the State railroads and from the taxes levied on passengers and freights was also reduced because of the absorption of the greater part of the railway service by the requirements of the War, the diminution of commercial traffic, and the occupation by the enemy of certain provinces. The general confusion of the first months of the War manifested itself in an unusual slackness in the payment of taxes, with the result that the actual receipts in 1914 were 674,000,000 rubles less than the estimates.[28] It must be noted in this connection that, as a result of an interpretation given by the Ministry of Finance to certain articles of the Fundamental Laws, the entire war expenditure was exempted from the control of the legislative chambers and was provided for from a special "war fund." The figures quoted above, therefore, refer merely to the "peace budget"; that is, no war expenditures were included in it. This duplication of the budget, or rather the existence side by side of two budgets—the "peace budget" which was voted by the legislature, and the much more important "war budget" which was not subject to any such control—presented one of the unusual features of Russian war finance.[29] The criticism of this system by members of the Duma produced no effect.[30]

War Expenditure

Simultaneously with the fall in revenue came the increase in expenditure. The most important was naturally expenditure growing out of the War. In addition to the outlay for the maintenance of the army and the navy, the Government made heavy disbursements in allowances to the families of mobilized men. In 1914 they amounted to 190,600,000 rubles; in 1915, to 623,-700,000 rubles; in 1916, to 1,106,800,000 rubles; and in 1917,

[28] Michelson, *op. cit.,* p. 89.
[29] *See below,* p. 98.
[30] Michelson, *op. cit.,* pp. 74–78.

to 3,000,000,000 rubles. The total sum thus spent during the War was something like 5,000,000,000 rubles. About 736,000,-000 rubles were spent during the same period on refugees. The appropriations for practically every department increased. The war expenditure of the Ministry of Transport was particularly heavy. It involved such items as the construction, repair, and operation of the railways, the purchase of rolling stock, new capital investments, and increases in the wages of labor. The latter item in 1917 necessitated an outlay of some 2,000,000,-000 rubles. We may also mention the construction and repair of roads and waterways, the expansion of commercial ports, purchases of foodstuffs, seeds, and fuel for the people, and measures for the promotion of factories and other enterprises working for the national defense. No official figures giving Russia's total war expenditure were ever published. We shall have therefore to rely upon the approximate estimates computed by M. Dementiev. In accordance with his data, the total war expenditure in 1914 was 1,655,400,000 rubles; in 1915, it increased to 8,818,400,000 rubles; in 1916, to 14,572,800,000 rubles; in 1917, for the first eight months, it was given as 13,-603,000,000 rubles; the total war expenditure from 1914 to September 1, 1917, thus reached 38,649,600,000 rubles.[31]

Taxation, Loans, Inflation

How was this expenditure met? In the field of public finance, just as in all other branches of State administration, the inherent weakness of Russia revealed itself during the War. An investigation of Russia's revenue and expenditure discloses this, that none of the war expenditure was covered by receipts from taxation. Inelastic and antiquated, the machinery of taxation was lacking in the essential features of modern fiscal systems. An income tax and a war profits tax were introduced as late as 1916, and of course the effects of these measures could not be felt at once. They also suffered from the defects of all hasty improvisations brought into operation under the conditions of a great war. The new taxes enacted after 1914 and the rise in the rates of existing taxes were barely sufficient to compensate for the loss of revenue resulting from the abolition of the liquor monopoly and the decline in other receipts. War expenditure therefore had to be covered from the two other sources which the Ministry of Finance had at its disposal: loans and the issue of paper money. This is exactly how they were covered. From the outbreak of the War to September 1, 1917, Russia concluded loans to the amount of 23,907,800,000 rubles of which

[31] *Ibid.*, pp. 215–220.

11,408,200,000 were consolidated domestic loans, 4,428,900,-000 treasury bills, and 8,070,700,000 foreign loans. Loans therefore provided 61.9 per cent of the funds required for the conduct of the War, and only 20.9 per cent were derived from foreign borrowing. The balance was to be provided by the issue of paper money.[32]

The printing press was set to work. The paper rubles in circulation at the outbreak of the War amounted to 1,633,000,000; by January 1, 1915, this increased to 2,946,000,000; by January 1, 1916, to 5,617,000,000; by January 1, 1917, to 9,097,000,000. On March 1, 1917, when the Empire was overthrown, the total of notes in circulation was 9,949,000,000 rubles; and when eight months later the Provisional Government was succeeded by the Bolsheviks, the volume of paper currency in circulation had reached the immense figure of 18,917,000,000. This, of course, meant inflation in its crudest form, with all the accompanying evils of the rapid depreciation of the ruble in home and foreign markets, and a rise in the cost of living.[33]

Industry and Agriculture

Professor Struve, the eminent Russian economist, says that in 1914–1915 the economic implications of war were not only misunderstood, but were also based upon fallacious assumptions none of which survived the test of events.

As regards Russia [he writes[34]], these fallacious assumptions were of two kinds: partly optimistic, partly pessimistic. It was believed that the economic backwardness of Russia and the inadequate development of her commerce and division of labor ought to render Russia less sensitive to the economic shocks of war. On the other hand, there was a widespread notion that war was bound to aggravate the impoverishment of the people and to tend to sap the strength of the nation. Both these assumptions, however, although in different degrees and in different senses, were belied by the results.

One of the current misunderstandings was the belief that articles of Russian export which, it will be remembered, was entirely discontinued with the outbreak of the hostilities, would greatly decrease in price. For instance in a paper read before the in-

[32] P. N. Apostol, "Credit Operations," in the volume *Russian Public Finance during the War* (Yale University Press, 1928), pp. 322–326, in this series of the "Economic and Social History of the World War."

[33] M. W. Bernatzky, "Monetary Policy," in the volume *Russian Public Finance during the War* (Yale University Press, 1928), p. 379, in this series of the "Economic and Social History of the World War."

[34] P. B. Struve, "Introduction" to the volume *Food Supply in Russia during the War* (Yale University Press, 1930), p. xiii, in this series of the "Economic and Social History of the World War."

fluential Moscow Agricultural Society in August, 1914, Prince Shakhovsky suggested that "it may be that wheat will for some time lose all its value for its holder because there will be no purchaser for it on the domestic market." And reports came from authoritative sources to say that industrialists, anticipating the shrinking of the market, were reducing their production by 25 or even 50 per cent "in nearly every class of manufacture."[35]

As soon as the confusion of the first weeks had subsided, it became clear that there was no ground for any such apprehension. In the market the new demands of the army successfully replaced the loss of foreign customers, and before long industry found itself deluged with orders. "Business as usual" was the generally accepted motto of this period, which lasted until the beginning of 1915. It was believed that industry ought not to concern itself with the War, but must perform its normal functions of supplying the population with the goods they needed as far as possible on the same scale as before the War. No interference with industrial freedom was contemplated at the time. The idea was generally accepted that the effects of war were limited to the area immediately adjoining the front, and that the commercial and industrial life of the country must be allowed to resume its usual course.

No doubt industry suffered considerable dislocation as a result of the operation of the various new factors: the mobilization of labor, especially of skilled workmen; the suspension of imports of raw materials and machinery on which it greatly depended; the disorganization of transport with the resulting difficulties in obtaining fuel and raw material; inflation and the general rise in prices and wages. In spite of this, many industries succeeded in increasing their output, and some industries, which were nonexistent in Russia before the War, came into being. Industries working entirely or mostly for the army, such as those producing manufactures of metals, textiles, and leather, were put in a particularly favorable position. These developments, however important and even necessary in themselves, had at the same time a detrimental effect upon the general economic conditions of the country by monopolizing for the use of the army most of the output of articles of general consumption. It is estimated that in 1916 about 70 or 80 per cent of the production of textiles went to the army. The share of the civilian population in the output of the leather industry was still smaller. The production of agricultural machinery and implements in 1915 and 1917 was reduced by almost 80 per cent as compared

[35] Demosthenov, *op. cit.*, pp. 246–247.

48

with the pre-war figure.[36] The resulting shortage in the commodities in which the farmers were particularly interested proved one of the fundamental factors in bringing about the shortage of food supplies. The peasants, receiving in exchange for their products nothing but rapidly depreciating paper money, which they could not exchange for the goods they needed, refrained from parting with their grain. The industrial backwardness of Russia, therefore, proved, as Professor Struve pointed out, far from being a safeguard against the economic blows of war. On the contrary it contributed more than anything else to the shortage of food supplies.

The anticipated impoverishment of the masses and the ruin of the economic machinery of the nation also failed to materialize. There is no doubt that certain social groups suffered considerable hardship, and that some of the national resources were gravely impaired. Nevertheless, until the Revolution and civil war the economic framework of the country remained fundamentally sound. If this was true of industry, it was still more true of agriculture. We have seen already that peasant farming was not adversely affected by the mobilization of men, although large estates suffered from the shortage of labor. The requisition of horses and the depletion of the supply of live stock, especially draft animals, also had a more detrimental effect upon large estates than upon peasant farming. This may be explained by the well-known fact that Russia had always had a surplus of horses and oxen, connected, no doubt, with the surplus of labor. As in the case of labor this surplus was to be found on peasant farms. The Agricultural Census of 1917 makes it plain that in 1916 the average number of deciatines per hundred horses in forty-eight provinces of European Russia was 344 on peasant land, and 568 on large estates. In spite therefore of the loss of some 2,600,000 horses, or about 10.2 per cent of the total number four years old and over, which were withdrawn from agriculture for the use of the army, its effects upon farming were far less detrimental than might have been expected.[37] The reduction in the supply of live stock which undoubtedly took place gave no ground for alarm. It is indeed maintained that "in some respects stock breeding was in a better condition in 1917 than at the outbreak of hostilities."[38]

The total area under crops (excluding Finland and Poland) suffered a reduction during the War of from 99,500,000 de-

[36] Ibid., pp. 412–414.
[37] Antsiferov and others, "Rural Economy," pp. 117–118, 123–126.
[38] Ibid., p. 180.

49

ciatines in 1913 to 95,700,000 in 1915, and 90,600,000 in 1916. This loss was largely due to the advance of the enemy, who in 1915 occupied wholly or in part seven Russian provinces. It will be recalled that in the territory free from enemy invasion a reduction in the area under crops was observed only on land belonging to large estates, while peasant farming made distinct and substantial progress.[39] From the point of view of national supplies of grain this was indeed unfortunate because large farming establishments were producing for the market, while peasant farms consumed a considerable portion of their produce. On the other hand, it must be remembered that the cereals harvested on peasant farms averaged about 87.7 per cent of the total crop and that it amounted to 78.5 per cent of the grain actually marketed.[40] The food supply of the country, in the last resort, depended on its peasant farmers.

This brings us to the crux of the problem of supply in Russia during the War. Far from resulting in the impoverishment of the masses, the War brought about a considerable if short-lived increase in their buying power, although undoubtedly it worked hardships in a great many individual cases. Among the groups whose standards of consumption were raised were, as we have seen, the soldiers. The peasants, too, found themselves unexpectedly in possession of new and substantial sources of income. Some of them are already familiar to us. They included savings resulting from the prohibition of liquor and allowances paid by the Government to the families of mobilized men. To this must be added the sums received for requisitioned horses, carts, and harness, and receipts from the sale of cattle which would not have been put on the market under normal conditions. The actual real increase derived from the new sources in the case of the average peasant income is estimated at about 18 per cent, allowance being made for the rise in the cost of living.[41] To this must be added savings resulting from prohibition which were not included in the computation. The increase in the monetary wealth of the rural community expressed in the rapidly depreciating paper ruble was, of course, much greater. It would also seem that the purchasing power of certain classes of the city population, for instance men and women employed by the establishments working for national defense, families of army officers, certain groups of manufacturers and traders who made large profits, etc., was also greatly strengthened. This led to a general increase in the demand for foodstuffs as well as for

[39] Ibid., pp. 142–143; see above, p. 41.
[40] Demosthenov, op. cit., p. 417.
[41] Antsiferov and others, "Rural Economy," pp. 135–137.

manufactured goods. On the other hand, the products of industry available for the market decreased as a result of the absorption by the army. The peasants therefore, in spite of the increased demand for farming produce, found little interest in exchanging their produce for paper money which rapidly depreciated, and for which they could buy in the cities none of the things they needed. The whole situation was further aggravated by the inadequacy of transport. To use the expression of Professor Struve, "here was not a case of anaemia but rather a pathological blood congestion of agriculture."[42] The weakness and inferiority of Russia's industry, which were held by some, at the outbreak of the War, to be one of her best safeguards against economic disturbances, proved the chief cause of her immense difficulties in organizing her food supply. In like manner the poverty and ignorance of the masses, so frequently extolled by the reactionaries as the corner stone of autocracy, proved a most favorable ground for the spreading of revolutionary ideas and spelled the doom of the monarchy.

The Organization of the Country for War

We have seen that the immensity of the problem of organization which confronted the country on the outbreak of the War was not realized at once and that for the first eight or nine months the prevailing attitude not only in official circles, but also in the community at large was "business as usual." The military reverses of the spring of 1915, accompanied by a calamitous shortage of munitions of war and military supplies, the disorganization of transport, and the depreciation of the ruble clearly indicated that this policy could not be continued without bringing disaster. Then, under the pressure of public opinion, a very real effort was made to mobilize industry. The summer of 1915 saw the creation of the four Special Councils—for National Defense, Transport, Fuel, and Food Supply.[43]

These councils represented an important step forward because they concentrated in the hands of a single authority wide powers for dealing with problems connected with the organization of the rear and the supply of the front, thus bringing to an end, at least in theory, the complete divorce between the front and the rear which we observed during the first period of the War. They marked the triumph of the idea that if war was to be brought to a victorious end the whole of the national resources must be taken under control. The composition of the

---

[42] Struve, *op. cit.*, p. xx.

[43] The Special Council on Refugees was organized a little later and played no part in the State control of industry.

councils, which included representatives of the legislative chambers and of the Unions of Zemstvos and of Towns, the two great war relief organizations,[44] was a distinct victory for the liberal circles which had gathered under the banners of the Duma.[45] The new policy was made possible by the fact that a parallel movement for the adaptation of all the country's economic machinery had arisen among the industrial and commercial classes. It became known as the "mobilization of industry" and found its expression in the formation of the war industries committees, an unofficial organization with headquarters in Petrograd and local committees all over the country. Its social basis was very broad and included not only representatives of commerce, industry, institutions of local government, and coöperative societies, but also of labor.[46] At the same time the Unions of Zemstvos and of Towns were appointing a Joint Committee, known by the abbreviated name of *Zemgor*, for the coördination of their efforts to meet the army's needs.[47] It appeared for a while in the second half of 1915 as if the country was on its way to achieve real unity and collaboration in its struggle against the enemy. These hopes were doomed to disappointment.

The economic policy of the Government during the War suffered from the lack of a definite plan, from opportunism, inconsistency, and incoherence. The initial period of almost unrestricted economic freedom was followed by the introduction of partial control and the splitting of the market into two sections, of which one continued to enjoy a large measure of freedom, while the other—embracing all army supplies—was put under a system of State control. It was only after the dismal failure of this method that the Government was gradually brought to the recognition of the necessity of uniform regulations for the market as a whole and was finally forced to introduce a number of State monopolies and even the rationing of consumption. These measures, which might have been helpful at an earlier stage, came too late. The disorganization of the country had in the meantime reached such a degree that the bureaucracy was no longer in a position to enforce the new policy. On the other hand, the measures of control themselves were often inconsistent and contradictory. Fixed prices were so frequently changed that instead of stabilizing production and supply they only added to the general confusion and stimulated

[44] *See below*, pp. 124 *sqq.*
[45] *See below*, Chapter V.
[46] *See below*, pp. 128–129.
[47] *See below*, p. 129.

speculation. Some of the new measures were enacted after the Revolution of March, 1917, and in the turmoil that followed simply remained a dead letter. It may well be questioned whether a rigid system of control, such as we find, for instance, in Germany or Great Britain during the War, could have been at all successful in a country like Russia, crippled by the handicaps of a backward economic organization and illiteracy. Coming, as they did, with infinite delays on the eve or even in the midst of a revolutionary upheaval, they were never given a fair trial.

The Economic and Political Factors

This rather sketchy outline of the effects of the War upon some of the more important aspects of the economic organization of Russia will, perhaps, justify the conclusion that, however grave might have been their consequences, they were far from being irreparable. Discussing the difficulty encountered by Russian farming, Professor Struve makes the following statement:

Essentially, however, this economic difficulty did not partake of the nature of a catastrophe. Although this is not a general history of Russia during the War, one may venture to suggest that the student of economic factors will not ascribe the political catastrophe that overwhelmed Russia in 1917 to the economic condition of the country in general and its food situation in particular. For an explanation of the Revolution, first and foremost, political forces should be considered. Herein lies the profound difference between Russia's war-time economy and that of the Central Powers, whose defeat was almost automatically prepared by the inexorable march of economic forces and, especially, by those of the food supply.[48]

This statement, if perhaps somewhat too extreme, contains nevertheless a substantial element of truth. The difference in the process which resulted in the breakdown of the Central Powers and of Russia is striking. What Russia was suffering from was not the exhaustion of her resources but the inability to make full and complete use of them. But if her stock of foodstuffs was not irreparably depleted, as was the case in Germany and Austria-Hungary, it nevertheless remains true that her industry was hopelessly unequal to the task, and that the shortage of manufactured goods together with the inadequacy of the railways resulted in the urban population's experiencing marked food difficulties in the second half of the War. The rural community suffered from the absence of textiles, ironware, agricultural

48 Struve, op. cit., p. xx.

machines and implements, and leather goods. The cities and industrial centers were short of fuel, flour, butter, eggs, milk, and vegetables. The economic hardships resulting from the disparity between agriculture and industry and from the disorganization of transport undoubtedly had an exceedingly important part in that general growth of discontent which finally resulted in the establishment of the Soviet Government. To say, therefore, that the political factor was, "first and foremost," responsible for the course of events does not seem to be wholly exact. The collapse of the Russian State was the result of the simultaneous action of many factors. It could hardly have been otherwise.

Chapter 3

The Eclipse of the Sovereign

War and Government

THE GOVERNMENT of practically every country that took an active part in the Great War went through a like process of readjustment necessitated by new conditions. On the one hand, the powers of executive officers were everywhere greatly increased and the effective control of the legislative bodies curtailed; on the other, the system of State controls expanding, as it did, to practically every aspect of national life, immensely broadened the social base on which rested the executive machinery of the Government. This undoubtedly made it easier even for countries with a long parliamentary tradition to become reconciled to the newly-acquired dictatorial powers of the executive.

The war history of Russia is no exception to the general rule. But under the peculiar conditions prevailing in Russia the same trends which, in countries with a larger experience in self-government, led to national unity had a very different effect. An important factor in the situation was the Emperor himself. His personality, his attitude toward the fundamental problems raised by the War, the influence exercised upon him by the Empress and her *entourage*,—played a decisive part in shaping the social history of his time. Some knowledge of these factors is therefore necessary for the understanding of the broader social movements.

The Emperor

It is obviously out of the question here to give a detailed character sketch of the late Tsar. We shall limit ourselves therefore to a few brief remarks bearing immediately on the social and political history of the country. Brought up under the strict rule of his father and the immediate influence of Pobedonostsev, that high priest and poet of autocracy, Nicholas II was fully imbued with the ideas of another age and was temperamentally unfitted for carrying the immense burden which devolved upon him after the death of Alexander III. He unreservedly shared the views enunciated by Count Uvarov, Minister of Education from 1833–1849, that "autocracy has always been and will always remain the principal condition of the existence and prosperity of Russia."[1] And he had an unlimited faith in the sacredness of the reactionary formula which reduced the essential elements of the Russian Empire to three: orthodoxy, autocracy, and nationality. This, of course, left no room for the development of liberal ideas and for the progress of the country along the lines of parliamentary government. We know that the manifesto of October 17, 1905, was issued by the Emperor under pressure and against what he considered his better judgment. In a very illuminating letter to his mother, dated October 19, 1905,[2] he describes his unwillingness to grant the concessions demanded by public opinion. And he makes no effort to disguise his disapproval of the *régime* limiting autocracy introduced by the manifesto. "My only consolation," writes the Emperor,[3] "is the hope that such is the will of our Lord." His dislike for Count Witte, the man who was the moving spirit and the framer of the proposed reform, was so strong that it defied even the moderating influence of years. The news of Witte's death caused the Emperor a joy which he did not try to conceal.[4] And he cherished the hope of getting rid of the legislative institutions which had been imposed upon him, and which he considered an illegitimate interference with his powers and therefore harmful to the country. In a conversation with F. A. Golovin, President of the Second Duma, which took place in the spring of 1907 shortly before the promulgation of

[1] *L'autocratie Russe: Constantin Pobiédonostsev, mémoires politiques, correspondance officille et documents inédits relatifs à l'histoire du règne de l'empereur Alexander II de Russie*, Paris, 1927, p. 15.

[2] *Lettres de Nicholas II et de sa mère*, Paris, 1928, pp. 75–82.

[3] *Ibid.*, p. 80.

[4] *The Letters of the Tsar to the Tsaritsa*, translated by A. L. Hynes from the official edition of the Romanov correspondence and now published for the first time in England, edited, with notes and an index, by C. E. Vulliamy and an introduction by C. T. Hagberg. London, 1929, p. 29.

the Election Law of June 3, 1907, the Emperor consistently developed the idea that the Duma was primarily a "platform for revolutionary propaganda."[5] And in October, 1913, he made a definite attempt to reduce the Duma and the State Council to the position of merely consultative bodies. In a letter to N. A. Maklakov, then Minister of the Interior, the Emperor directed him to submit the question of the revision of the statute establishing the legislative chambers to the Council of Ministers. "The presentation to the sovereign," he wrote, "for his choice and approval of both the majority and the minority opinions will be a welcome return to the former peaceful course of legislation which, moreover, is in accordance with the Russian tradition."[6] But even Maklakov, this most conservative and devoted servant of the throne, thought that the suggestion of his Imperial master was both illegal and impracticable, and had no chance of being accepted by the Council of Ministers. The matter therefore was not discussed by the Council and became known only after the Revolution. Maklakov scrupulously kept the secret entrusted to him.[7]

In spite of his dislike for anything approaching a constitutional system of government, before the War the Emperor interfered but little with the normal working of the Duma. The immense outburst of public activity, free from the fetters of bureaucracy, which took place during the War was a move in a direction of which he strongly disapproved. And this led to conflicts and mutual distrust.

Two other important influences must be mentioned here: the Emperor's devotion to his family, and especially to his wife, which created in the Imperial court an atmosphere of artificial isolation and aloofness, and his profound piety. Both must be taken into account because they made possible the immense growth of the influence of the Empress and brought to the steps of the throne a long *cortège* of most unexpected people, headed by the notorious Rasputin.

Shy and reserved in his relations with those not belonging to his small and intimate circle, Nicholas II found relaxation only among the members of his family. In his letters to the Empress written during the War, to which we shall have to make frequent reference, he speaks continuously of his desire to return home and spend a quiet evening with his wife and children. The unfortunate effect of this excessive devotion to his family was

[5] Evidence of Golovin in *Padenie Tsarskago Rezhima*, V, 372–373.
[6] *Monarkhya Pered Krusheniem (Monarchy Before Its Downfall)* papers of Nicholas II and other documents edited by V. P. Semennikov, Moscow-Leningrad, 1927, p. 92.
[7] *Ibid.*, pp. 94–95; also evidence of Maklakov in *Padenie Tsarskago Rezhima*, V, 195 *sqq.*, and evidence of Rodziankoin *ibid.*, VII, 148.

his estrangement from not only the broad masses of his people, but even from the higher bureaucracy and aristocracy which formed the upper levels of the society of the capital. "The characteristic feature of the Imperial family," wrote Protopopov who, for a time, was very close to the court of Tsarskoe Selo,[8] "is their inaccessibility to the outside world and their atmosphere of mysticism."

It also seems that it was the Emperor's habit to permit the members of his *entourage* to discuss with him nothing but matters relating to the activities of which they had the immediate charge. Such is the evidence of General Dubensky who spent a considerable time at Imperial Headquarters and had excellent opportunities to observe the Emperor. He found, for instance, that no conversation dealing with problems of general importance was tolerated at the Emperor's table: "One could merely answer questions."[9] On the other hand, some of the higher officials whose duty it was to keep the Emperor well informed not infrequently refrained from communicating to him news of a disturbing nature. Guchkov, the well-known leader of the Octobrist Party and former President of the Third Duma, whose evidence on this point is of particular value, gives several interesting instances of the complete ignorance of the actual situation in which the Sovereign was intentionally kept by men holding responsible offices.[10] The result was that the Emperor was entirely out of touch with the general trend of public opinion and had to depend for his information and guidance on the small circle that had grown up at Tsarskoe Selo around the Empress Alexandra Feodorovna.

The Empress

Few historical figures have passed off the stage leaving behind so great a train of disaster and suffering as the last Empress of Russia. It would almost seem as if some merciless fate, not unlike one of the terrible deities of Greek tragedy, were following her every movement and feeling, and turning them to the worst possible advantage. An ardent believer in the Orthodox Church, a devoted mother and wife, a righteous Empress dreaming of nothing but the happiness of her people, a faithful ally— the Tsaritsa became one of the instruments that undermined the Church, brought unparalleled misery and finally death to her children and husband, broke down the autocratic system of

---

[8] Evidence of Protopopov in *Padenie Tsarskago Rezhima*, IV, 9.
[9] Evidence of Dubensky in *Padenie Tsarskago Rezhima*, VI, 396–397.
[10] Evidence of Guchkov in *Padenie Tsarskago Rezhima*, VI, 256–258; also evidence of Rodzianko in *ibid.*, VII, 126.

which she was so staunch a supporter, and necessitated the conclusion of a separate peace with the enemy.

Born in Germany and brought up at Kensington Palace by her grandmother, Queen Victoria, the consort of Nicholas I found in the mystical traditions of the Russian court a favorable ground for the development of the religious exaltation of her nature, an exaltation made up of a singular mixture of German romanticism, English puritanism, and Russian autocracy. Still more than Nicholas II did the Empress hate liberalism and believe in the mystical union of the autocrat of All the Russias with the people, blessed by the Orthodox Church. The strength and simplicity of the Empress' faith was most striking, but it often degenerated into superstition. "Faith and religion play such a strong part in my life," she wrote to the Emperor in April, 1916,[11] "... and the love of Christ too—and it has always been so closely linked with our lives these twenty-two years. First the question of taking the orthodox faith and then our two friends[12] sent to us by God."

This religious fervor and mysticism, coupled with her ardent desire for the heir that was so long refused to her, opened the door for the advances of unscrupulous adventurers who took advantage of the simple faith of the Emperor and the Empress to achieve their personal aims. Rasputin was only one of several "men of God," as the Empress called them, who gained admittance to the Imperial court.[13] The reason for his extraordinary influence is well known. The long-hoped-for heir, the Grand Duke Alexis, proved a terrible disappointment. The child was suffering from a rare and incurable disease—haemophilia—which manifests itself in severe bleeding at the slightest bruise. The disease was one found in the male line of the House of Hesse, and the boy Alexis owed it to his mother. It is easy to imagine how tragic a discovery this was for the Empress. Rasputin who, we are told, was endowed with considerable hypnotic powers, and had even, according to Beletsky, been trained by a professional medium,[14] succeeded on several occasions in stopping the bleeding when the resources of science had been powerless. He was naturally held by the mystically-inclined and superstitious Empress to be the savior, the "man of God" sent by

[11] *The Letters of the Tsaritsa to the Tsar 1914–1916*, with an introduction by Sir Bernard Pares, London, 1923, p. 321. The language used by the Emperor and the Empress was English. In spite of the Empress' excellent command of the spoken language, her grammar and spelling were defective and the wording sometimes very quaint.
[12] M. Philippe and Rasputin.
[13] M. V. Rodzianko, *The Reign of Rasputin: an Empire's Collapse*, London, 1927, Chapter I; also evidence of Beletsky in *Padenie Tsarskago Rezhima*, IV, 499 sqq.
[14] Evidence of Beletsky in *Padenie Tsarskago Rezhima*, IV, 501.

Providence to protect the life of the future Emperor of Holy Russia. The Empress seems to have had a real *idée fixe* that his removal would mean the death of her boy.[15] The very coarseness of Rasputin's manners, his complete lack of education, his obscure pronouncements and messages, which often made little sense to any ordinary person, only increased his prestige in the eyes of his Imperial patrons. Even the protests which were raised at his presence in the palace and his shameful and disgraceful behavior contributed to that aura of martyr and saint with which the imagination of the Empress surrounded him. "Last night Gospels," she wrote to the Tsar,[16] "made me think so vividly of Gregory [Rasputin] and his prosecution for Christ and our sakes—everything had a double meaning." He was held to be the living embodiment of the third element of the sacred formula: orthodoxy, autocracy, and nationality. He personified the Russian people, uneducated and coarse, but divinely inspired and devoted to the throne.

At the beginning Rasputin's influence was not felt in public affairs, and it was only in the years immediately preceding the War that he began to attract a great deal of public attention. This was, especially, in connection with certain scandals in church administration in which he took a prominent part. The matter went so far that there was an interpellation in the Duma, and Guchkov delivered a speech discussing Rasputin's activities, which the Empress never forgave.[17] Nevertheless, in spite of Rasputin's presence in the palace and the reflection it undoubtedly cast upon the dynasty and the whole *régime*, his influence in politics remained practically negligible until the outbreak of the War, or to be more exact, until the assumption by the Emperor of the command of the army, which took place in August, 1915. It was only as a result of the new situation created by the War that he grew into a factor of national importance, and his doings and opinions acquired an interest and significance which relegated to the background even the struggle against Germany.

The Problem of the High Command

The command of the army was a question in which the Emperor was deeply interested. His general conception of the duties of kingship naturally included that of army leader in a national emergency. Old Goremykin told the Council of Min-

[15] Evidence of Dzhunkovsky in *Padenie Tsarskago Rezhima*, V, 106.
[16] *Letters of the Tsaritsa to the Tsar* p. 321.
[17] Rodzianko, *The Reign of Rasputin: an Empire's Collapse*, Chaps. II and III; also evidence of Guchkov in *Padenie Tsarskago Rezhima*, VI, 250–252.

isters that the Emperor "had never forgiven himself for not having led the army in the Japanese War."[18] And there seems to be evidence to show that he seriously contemplated this step at the outbreak of the Great War.[19] Better counsels however prevailed at that time, and he was persuaded to remain in Petrograd and appoint the Grand Duke Nicholas Nikolaevich Commander-in-Chief.[20] However unfortunate this choice may have been, it probably was unavoidable, and it certainly was better than exposing the sovereign to the consequences of being immediately responsible for the conduct of a war, the issue of which was still highly problematical. And then it was fully understood by the Council of Ministers that the departure of the Tsar for the army would mean a further disorganization of the machinery of the Government, already sorely tried by the War. It was realized that the place left vacant in Petrograd must be filled by somebody, and that the absence of the Emperor would result in an immense increase in the influence of the Empress and her friends, especially Rasputin.[21] This is exactly what happened.

The decision of the Emperor to assume the command of the army may be traced, on the one hand, to his own conception of the duties of the sovereign, and, on the other, to the influence of the Tsaritsa, whose grasp upon him seems to have increased with the progress of the War. It will be remembered that the first year of hostilities ended for Russia with heavy military reverses. If the terrible losses in East Prussia did not come entirely as a surprise to the High Command, and the whole operation was undertaken for the avowed purpose of relieving the pressure on Paris—a purpose which was achieved, at a terrible price, it is true—the same cannot be said of the advance of the Russian troops in Galicia. This rash and unfortunate operation by an army which was sadly lacking in munitions of war certainly added little to the reputation of the military leaders behind the line. Its moral effects upon the country were disastrous. There was always a kind of vague and sentimental feeling in Russia for the Slavs living under the Austrian "yoke." And their "liberation" by Russian troops was received with immense enthusiasm, which turned into bitter disappointment when all

[18] A. N. Yakhontov, *Tyazhelie Dni (Fateful Days)*, minutes of the secret sessions of the Council of Ministers from July 15 to September 2, 1915, published in *Arkhiv Russkoi Revolutsii (Archive of the Russian Revolution)*, (Berlin, 1926), XVIII, 54 (*see below*, p. 72, n. 1); also evidence of Rodzianko in *Padenie Tsarskago Rezhima*, VII, 118.

[19] Yakhontov, *op. cit.*, p. 54.

[20] *See below*, pp. 194 *sqq.*

[21] Evidence of Prince Shcherbatov in *Padenie Tsarskago Rezhima*, VII, 220.

the conquered territory had to be abandoned to the enemy. The general policies of the High Command were open to serious criticism. These considerations alone, one will readily admit, would have been sufficient to revive the Tsar's romantic determination "to be among his troops, and either to lead them to victory, or perish with them."[22]

The Attitude of the Empress

But there was also the second influence which we have mentioned and which undoubtedly had an important part in bringing the Emperor's fateful decision, the influence of the Empress. A woman of delicate health who suffered from a weak heart, she took an immediate and active part in war work. Some of the Imperial residences were converted into hospitals, and the Empress and her daughters did the actual nursing, being present even at operations. Alexandra Feodorovna also directed the work of the various charitable organizations, such as the Red Cross, the relief of prisoners of war, etc. This unaccustomed physical exertion coupled with the immense anxiety through which everyone had to live in these trying years, an anxiety aggravated in the case of the Empress by a feeling of crushing responsibility, offered a favorable ground for the intensification of that attitude of mystical and religious exaltation to which she was always so strongly inclined. She felt that she had a special mission—that of saving Russia, a mission she was to fulfil under the guidance of the "man of God," Rasputin. She was to safeguard the sacred principle of autocracy which was menaced from all sides. Her suspicions and apprehensions centered upon the Grand Duke Nicholas Nikolaevich. His popularity with the army, she imagined, might prove a real danger to the throne or, at least, to its present occupant. "Forgive me," she wrote to the Emperor in April, 1915,[23] ". . . but you know you are too kind and gentle . . . be more decided and sure of yourself—you know perfectly well what is right, and when you do not agree and are right, bring your opinion to the front and let it weigh against the rest. They must remember more who you are and that first they must turn to you. Your being charms

[22] Yakhontov, *op. cit.*, p. 54. It may be interesting in this connection to quote Professor Joseph Redlich on the Emperor Francis Joseph's decision to lead his troops in 1858: "For the young Emperor to lead his troops in person in great battles that loomed ahead was a matter of simple duty. The immense responsibility he had assumed was, for him, overshadowed by his sense of the obligation of the supreme war lord of sharing the dangers of the fray with his officers and men. Such sense does him honor as an officer, but again reveals a lack of any profounder comprehension of his position as a sovereign." (Redlich, *Francis Joseph of Austria*, New York, 1929, p. 265.)

[23] *Letters of the Tsaritsa to the Tsar*, p. 62.

every single one, but I want you to hold them by your brain and experience. Though Nikolasha [the Grand Duke Nicholas Nikolaevich] is highly placed, you are above him. The same thing shocked our Friend [Rasputin], as me too, that Nikolasha words his telegrams, answers to governors, etc., in your style—his ought to be more simple and humble and other things." The idea of the Emperor not being sufficiently autocratic is a dominating note in the Empress' letters. "Remember that you are the Emperor,"[24] "if you could only be severe . . . it is so necessary,"[25] "be more autocratic . . . show your mind."[26] "You are and must remain autocratic Emperor, we are not ready for a constitutional government,"[27]—such are the counsels which were daily sent to the Tsar. On the other hand, the dislike of the Grand Duke appears more and more clearly. "I have absolutely no faith in N. [Nicholas Nikolaevich]," the Empress wrote on June 16, 1915,[28]—"I know him to be far from clever and having gone against a man of God; his work cannot be blessed, nor his advice be good." And she is still more outspoken on June 25 when she writes that "Nikolasha knows my will, and fears my influence (guided by Gregory) upon you; it is so clear."[29]

These exhortations fell on ground which was already well prepared, and although the references to the Grand Duke Nicholas Nikolaevich made by the Tsar are invariably friendly[30] he nevertheless decided to assume the command of the army, and stuck to his decision with the obstinacy which was typical of him. On August 23, 1915, he took over the supreme command from the Grand Duke. On this occasion he received from the Empress a letter which is a highly eloquent and characteristic document: ". . . You showing your mastery, proving yourself the autocrat without whom Russia cannot exist . . .," she wrote on August 22.[31] "It will be a glorious page in your reign and Russian history . . . and God who is just and near you will save your country and throne through your firmness. . . . God anointed you at your coronation, he placed you where you stand and you have done your duty, be sure, quite sure of this. . . . Those who fear and cannot understand your actions will be brought by events to realize your great wisdom. . . . All is for

[24] Ibid., p. 79.
[25] Ibid., p. 86.
[26] Ibid., p. 94.
[27] Ibid., p. 100.
[28] Ibid., p. 97.
[29] Ibid., p. 111.
[30] The Letters of the Tsar to the Tsaritsa, pp. 26, 43, 54, 61, 71.
[31] Letters of the Tsaritsa to the Tsar, pp. 114–115.

the good as our Friend says, the worst is over." And the Emperor answered this message with an affectionate letter in which he said that he took up "this new heavy responsibility" with a feeling like the one he had after Holy Communion. "I know of no more pleasant feeling," he wrote,[32] "than to be proud of you, as I have been all these past months when you urged me on with untiring importunity, exhorting me to be firm and to stick to my own opinions." And he remarked that "a new clean page begins, and only God Almighty knows what will be written on it!"

The Aspirations of the Empress

A "new clean page" was indeed open, but it brought little of that glory the Empress was expecting. We have already said that the immense strain of the War provided favorable ground for the development of the state of morbid religious ecstasy in which the Empress was living. Now that the country and the throne were in danger they certainly needed, more than ever, divine protection and divine guidance. And she was sure that both were dispensed through the instrumentality of Rasputin. Her letters to the Tsar are full of references to "our Friend," and the few instances we are quoting here will give an idea how complete was her faith in him. "Hearken unto our Friend," the Empress wrote on June 10, 1915,[33] "believe him, he has your interest and Russia's at heart—it is not for nothing God sent him to us—only we must pay more attention to what he says, his words are not lightly spoken, and the gravity [?] of having not only his prayers but his advice is great." "You remember," she wrote a few days later,[34] "dans *Les Amis de Dieu* it says a country cannot be lost whose sovereign is guided by a man of God. Oh, let him [Rasputin] guide you more." "I fully believe in our Friend's words that the glory of your reign is coming, ever since you stuck to your decision, against everybody's wish—and we see the good results."[35] And as time went on the unbounded confidence of the Empress in her prophet was if possible growing. "Do listen to him [Rasputin]," she writes on September 7, 1916,[36] "who only wants your good and whom God has given more insight, wisdom and enlightenment than all the military put together. His love for you and Russia is so intense and God has sent him to be your help and guide

[32] *The Letters of the Tsar to the Tsaritsa*, pp. 70–72.
[33] *Letters of the Tsaritsa to the Tsar*, pp. 86–87.
[34] *Ibid.*, p. 100.
[35] *Ibid.*, p. 167.
[36] *Ibid.*, p. 394.

and he prays so hard for you." "How I wish," she writes on October 12, 1916,[37] "you could have come for two days only, just to have got our Friend's blessing, it would have given you new strength—I know you are brave and patient, but human, and a touch of his on your chest would have soothed much pain and given you new wisdom and energy from above, these are no idle words, but firm convictions."

So long as the religious exaltation of the Empress manifested itself merely in sending ikons to the soldiers, attending church services, burning candles, and presenting the Emperor with such valuable talismans as a cane or a comb first used by Rasputin,[38] a bottle of wine from his birthday celebration to drink his health with "as we did,"[39]—there was no special ground for alarm. But with the departure of the Emperor to Headquarters at the end of August, 1915, the energies of the Empress were directed into a new channel. She was no longer satisfied with suggesting such relatively innocent measures as the organization of church processions[40] or the passing on of Rasputin's illiterate telegrams, messages, and blessings.[41] Her new rôle appeared to her "to be the medicine of the muddled minds after the microbes from town [Petrograd],"[42] and also the supreme adviser and guide (with the help of Rasputin) of the autocrat of All the Russias. The more servile among the ministers immediately scented the change and hastened to fall in with it. "Poor old man [Goremykin] came to me," writes the Empress on September 7, 1915,[43] "as a *soutien* and because he says I am *l'énergie*." "Try to heed to what I say," she writes two days later,[44] "it is not my wisdom, but a certain instinct given by God beyond myself so as to be your help. . . . I long to poke my nose into everything . . . to wake people up, put order into all, and unite all forces." As may be easily imagined, this interference was far from meeting with general approval and bringing about the union of all forces that the Empress was hoping for. "Some are afraid I am meddling in state affairs (the Ministers)," the Empress wrote on September 17,[45] "and others look upon me as the one to help as you are not here (Andronikov, Khvostov, Varnava, and some others). That shows who is devoted to you in the real sense of

[37] *Ibid.*, p. 421.
[38] *Ibid.*, pp. 94, 117.
[39] *Ibid.*, p. 262.
[40] *Ibid.*, pp. 90–91, 96, 97–98, 111.
[41] *Ibid.*, pp. 35, 50, 346.
[42] *Ibid.*, p. 138.
[43] *Ibid.*, p. 145.
[44] *Ibid.*, pp. 152–153.
[45] *Ibid.*, p. 171.

the word—they will seek me out and the other will avoid me—
is it not true?"

The Effacement of the Tsar

These extravagant ambitions of the Empress met with no
opposition on the part of the Tsar. Not only does he read the
messages of Rasputin, drink to his health from the little bottle
"to the last drop,"[46] visit holy ikons,[47] and eat the apple given
to the Empress by an aged nun ("found it excellent"),[48] but
what is infinitely more important seems genuinely relieved to
have the burden of government shifted from his weak shoulders
to those of his exalted and determined consort. In a letter dated
August 25, 1915, written immediately after the Tsar assumed
the leadership of the army, he makes a direct appeal to the
Tsaritsa:[49] "Will you not come to the assistance of your hubby
now that he is absent? What a pity that you have not been
fulfilling this duty long ago or at least during the War." "Yes,
truly," he writes on September 23, 1916,[50] "you ought to be my
eyes and ears there in the capital, while I have to stay here.
It rests with you to keep peace and harmony among the ministers—thereby you do a great service to me and to our country. . . . I am so happy to think that you have found at last a
worthy occupation! Now I shall naturally be calm, and at least
need not worry over internal affairs." And again next day: "You
will really help me a great deal by speaking to the ministers and
watching them."[51] "I read and re-read your dear letter many
times, especially that part in which you tell of your conversation
with Sturmer and Protopopov," writes the Emperor on November 1, 1916.[52] "There is nothing to forgive you for, on the
contrary, I must be deeply grateful to you for so far advancing
this serious matter by your help."

This attitude of the Emperor is in part puzzling because he
did not seem to share the unbounded faith of the Empress in
the divine guidance of Rasputin. No doubt, he was himself
under the influence of the latter; but we nevertheless find certain
indications that the "man of God" did not enjoy his full confidence. On two or three occasions he communicates military
news to the Empress with the explicit provision that it is exclu-

---

[46] *The Letters of the Tsar to the Tsaritsa*, p. 136.
[47] *Ibid.*, p. 192.
[48] *The Letters of the Tsar to the Tsaritsa*, p. 309.
[49] *Ibid.*, pp. 71–72.
[50] *Ibid.*, p. 269.
[51] *Ibid.*, p. 270.
[52] *Ibid.*, p. 289.

sively for her own information and should not be communicated to anyone, not even to "our Friend."[53] And in one of his letters he goes so far as to suggest that "our Friend's opinions of people are sometimes very strange."[54] The real explanation of the Emperor's attitude lies probably, on the one hand, in his complete devotion to his wife, whose will undoubtedly dominated him, and on the other in his recognition of the fact that he knew little or nothing of some of the problems he had to deal with. "I never was a business man and simply do not understand anything in these questions of supplying and provisioning," he frankly admits.[55] His approach to the problems of statecraft was remarkably naïve. Liberal reforms and the expansion of local government were naturally entirely out of the question. It was taken for granted that the system itself was perfectly sound. The only method therefore of solving the immense difficulties raised by the War, difficulties which could not be denied, was to be sought in entrusting the control of the Government to the right men. The Emperor was continually complaining of the lack of men,[56] and the Empress endeavored to help him make the important discovery that would cure all evils.

The Empress at the Helm

We know already that the Empress was only too anxious to replace her husband at the helm of the ship of State, in full agreement with his own wishes. Her motives were perfectly sincere and, from her own point of view, highly honorable. "We have been placed by God on a throne," she writes on December 14, 1916,[57] "and we must keep it firm and give it over to our son untouched—if you keep that in mind you will remember to be the sovereign—and how much easier for an autocratic sovereign than for one who has a constitution." And the Empress was firmly convinced that her views were shared by those people who constituted real Russia. "Why do people hate me?" she asks in a letter of December 4, 1916.[58] "Because they know I have a strong will and when I am convinced of a thing being right (when besides blessed by Gregory) do not change my mind and that they can't bear. But it's the bad ones . . . those who are good and devoted to you honestly and purely love me, look at the simple people and the military."

Strong in this belief, with the divinely-inspired support of

[53] *Ibid.*, pp. 200, 202–203, 270.
[54] *Ibid.*, pp. 256–257.
[55] *Ibid.*, p. 266.
[56] *Ibid.*, pp. 145, 246–247, 248.
[57] *Letters of the Tsaritsa to the Tsar*, p. 456; *see also* pp. 440–441.
[58] *Ibid.*, pp. 442–443.

Rasputin, and the further support of the complaisant and encouraging attitude of the Emperor himself, the Tsaritsa proceeded to use her influence to remove all members of the Cabinet of whom she did not approve. She seems to have completely overcome that shyness which sometimes used to make intercourse with her difficult.[59] "I am no longer the slightest bit shy or afraid of ministers and speak like a waterfall in Russian!" she writes to the Tsar on September 22, 1916.[60]

The burden of the Imperial displeasure was first felt by the ministers who opposed the Emperor's plan to take command of the army. And all who did not show sufficient willingness blindly to accept the guidance of the "man of God" were summarily dismissed and replaced by certain extraordinary individuals whose presence in high offices in time of war was not only a disgraceful scandal but also a national danger. More will be said of this in the next chapter. It may suffice here to say that after the middle of 1915 the fairly honorable and efficient group who formed the top of the bureaucratic pyramid degenerated into a rapidly changing succession of the appointees of Rasputin. It was an amazing, extravagant, and pitiful spectacle, and one without parallel in the history of civilized nations.

As to the leaders of the Duma, the zemstvos, and the semi-official organizations, such as the war industries committees, they were simply considered to be criminals. The news of the illness of Guchkov filled the Empress with joy.[61] And she bluntly suggested that Prince Lvov, Miliukov, Guchkov, and Polivanov should all be sent to Siberia![62]

The ministers, including those who had received the sanction of Rasputin, continued to feel the directing hand of the Empress even when they visited Headquarters. In a letter of September 27, 1916, the Empress sends her husband a list of six questions which he is to discuss with Protopopov, the new Minister of the Interior, and she indicates in certain cases what he is to tell him.[63] This procedure does not seem to have appeared to the Emperor as unusual. In his account of the interview with Protopopov he tells her: "Your little list with the questions was before me"; and he adds rather apologetically that he did not touch upon one of the questions: "It was getting late, and the guests in the other room were very noisy!"[64]

[59] See for instance Sir John Hanbury-Williams, The Emperor Nicholas II as I Knew Him (London, 1922), pp. 92–93; also Maurice Paléologue, La Russie des Tsars pendant la guerre (Paris, 1921), I, 5, 18–19.
[60] Letters of the Tsaritsa to the Tsar, p. 409.
[61] Ibid., pp. 250, 252, 257.
[62] Ibid., p. 456.
[63] Ibid., pp. 416–417.
[64] The Letters of the Tsar to the Tsaritsa, p. 275.

The influence of Rasputin was now extending itself not only into the field of civil government, but was also infringing on purely military matters;[65] and there are reasons to believe that at least on one occasion his advice was followed, although there is still some obscurity here.[66]

It would be an injustice to Nicholas II not to note the fact that he made several attempts to free himself from the effectual tutelage established over him from Petrograd. Some of the appointments were made by him not only without the approval of the Empress, but even against her wishes. A notable instance was the appointment of Samarin as Procurator of the Holy Synod, in 1915, and, at the end of 1916, the appointment of Trepov as President of the Council of Ministers. The Emperor even expressed himself in the latter case with a vigor which was rather out of keeping with his ordinary attitude. "I beg you not to drag our Friend into this," he wrote to the Empress, when referring to Trepov.[67] "The responsibility is with me, and therefore I wish to be free in my choice." But his revolt was short-lived. Both Samarin and Trepov remained in office only for a few weeks, and were replaced by men who enjoyed the confidence of the Empress. With reluctance and regret the student of the political situation in Russia during the War sees himself forced to conclude that by the end of 1916 Rasputin was the undisputed master of the destinies of the country.

Rasputin's Political Views

Little need be said about Rasputin's political views for the simple reason that he had none. An illiterate and depraved peasant, he was incapable of discussing any subject of general interest, and world politics were entirely beyond his grasp. If the question has been raised here at all, it is because the opposite view has occasionally been advanced by competent writers. For instance Rodzianko, the former President of the Duma, who made a very detailed although obviously prejudiced study of the question, stated in an article published in 1922 that "there was not the slightest doubt" that Rasputin and his friends were collaborating with the German general staff.[68] In a publication issued at a later date[69] Rodzianko changed his view so far as to

[65] *Letters of the Tsaritsa to the Tsar,* pp. 377, 379, 382, 411, 412.
[66] *The Letters of the Tsar to the Tsaritsa,* pp. 272–273.
[67] *Ibid.,* p. 298.
[68] M. V. Rodzianko, *Gosudarstvennaya Duma i Fevralskaya 1917 Goda Revolutsya (The Duma and the Revolution of February, 1917),* in *Arkhiv Russkoi Revolutsii,* VI, 44; *see also* evidence of Rodzianko in *Padenie Tsarskago Rezhima,* VII, 128.
[69] Rodzianko, *The Reign of Rasputin: an Empire's Collapse,* pp. 238–240.

admit that Rasputin himself was entirely incapable of holding any political opinions, but he nevertheless maintained that he was a convenient tool of certain sinister agents working for Germany. Rodzianko however produced no evidence to support his contention, and it would seem that the "strict correlation in all the acts of the Rasputinites" which he pretended to have observed was merely the product of his imagination. The less romantic but far more detailed evidence of Beletsky, the former head of the State Police Department, who had exceptional opportunities of learning all about Rasputin, inspires greater confidence.[70] It appears from his narrative that the man's *entourage* consisted merely of the unscrupulous seeking their own personal advantage. Rasputin's influence was due not to his connection with mysterious and powerful German agents, but to the simple fact that he chanced to strike a responsive chord in the heart of the mystically inclined Tsaritsa, and to the medieval conditions existing in the Russian court.

The Fall of the Dynasty

The amazing transformation which the power of the Tsar suffered during the War was, of course, an open secret. Rumors, often cruel and absurd, were freely circulated in all classes of society, from the salons of the grand duchesses and the messrooms of the regiments of the guards down to the remotest corner of the vast realm. Distorted and exaggerated, they were repeated in roadside inns and peasant cottages. In these rumors the name of the Empress was invariably coupled not only with that of Rasputin, whose relations with her were given a color wholly unwarranted, but also with those of her German relatives and of the enemies of Russia in general. There was a firmly established belief in the existence of a pro-German party of which Alexandra Feodorovna was reputed to be the leader. This legend, which is not yet completely dead, seems to have been given some semblance of reality by the large number of officials closely connected with the Imperial household and government circles who bore German names. The influential conservative newspaper *Novoe Vremya* amused itself and its readers by publishing long lists of the members of Russian embassies and by pointing out that in some of them there were to be found either no Russian names, or very few. No consideration was given to the fact that many of the suspected families had been in the service of the Russian Crown for generations,

---

[70] Evidence of Beletsky in *Padenie Tsarskago Rezhima*, IV, 281 *sqq.*, 351 *sqq.*; also evidence of Miliukov in *ibid.*, VI, 356.

and were probably among the most faithful servants of the Tsar. Among them was, for instance, the venerable Count Fredericks, Minister of the Imperial Household since the days of Alexander III. The Tsaritsa herself was almost invariably referred to as *Nemka*—the German—recalling to mind the similar situation of Marie Antoinette, known in her day as *l'Autrichienne*. The foolish policy of prosecuting nonofficial organizations and the Duma was held to be treason to the country. The wave of popular indignation reached its highest point when in November, 1916, open accusations against Sturmer, then Prime Minister, and the Empress herself were made by M. Miliukov from the tribune of the Duma.

It was clear to everyone except the Tsar and the Tsaritsa that the existing situation could not last much longer. Innumerable warnings were given to the Tsar by the President of the Duma, by members of the Imperial family, by representatives of war industries committees and the Unions of Zemstvos and of Towns, even by such conservative bodies as the associations of the nobility and the State Council. But the general demand for a government "enjoying the confidence of the nation" was invariably rejected.

Then in December, 1916, came what must have been for the Empress a crushing blow—the murder of Rasputin in the house of Prince Yusupov, by Purishkevich, a conservative member of the Duma, with the active participation of the Grand Duke Dimitry Pavlovich. The news of the disappearance of the evil spirit of the monarchy was received with feelings of immense relief all over the country, and grew into an event of national importance; but it did little to clear the unbearable atmosphere of the court. Strong in their almost unbelievable ignorance of the world in which they were living, and drawing their inspiration from those small closed circles to which few had access, the Emperor and the Empress moved blindly toward the doom which they had brought upon themselves.

And when, at the end of February, 1917, the Revolution actually came, they found nobody to defend them. With the extraordinary obstinacy of a really weak man the Emperor refused to grant concessions until it was too late. And then, under the pressure of events and on the advice of Rodzianko and the military leaders, he abdicated for himself and his son. His reserve and composure throughout these trying days amazed all those who had an opportunity to observe him. It almost seemed as if he was above ordinary human emotions. On March 3, 1917, the day following his abdication, on the Imperial train which bore him into captivity, he made the following entry in his diary: "I had a long and sound sleep. Woke up beyond Dvinsk. Sunshine and frost. . . . I read much of Julius Caesar."[71]

The rule of the Romanovs had been brought to and end.[72]

Chapter 4

The Breakdown of the Bureaucratic System

Headquarters and the Government

WE HAVE SEEN in Chapter 1 that in the course of the nineteenth century Russia gradually built up a mechanism of bureaucratic government which, while suffering from grave imperfections, was nevertheless fairly efficient and reasonably honest. This especially applied to its upper levels. That a government of this type, lacking, as it does, flexibility and elasticity, finds it extremely difficult to readjust itself to the rapidly changing conditions of a great war is a foregone conclusion. In the case of Russia, however, the inevitable upheaval was aggravated by certain peculiar developments inherent in the conditions of the country. The strain they imposed on the venerable structure based on the reforms of Speransky was far beyond its powers of endurance. The result was that a process of rapid disintegration set in that eventually led to its complete collapse.

[71] *Dnevnik Nikolaya Romanova (The Diary of Nicholas Romanov)* in *Krasni Arkhiv (Red Archive)*, Moscow-Leningrad, XX, 137.

[72] The account given in these pages about the rôle of the Emperor and the Empress in the collapse of the monarchy under the strain of the War may appear too harsh and unsympathetic. This may be due to the fact that we have intentionally limited ourselves to those aspects of the character of the Tsar and the Tsaritsa which had a direct and immediate bearing upon the political and social development of Russia. There is no task less pleasant than to be forced to pass a severe judgment upon a man whose mistakes, due to honest aberrations, have been paid for in terrible sufferings and a most tragic death. There is no doubt at all that for the concerns of private life Nicholas II and his wife were endowed with an unusually large share of high moral qualities. Nowhere were these displayed with greater dignity, and at no time did they command greater respect, than during the period which followed the Emperor's abdication. An eloquent story of the ordeal of the Imperial family after the Revolution will be found in Count Paul Benckendorff, *Last Days of Tsarskoe Selo* (London, 1927), and in Pierre Gilliard's excellent volume, *Le tragique destin de Nicholas II* (Paris, 1922). An account of the murders at Ekaterinburg is supplied by N. Sokoloff, *Enquête judiciaire sur l'assassinat de la Famille Impériale Russe* (Paris, 1924), and by Robert Wilton, *The Last Days of the Romanovs* (London, 1920).

One of the most important factors, one which deeply undermined the position of the Cabinet, was the lack of a definite line of demarcation between the powers of the military and civilian authorities. The "Law Dealing with the Administration of the Army in the Field in Time of War" which regulated this relationship was hastily enacted during the crisis, and received the Imperial sanction virtually on the eve of the general mobilization, on July 16 (29), 1914. In accordance with the provisions of this Law, the territory adjoining the front, as also the whole area where auxiliary army organizations were located, was exempted from the jurisdiction of the civilian authorities, and was put under the control of the Commander-in-Chief, who was responsible to the Emperor alone. The civilian authorities in the "military zone" which, with the retreat of the Russian army in 1915, included a considerable part of the Empire and extended even to the city of Petrograd, were to take their orders from the representatives of the military Headquarters and were not permitted even to question their legality. Similar powers were vested in the general officers commanding separate "fronts." They included the power of dismissing all members of the civilian administration employed whether by the central government, or by the zemstvos and municipalities. While conferring these wide and important powers upon the Commander-in-Chief and the principal military officers, the Law of July 16 contained no provision as to the relationship between the military and the civilian authorities. The Council of Ministers and its President were not even mentioned in the Law, and no indication was given as to how questions of national importance which might arise within the territory controlled by the Commander-in-Chief should be settled. The military authorities were not obliged to communicate to the respective ministers the measures they deemed it necessary to enact, and the latter were confronted with a mere *fait accompli*, thus excluding the very possibility of a coherent and comprehensive policy.[1]

[1] A. N. Yakhontov, *Tyazhelie Dni (Fateful Days)*, minutes of the secret sessions of the Council of Ministers from July 15 to September 2, 1915, in *Arkhiv Russkoi Revolutsii*, XVIII, 10, quoting a memorandum presented to the Council of Ministers by M. Lodizhensky; *ibid.*, p. 17; also evidence of Rodzianko in *Padenie Tsarskago Rezhima*, VII, 118 *sqq.* The semiofficial minutes published by M. Yakhontov, assistant secretary to the Council of Ministers, are among the most interesting and important documents dealing with Russia's war government. M. Yakhontov attended, in his official capacity, the meetings of the Council of Ministers, and assisted his chief, I. N. Lodizhensky, secretary general of the Council, in preparing the minutes or, as they were officially described, the "Journal" of the deliberations of the Council, a document which was always read at the following meeting, was signed by the members, and submitted to the Emperor. Realizing the immense importance of the discussions that took place before him, M. Yakhontov did not limit himself to a purely formal *résumé* of the proceedings; he also took very detailed notes of

The wide powers given by the Law of July 16 to the Commander-in-Chief were used without discrimination and inevitably led not only to bitter conflicts between the military and the civilian authorities, but also to complete confusion. The memorandum of M. Lodizhensky submitted to the Council of Ministers in the summer of 1915 gives the following highly interesting and characteristic instance.

Without the previous knowledge of the Council of Ministers [says the memorandum], a number of measures were carried out [by Headquarters] dealing with the deportation to the interior of German settlers and Jews, and also imposing upon them the duty of providing hostages. The attention of the chief of staff of the army has been drawn to the opinion of the Council of Ministers that the application of such wholesale measures against the Jews was inadmissible from the point of view of internal peace; and that such measures must produce an unfavorable effect abroad and create obstacles to our borrowing in foreign markets. The chief of staff, on the other hand, has instructed the chief of his civilian chancery ... to inform the secretary general of the Council of Ministers that "all repressive measures taken against the Jews, who had sufficiently proved their antagonism to the interests of our country" were considered by General Yanushkevich to be "very mild" and that he would not hesitate to use much more rigorous methods. ... Neither the economic condition of the destitute Jews with all its consequences for the population of the localities where they finally settled down, nor the reaction of public opinion in Allied countries, nor even the

---

the speeches delivered, and sought to preserve their individual character as well as the general atmosphere of the debate. He succeeded to an extraordinary degree, and in the vast mass of documents, memoirs, and various publications dealing with the approaching downfall of hte Empire his account stands out as a source of primary importance. The taking of detailed notes of the impassioned and often not too orderly debates of the Council was in itself no mean achievement, and in performing this difficult task M. Yakhontov has given another evidence of that keen sense of duty and comprehension of historical values not uncommon among the higher Russian bureaucracy. We have another example of it in the so-called "Diary" of the Russian Ministry of Foreign Affairs prepared by Baron M. Schilling, *chef de cabinet* of M. Sazonov, which is familiar to all students of the question of responsibility for the War (*How the War Began in 1914*, being the diary of the Russian Foreign Office with a Foreword by S. D. Sazonov and an Introduction by Baron M. F. Schilling [London, 1925]). But while the records of Baron Schilling remained at the Ministry of Foreign Affairs in Petrograd and, as we are told by Baron Schilling, only a few of them have been published by the Soviet Government and subsequently translated into foreign languages (a new instalment of Baron Schilling's records covering the years 1915–1916 was published in *Krasni Arkhiv*, vols. XXXI–XXXII), M. Yakhontov succeeded in taking his notes abroad and edited them himself, a work for which he deserves the gratitude of the historians. The accuracy of his narrative has never been questioned by the many actors of the events he describes who are still alive and residing outside Russia. On the contrary, we are told by M. Yakhontov (p. 8) that several former members of the Council of Ministers, who were given an opportunity to read his account before it was published, expressed their satisfaction and approval in very flattering terms. M. Yakhontov's account will frequently be quoted hereafter, and it is the author's sincere regret that it cannot be reproduced in full.

opinion of financial circles, which were largely influenced by the Jews, but the practical difficulties which were inevitably encountered by the civilian authorities in carrying out this mass deportation of the Jews formed a real obstacle to the further extension of the policy of repressions.[2]

We shall have another opportunity to discuss the policy of Headquarters toward the Jews and the enforced removal of the population from the front-line zone in general, a policy which was inspired by the criminal folly of reënacting the "retreat of 1812" and leaving to the enemy a desert.[3] The instance given above illustrates the manner in which Headquarters looked upon suggestions from the Council of Ministers for dealing with questions of national importance.

The Russian method of settling difficulties by appointing military officials with practically unlimited powers was freely used from the very beginning of the War. An instance of its effect upon the general war organizations of the country may be found in the nomination of the aged Prince Alexander P Oldenburg (he was seventy in 1914) as head of the Army Medical Service. General Sukhomlinov, Minister of War in 1909–1915, makes the following comments on this appointment in his letters to his close friend, General Yanushkevich, chief of staff of the army. "The appointment of Prince Oldenburg," he wrote on September 7, 1914,[4] "has here [in Petrograd] produced a most unfavorable impression; the general feeling is that now disorder will reign supreme in the rear and that a breakdown is unavoidable." Prince Oldenburg, who confessed that he was "old" and his memory "rather weak," while General Belaev described his conversation as "raving,"[5] was endowed with immense if rather erratic energy. He firmly believed in the theory that "with good will everything can be done in an hour."[6] His sudden appearance in most unexpected places, his utter contempt for railway schedules and the orders of the Minister of Transport coupled with a rather violent temper succeeded, if we are to believe Sukhomlinov, in "uniting everyone against him" —and this a few weeks after the outbreak of the War! It was thus that he achieved his chief purpose of bringing about "general coöperation." The only course open to the Minister of Transport, Sukhomlinov suggested, was to ask the Prince to take over the management of his department.[7]

[2] Yakhontov, op. cit., pp. 11–12.
[3] See below, pp. 197 sqq.
[4] Perepiska V. A. Sukhomlinova (Correspondence of V. A. Sukhomlinov) in Krasni Arkhiv, I, 244.
[5] Ibid., p. 244.
[6] Ibid., p. 246.
[7] Ibid., p. 256; see also ibid. in Krasni Arkhiv, II, 161, and III, 30.

By the middle of the summer of 1915, that is, on the eve of the assumption of the command of the army by the Emperor which, it will be remembered, was a turning point in the war history of Russia, the divorce between the military authorities and the Cabinet was complete. The account of M. Yakhontov gives a very clear idea of the feelings of the ministers. At the meeting of the Council on July 16, 1915, complaints were made that the Commander of the Sixth Army, whose jurisdiction included the City of Petrograd, had issued orders dealing with the most essential aspects of the life of the capital without even bringing them to the notice of the Council of Ministers or of the Minister of the Interior. This led to a memorable discussion in which the position of the Cabinet was clearly stated. "Disorganization is assuming such proportions," said A. V. Krivoshein, Minister of Agriculture, "that one begins to fear for the future. Sometimes while listening to local reports one imagines one-self in a lunatic asylum." This view is fully shared by his colleague at the Ministry of the Interior, Prince Shcherbatov.

> My brief experience at the Ministry of the Interior[8] [he said], has led me to the conclusion that the present situation cannot last. The governors of provinces deluge me with requests and telegrams depicting the impossible position created by the military authorities. Their slightest objections are met with severe rebukes and threats,— sometimes, of imprisonment. It is impossible to find out whose orders should be executed. They come from everywhere and are often contradictory. The result is complete confusion and disorganization.[9]

Prince Shakhovskoy, Minister of Commerce and Industry, emphasized the grievances of his department.

> It is particularly important [he said] to put an end to the extravaganzas of Headquarters in dealing with labor. While accusing industrialists of slackness, of neglecting to increase output, and of giving more attention to private gain than to patriotic duty, the military authorities employ at the same time methods of terror against the workers. At the slightest misunderstanding they make use of courts martial, armed force, the suspension of exemptions from military service, and other penalties. Insignificant squabbles are exaggerated into almost revolutionary events.

And S. V. Rukhlov, a staunch conservative and Minister of Transport, added his voice to the general chorus when he stated that "all plans, arrangements, and schemes were destroyed by

[8] June–September, 1915.
[9] Yakhontov, *op. cit.*, pp. 18–19.

the interference of some soldier of the rear." "However great may be the genius of the chief of staff of the army [Yanush-kevich]," declared Krivoshein, "he nevertheless cannot replace the Council of Ministers or, as things are now, the whole machinery of the government of the Russian Empire."[10]

These quotations will suffice to give an idea of the relationship which existed between the Cabinet and Headquarters. Undoubtedly similar problems arose in other countries, especially in France, but seldom do we find elsewhere a statement like the one made by Prince Shcherbatov at the meeting of the Council of Ministers of August 11, 1915.

> I have repeatedly drawn the attention of the Council to the fact [he said][11] that even in Petrograd, the capital of the Empire, which sets the example for the whole country, the Minister of the Interior is a mere "man in the street" who is permitted to act only so far as this does not interfere with the fanciful orders of the military authorities.

And when the Minister of War informed the Council that Headquarters was busy preparing a plan for the extension of the "military zone" to the line of Tver-Tula, the same minister exclaimed:

> The rear of the "theatre of war" presents a revolting picture of anarchy, lawlessness, and paralysis of power. We cannot allow the central provinces to be torn to pieces by the "red" Danilov [the quartermaster general] and his hordes of heroes of the rear.[12]

It may also be worth noting that in their attitude toward military authority the members of the Cabinet displayed a unanimity which was by no means characteristic of the deliberations of that august body.

The contemptuous and arrogant attitude of the High Command toward the civilian authorities not only created immense difficulties in the carrying out of the functions of government but, what is particularly important in a country of low educational standards like Russia, greatly undermined the prestige of the civilian administration. "Moans about the responsibility of the rear [for general disorganization and military reverses] continue to come from there [Headquarters]," said on July 30, 1915, General Polivanov, Minister of War,[13] "and they are like water on the wheel of the mill of anti-government propaganda."

[10] Yakhontov, *op. cit.*, pp. 20–21.
[11] *Ibid.*, p. 64.
[12] *Ibid.*, p. 73.
[13] *Ibid.*, p. 30.

The Problem of High Command

The decision of the Emperor to assume the leadership of the army took the Council of Ministers entirely by surprise. We have already described the influences which were brought to bear upon him and his own view of the duties of a sovereign. None of the members of the Cabinet was taken into his confidence except the president of the Council, J. L. Goremykin, a man of seventy-five, whom Baron Nolde properly describes as the "worst product of the Russian bureaucracy."[14] The presence of a man of his age, failing health, and antediluvian views at the head of the Government of a vast Empire in time of a national emergency was in itself a condemnation of the whole system. As far back as 1896 Pobedonostsev wrote to Nicholas II that Goremykin needed a rest, otherwise "he would not last throughout the winter."[15] This did not prevent him from heading the Government twenty years later, during the Great War. His conception of his duty toward his country and his sovereign can be best given in his own words:

I am a man of the old school and an Imperial command is for me a law.[16] [And again]: To me His Majesty is the anointed one, the rightful sovereign. He personifies the whole of Russia. He is forty-seven and it is not just since yesterday that he has been reigning and deciding the fate of the Russian people. When the decision of such a man is made and his course of action determined, his faithful subjects must accept it whatever may be the consequences. And then let God's will be fulfilled. These views I have held all my life and with them shall I die.[17] [And again]: In my opinion the will of the Tsar is the will of the Russian people; the Tsar and the Russian people are inseparable.[18]

These views were fully in harmony with those held by Nicholas II and the Empress. Goremykin also kept in constant and intimate touch with Rasputin.[19] Little wonder therefore that he was *persona grata* at the court of Tsarskoe Selo and that the Empress wrote in one of her letters:[20] "He [Goremykin] sees and understands all so clearly, that it is a pleasure speaking to him." This undoubtedly was the reason why of all the ministers

[4] Nolde, *L'ancien régime et la révolution russes*, p. 105.
[5] *Pisma Pobedonostseva k Alexandru III s Prilozheniem Pisem k Velikomu Knyazu Sergeyu Alexsandrovichu i Niko layu II*, II, 316–317.
[6] Yakhontov, *op. cit.*, p. 54.
[7] Yakhontov, *op. cit.*, p. 94.
[8] *Ibid.*, p. 96.
[9] *Letters of the Tsaritsa to the Tsar*, pp. 98, 219.
[10] *Ibid.*, p. 103.

Goremykin alone had been informed of the proposed change in the command of the army.

The news itself was brought to the attention of the Council in a dramatic fashion. At the meeting of August 6, 1915, Polivanov, Minister of War, made his usual report on the conditions at the front. It will be remembered that at that time the Russian army was in full retreat from Galicia.

The situation at the front is getting worse and more complicated [Polivanov said].[21] Under the conditions prevailing at the front and in the rear an irreparable catastrophe may be expected at any time. The army is no longer retreating but simply fleeing. Self-confidence is completely undermined. The slightest rumor about the enemy, the appearance of an insignificant German detachment leads to panic and the flight of whole regiments. The burden of saving the country has been carried thus far exclusively by the artillery which lives up to expectations and is not sparing itself. But its ranks are depleted, munitions are lacking, guns are worn out. Headquarters has completely lost its head. Contradictory orders, absence of a plan, feverish changes of commanding officers, and general confusion upset even the most courageous men. . . . The confusion at Headquarters is no longer a secret and still further demoralizes the army.

After this not too reassuring survey of the military situation Polivanov announced to the Council that he was intentionally breaking his promise to keep silent and intended to disclose an official secret. "I feel it my duty to warn the Cabinet," he said,[22] "that this morning His Majesty informed me of his decision to remove the Grand Duke and to assume in person the leadership of the army." This statement produced general consternation. It must be said here that while the relations between the Government and Headquarters were anything but friendly, the blame for the mismanagement of the army and of the "military zone" was laid at the door of General Yanushkevich, chief of staff of the army, and General Danilov, quartermaster general. The Grand Duke himself was not directly attacked, and he even enjoyed, it would seem, a certain popularity with the ministers. At any rate it was generally realized that his presence at Headquarters was practically unavoidable and that it was infinitely better than the only possible alternative, the one the Emperor had just decided upon.

Continuing his statement Polivanov informed the Council that he had used all his powers to persuade the Emperor to alter his decision.

[21] Yakhontov, *op. cit.*, p. 52.
[22] *Ibid.*, p. 53.

78

I took it upon myself [he said] to emphasize the danger in the sovereign's assuming command of the army at a moment when it is demoralized as a result of continuous reverses and a long retreat. I explained that at the present time the supply of the army is in hopeless condition and that the effects of the measures taken will not be felt for some time. I did not refrain from pointing out the possible consequences in the internal life of the country in case the personal command by the Tsar did not bring an improvement in the situation at the front and halt the advance of the enemy. And I stressed the fact that under the existing conditions there was no hope of obtaining even a partial success, and that it was still more futile to expect to check the victorious advance of the Germans. It would be terrible to contemplate the impression that would be made upon the country if the Emperor should have to issue in his own name the order for the evacuation of Petrograd or, God forbid, of Moscow. His Majesty listened to me attentively and replied that all this had been considered by him, that he realized the difficulties of the present, but that nevertheless his decision was final.[23]

In the discussion that followed other points were brought out. Sazonov, the Minister of Foreign Affairs, bitterly attacked Goremykin's contention that he did not consider it possible to disclose information which the Emperor had ordered him to keep secret.

There are circumstances [said Sazonov], when it is the duty of a subject to be insistent with the Tsar in the name of national interests. . . . It is no use denying that the firmness of the Emperor's character and the influences to which he is subject inspire little confidence abroad. The whole thing is so terrible that my ideas are in confusion. Into what an abyss is Russia being dragged!

Krivoshein declared that "the fate of the dynasty, of the throne itself, was at stake." Prince Shcherbatov expressed his conviction that the decision of the Emperor would be ascribed to the influence of Rasputin. And P. L. Bark, Minister of Finance, emphasized the probably disastrous effect the change would have upon Russia's credit. The ministers, with the exception of Goremykin, considered it necessary again to approach the Emperor and to endeavor to persuade him to change his decision. In this atmosphere bordering on despair a dramatic appeal made by Goremykin had the echo of an anachronism. "I call upon you, gentlemen," he exclaimed, "in the face of events of extraordinary importance, to bow to the will of His Majesty, to lend him your full support in the moment of trial, and to devote

[23] *Ibid.*, p. 53.

all your powers to the service of the Sovereign." This appeal had little effect.[24]

However grave were the national problems raised by the decision of the Emperor the importance of which was fully realized by the members of the Cabinet, there was one particular aspect of the situation in which they were immediately concerned. The decision of the Tsar was taken without any consultation with his ministers, and could not but be interpreted as a lack of confidence on the part of the Sovereign. In an autocratic country like Russia, where the members of the Cabinet were selected by the Tsar and held office at his pleasure, such an attitude was of immense importance, and, psychologically, had far-reaching effects upon them. We have already seen that the Council of Ministers was openly snubbed by the military authorities. It was now given a convincing proof that it did not enjoy the confidence of its Imperial master. Prince Shcherbatov clearly expressed the general feeling when, at the meeting of August 9, 1915, and deploring the "fatal" decision of the Tsar, he exclaimed: "Under these conditions I can no longer assume responsibility for the Ministry of the Interior."[25]

"A Government Hanging in the Air"

The steps taken by the Council of Ministers to induce the Tsar to reconsider his decision were futile and rather pathetic in their helplessness. Their failure, together with abundant evidence from all sides, strengthened the conviction of the ministers that their position was growing absolutely unbearable. Demands for a fundamental change in the whole system of government were reaching the Council of Ministers from everywhere. Early in August, Guchkov, then chairman of the Central War Industries Committee,[26] communicated to the President of the Council of Ministers a resolution adopted by that body calling in no uncertain terms for a complete change of policy. Goremykin dealt with this resolution by declaring that the contents of the communication were so abhorrent that he did not propose to answer it. But this, of course, was far from settling the question. "What is the position of a government," asked Sazonov, "that Messrs. Guchkov and the unofficial organizations dare to address in this manner? It appears that in their opinion the Cabinet has no authority." And P. A. Kharitonov, the State Controller, sadly remarked: "The country has no confidence in the Government. The army and the popu-

[24] Yakhontov, *op. cit.*, pp. 54–56.
[25] *Ibid.*, p. 58.
[26] *See below.*

ation are relying upon the Duma and the war industries committees, not upon us." And Sazonov summed up the feelings of his colleagues when he said that "the Government was hanging in the air and had no support either from above or below."[27]

The recognition of this fact, of course, was not limited to ministerial circles. On August 11, 1915, Rodzianko, the President of the Duma, having learned the proposed change in the command of the army, called upon the President of the Council of Ministers in a state of great excitement. He insisted that the Cabinet should intervene in the matter. Goremykin's reply, as may well be imagined, did not satisfy him. "I begin to believe those who say that Russia has no government," Rodzianko exclaimed and dashed out of the room without even taking leave of his host. And the comment of Goremykin that "it was not worth while to spend one's time on such lunatics as M. Rodzianko" was but slight consolation to his colleagues.[28]

The whole matter was again brought to the fore as a consequence of a resolution adopted by the Municipal Council of Moscow demanding a government enjoying the confidence of the country, expressing its appreciation of the Grand Duke Nicholas Nikolaevich, and begging the Emperor to receive a deputation which would lay before him the grievances of the country. The resolution was transmitted by telegraph directly to the Tsar. The Cabinet was entrusted with the drafting of a reply. Goremykin was naturally of the opinion that "the simplest thing to do was not to answer such chatter-boxes when they ventured into a sphere beyond their competence."[29] But the other ministers took a very different view. Polivanov pointed out that "there was nothing forbidden or revolutionary in the resolution. A government that enjoyed the confidence of the country was merely what it normally should have." Sazonov, Samarin, and Kharitonov expressed themselves in favor of the Emperor's granting an audience to the delegation. Krivoshein pointed out the impossible position of a cabinet to whom no one pays any attention, a position impossible not only from the point of view of the ministers themselves and their feelings, but from that of national defense and the administration of public affairs. The petition of the Municipal Council of Moscow would be followed by thousands of petitions from all over the country, and all alike would go over the head of the ministers. There must be either a military dictatorship, or a recognition of public opinion. The present Government must be replaced by another

[27] Yakhontov, *op. cit.*, pp. 59, 64.
[28] *Ibid.*, p. 63.
[29] Yakhontov, *op. cit.*, p. 82.

enjoying public confidence. Warnings were coming from everywhere that the present situation could not last.[30]

Arguments of any kind had little effect upon the President of the Council, and when the discussion of a reply to the Moscow telegram was resumed at the next meeting of the Council, on August 21, he advanced the opinion that "it would be sufficient to convey the thanks of His Majesty for the expression of devotion on the part of the Municipal Council." But it was no longer in his power to control the revolt of his colleagues, and the debate that followed presents one of the most pathetic and eloquent pages in the history of any government. Sazonov sternly rejected this suggestion by Goremykin.

The thing that matters [he said] is not the expression of devotion but the fact that the telegram is written with the blood of Russians who are suffering for their country. The best thing we can do is to accede to the wishes of the Moscow Municipal Council, which are perfectly valid. No one can seriously maintain that a government should not be strong and should not enjoy the confidence of the country.

Later in the debate Sazonov made the following statement:

It is our duty at this critical moment, when the future of Russia is at stake, to tell the Tsar frankly that under existing conditions we cannot govern the country, that we cannot serve conscientiously, and that we are doing harm to our country.

And replying to Goremykin's interjection that this meant an ultimatum to the Tsar, Sazonov added:

In Russia we do not know of such a thing as an ultimatum. We can only implore His Majesty as his faithful subjects. Don't let us argue about words. The contents are far more important at the present terrible moment. It is not a question of an ultimatum, but of making a last attempt, before it is too late, to open the eyes of the Tsar to the menace to Russia of his decision, to warn him of the deadly danger, and to tell him honestly that the Cabinet cannot perform its functions while it does not enjoy the confidence of the Sovereign.

Prince Shcherbatov supported a suggestion by Admiral Grigorovich, Minister of the Navy, that a written appeal should be sent to the Emperor.

We must present to His Majesty a written report and explain that a government that enjoys the confidence neither of the Sovereign,

[30] Ibid., pp. 84-85.

82

nor the army, not the towns, nor the zemstvos, nor the nobility, nor the merchants, nor the working men—such a government cannot perform its duties or even exist. We are here playing the part of Don Quixote.[31]

In the debate that followed Goremykin took the position that the agitation against the removal of the Grand Duke was almost a revolutionary movement. This interpretation brought a severe rebuke from Sazonov who declared that there was undoubtedly a complete divergence of opinion between the President of the Council and the majority of his colleagues. "I beg you to inform the Emperor," replied Goremykin, "that I am not fitted for my position and that it is necessary to appoint a man of more modern views in my place. I shall be grateful to you for the service." An answer to his request came from Prince Shcherbatov.

The problem of the government is a much broader one [he said]. We are none of us fitted to govern Russia under the present conditions. Where a bass voice is needed it does no good to substitute tenors for it. I and several of my colleagues are prefectly well aware that it is impossible for us to work when indications from above are obviously against the spirit of the time. We need either a dictatorship, or a policy of conciliation. I do not consider myself to be fitted for either.[32]

The other ministers expressed themselves in the same sense and, with the exception of A. A. Khvostov, Minister of Justice, and Goremykin, upheld the proposal to send the Tsar a written appeal. "The country does not believe," said Shcherbatov, "that the Council of Ministers, the closest servants of the Tsar, are incapable of keeping him from taking the fatal step. We have implored him by word of mouth. Let us now try, for the last time, to implore him in writing. The future historian will absolve us from the charges that are being heaped upon us to-day." And as Goremykin refused to have anything to do with the proposed appeal, firmly holding his opinion that "the will of the Tsar must be obeyed like the Gospel" (to which Sazonov replied: "Then the only way out—is to go and drown ourselves"). It was finally decided that the *démarche* agreed upon should take the form of a letter to the Emperor. The letter was drafted and dispatched the same day, August 21. It was signed by Krivoshein, Kharitonov, Sazonov, Bark, Shcherbatov, Samarin, Ignatiev, Shakhovskoy. Polivanov, Minister of War, and Grigorovich, Minister

---

[31] *Ibid.*, pp. 89–91.
[32] Yakhontov, *op. cit.*, pp. 92–93.

of the Navy, did not sign, but informed the Emperor that they were in full agreement with their colleagues. The letter asked for a reconsideration of the Tsar's decision to dismiss the Grand Duke and pointed out the divergence of opinion within the Council of Ministers which "was inadmissible at any time, but to-day was simply fatal."[33] The Empress wrote to the Tsar that Goremykin was "shocked and horrified by the ministers' letter" and that he "finds no word for their behavior."[34]

The letter had no effect. On August 23 the Emperor went to Headquarters and assumed command of the army, a fact of which the Council of Ministers was still unaware on the 24th.[35] Once more to use the Tsar's own expression, he had opened a "clean page."

The Sovereign's Displeasure

The dominating feature of the period that followed the crisis in the summer of 1915 was the rapidly growing influence of the Empress in the administration of the affairs of State. The Tsar was openly displeased with the stubborn opposition of his Cabinet to the change in high command.

The behavior of some of the ministers continues to amaze me [he wrote to the Empress on September 9, 1915]. . . . What matter? so much the worse for them! They were afraid to close the Duma—it was done! I came here [came to Headquarters] and replaced N. [Nicholas Nikolaevich], in spite of their advice; the people accepted this move as a natural thing and understood it, as we did. The proof —numbers of telegrams which I received from all sides, with the most touching expressions. All this shows me clearly one thing: that the ministers, always living in town, know terribly little of what is happening in the country as a whole. Here I can judge correctly the real mood among the various classes of people.[36]

And the Empress emphasized the same note by writing three days later: "The ministers are rotten. . . . I am more than disgusted with those cowards."[37] It was clear to everyone that

[33] *Ibid.*, pp. 93–98. That the tension within the Council of Ministers had reached its limit may be illustrated by the following fact. "When the meeting [of September 2] was over," Yakhontov writes, "and Goremykin was leaving the hall, the Minister of Foreign Affairs declared: 'I don't want to take leave of that madman or shake hands with him.' He then went with unsteady steps towards the entrance, and I followed him to support him if he collapsed. Sazonov did not notice anything around him and was almost unconscious. In the ante-room he shouted: '*Il est fou ce vieillard*' and dashed out." *Ibid.*, p. 128.

[34] *Letters of the Tsaritsa to the Tsar*, p. 117.

[35] Yakhontov, *op. cit.*, p. 103.

[36] *The Letters of the Tsar to the Tsaritsa*, p. 85.

[37] *Letters of the Tsaritsa to the Tsar*, p. 159.

hanges in the Cabinet could not be delayed much longer. They
ook, however, the opposite direction to that suggested by the
etter of the eight ministers.

It can be no exaggeration to say that the group of men who
nominally presided over the destinies of the Russian Empire in
the middle of 1915 was, with the notable exception of Goremykin and, perhaps, two or three others, far above the ordinary
level. For a Russian Imperial Government it was, indeed, a very
liberal-minded body, inspired with a very genuine desire to
serve its country to the best of its abilities. The ministers were
not lacking in moral courage and were willing to make the sacrifice of their official position in order to bring about what they
considered to be the necessary reforms.

Changes carried out in the composition of the Cabinet in the
spring and early summer of 1915 removed some of the more
objectionable ministers. General Sukhomlinov, who was held
responsible for Russia's complete unpreparedness for war, was
replaced by General Polivanov whom General Sir Alfred Knox,
British Military Representative in Russia during the War and
one of the keenest observers of Russian conditions, describes
as "undoubtedly the ablest military organizer in Russia."[38] The
reactionary Minister of the Interior, N. A. Maklakov, was replaced by Prince N. B. Shcherbatov, a member of the liberal
nobility of the Province of Poltava. N. G. Shcheglovitov, the
notorious leader of the extreme Right, was succeeded as Min-
ster of Justice by the honest and moderate A. A. Khvostov.[39]
The no less notorious V. K. Sabler, Procurator of the Holy
Synod, was dismissed and A. D. Samarin, a well-known church-
man and an outstanding representative of those Moscow nobles
who were in a traditional opposition to the Petrograd bureaucracy and for whom the Empress had so cordial a dislike, was
appointed his successor. It is notable that the two most important of these appointments—those of Polivanov and Samarin—
were decided upon by the Emperor[40] during his visits to Headquarters and in spite of the objections of the Empress, which he
anticipated and which were not slow in coming.[41]

Among the ministers who joined the Cabinet at an earlier
date and were still in office during the crisis of 1915 were Count
Paul Ignatiev and Sazonov. Count Ignatiev, a former chairman
of the executive board of the Kiev zemstvo, very properly con-

[38] Major-General Sir Alfred Knox, *With the Russian Army, 1914–1917,* two volumes
New York, 1921), p. 412.
[39] Rodzianko calls him "a very honorable man." *Padenie Tsarskago Rezhima,* VII,
28.
[40] *The Letters of the Tsar to the Tsaritsa,* pp. 57, 60.
[41] *Letters of the Tsaritsa to the Tsar,* pp. 90–91, 95, 96, 97–98, 108, 110.

sidered himself an outsider in the Bureaucratic circles of the capital.[42] With remarkable enthusiasm and great ability he devoted himself to the work of national education, first, at the Ministry of Agriculture, and, from the beginning of 1915, as Minister of Education. His broad general outlook and his enlightened educational policies, which were partly inspired by the views of John Dewey, made his appearance on the bureaucratic horizon of Petrograd something of a sensation. If under the conditions prevailing during the War only a few of his proposals were carried out, this was certainly not due to his lack of courage or vision.[43]

Sazonov, Minister of Foreign Affairs, on whom so many undeserved accusations have been piled in the course of the last ten years by overzealous and not-too-scrupulous historians in search of the causes of the Great War, was a man of high moral character, considerable ability, and keen sense of duty. His long and distinguished career in foreign countries, especially his protracted stay at the Russian Embassy in London, had brought him into close contact with the great European democracies. We have seen that he made no secret of his preference for a constitutional form of government and the arbitrariness and chaos prevailing in Russia were abhorrent to him. As to his alleged planning of a European war, that is fortunately entirely outside our subject and may be left with profit to more imaginative writers.

That such men as the above found themselves under the leadership of the senile and obstinate Goremykin and were compelled to accept the orders of a misguided monarch living in a different age was not only a personal tragedy for all them, a tragedy of which we have given a few glimpses, but also a national calamity. Their courageous action in the summer of 1915 was, as they well realized, their doom. It was merely a matter of time before they were dropped from the Cabinet one by one and replaced by men willing to accept the guidance of the "man of God" or act as mere figureheads incapable of independent thinking.

Of the ministers who signed the letter of August 23 to the Tsar, or declared themselves in agreement with its contents, the first to go were Samarin and Prince Shcherbatov, whose tenure of office lasted merely a few weeks. They were dismissed in September, 1915. In October they were followed by Krivoshein; in January, 1916, by Kharitonov; in March, by Polivanov; in

[42] See his evidence in *Padenie Tsarskago Rezhima*, VI, 1–26.
[43] For a detailed discussion of Count Ignatiev's work *see* Odinetz, *op. cit.*, pp. 97 *sqq.*

uly, by Sazanov. Ignatiev survived until December, 1916. Of the three signatories of the letter who remained in office until the downfall of the monarchy—Grigorovich, Bark, and Shahovskoy—two, Bark and Shakhovskoy, it may be surmised, owed their good fortune to their friendly relations with Rasputin.[44] The letters of the Empress leave no room for doubt that these changes were largely due to her influence. Her hatred of Polivanov was particularly intense. "Any honest man better than him," she writes on March 12, 1916.[45] "A greater traitor" than Sukhomlinov.[46] And the Emperor was quickly converted to this point of view. "After Polivanov's removal I shall sleep in peace, and all the ministers will feel relieved as well," he writes to the Empress.[47] But General Knox took a very different view. He believed that Polivanov's dismissal "was a disaster."[48] And the public opinion of the country sided with the English general.

Ministerial "Leap-frog"

The intensity of the crisis in the summer of 1915 convinced even the Emperor that the leadership of the Cabinet could not continue to remain in the hands of the senile Goremykin.[49] But the latter enjoyed the confidence of the Empress and Rasputin, and their support made it possible for him to continue in office until the beginning of 1916. The Empress still maintained in September, 1915, that it was much better to "clear out ministers who strike and not change the President who with decent, energetic, well-intended coöperates[?] can serve still perfectly well."[50] But in November she was forced to realize that public feeling had reached a stage when some concessions were imperative. So she admitted that it might be better for Goremykin to go before he was compelled to do so by a scandal in the Duma.[51] And this in spite of the authoritative opinion of Rasputin that Goremykin is "very wise and when others make a row and say he sits *ramoli* with his head down—it is because he understands

Letters of the Tsaritsa to the Tsar, pp. 84–85, 356–357. It appears from the correspondence of the Emperor and the Empress that Bark's position was far from safe. The Empress vigorously advocated Count Tatishchev as his successor and it would seem that the sudden disgrace of A. N. Khvostov, then Minister of the Interior, whose candidate Tatishchev was, prevented this scheme from materializing. *Ibid.*, pp. 219, 241; *see also* evidence of A. N. Khvostov in *Padenie Tsarskago rezhima*, VI, 89–91; also evidence of Beletsky in *ibid.*, IV, 250–258.
Letters of the Tsaritsa to the Tsar, p. 297.
Ibid., p. 302.
The Letters of the Tsar to the Tsaritsa, p. 155.
Knox, *op. cit.*, p. 412.
The Letters of the Tsar to the Tsaritsa, p. 91.
Letters of the Tsaritsa to the Tsar, p. 145.
Ibid., p. 210.

that to-day the crowd howls, to-morrow rejoices, that one need not be crushed by the changing waves."[52]

That the indignation with the existing political situation in general and with the President of the Council of Ministers in particular was approaching the breaking point may appear from the fact that on December 19, 1915, the President of the Duma took the unprecedented step of sending a letter to Goremykin demanding his resignation.

If you feel that you lack the necessary strength to carry the burden of government and to use every means to lead the country to victory [wrote Rodzianko], you must have the courage to confess it and to make room for younger men. The decisive moment has arrived, terrible events are approaching. . . . Do not lose any time, the country is in danger.[53]

In January, 1916, Goremykin was dismissed, but his disappearance from the political stage brought no relief to the situation. His successor was the notorious Boris Sturmer, then sixty-eight years old, a bureaucrat of a still worse type than his predecessor. Goremykin, with all his faults, was personally an honest man. This could hardly be said of Sturmer who was openly accused, and it seems not without some foundation, if not of actual dishonesty, at least of extremely dubious dealings. He was surrounded with men of the most objectionable type, such as the unscrupulous adventurers Manasevich-Manuilov and Prince Andronikov. "He [Sturmer] always gave me the impression of being a man of extremely limited mental gifts, of one who was suffering from an acute state of sclerosis due to advanced age," testified N. N. Pokrovsky, a member of Sturmer's Cabinet and later his successor as Minister of Foreign Affairs.[54] "For instance, he could never formulate an idea without writing it down. In order to express his opinion he had to put down on paper the simplest remarks. . . . His character, his mental condition, his intellectual equipment, I think, prevented him from directing anything." But the Empress thought that he was "a right man" and that he "would work well with the new energetic ministers."[55] Then, of course, "he very much values Gregory which is a great thing;"[56] and "completely believed" in Rasputin's "wonderful, God sent wisdom."[57] The result was

[52] Ibid., p. 219.
[53] Rodzianko, Gosudarstvennaya Duma i Fevralskaya 1917 Goda Revolutsya, p. 36.
[54] Evidence of Pokrovsky in Padenie Tsarskago Rezhima, V, 338–339.
[55] Letters of the Tsaritsa to the Tsar, p. 251.
[56] Ibid., p. 256.
[57] Ibid., p. 428.

hat Sturmer, even more than Goremykin, became an instrument of the personal rule of the Empress. He made his reports to her regularly every week.[58] And he frequently communicated with he Empress through her friend and adviser, Madame Vyrubov.

It is impossible to speak of Sturmer's political program because he had none and his position as an appointee of Rasputin and the Empress excluded the very possibility of his having one. He practically admitted this himself.[59] It seems hard to believe hat a man with such qualifications was put at the head of the Government of the Empire in the middle of the second year of he War and remained there for almost a year! In addition to he office of President of the Council of Ministers, Sturmer held n March–June, 1916, the portfolio of the Interior which he esigned in July in order to succeed Sazanov at the Ministry of Foreign Affairs, a department about which he knew virtually nothing. No wonder that the news of his appointment was received with consternation not only at home, but also in Allied countries. The wish of the Emperor that Sturmer's appointment "should come like a thunder clap"[60] was undoubtedly fulfilled, although one may well doubt whether the effect actually produced was the one intended by the Sovereign. Sturmer's political career was brought to an end by the speech delivered in the Duma by Miliukov in November, 1916, in which both he and he Empress were accused of treason.

His successor was chosen by the Emperor himself against the will of the Tsaritsa, who did not try to conceal her disapproval of his choice.[61] A. F. Trepov, the new President of the Council of Ministers, was a man of strong conservative views, but sufficiently independent not to accept the guidance of Rasputin. His plan was to persuade the Emperor to allow him to prepare his own list of ministers which would then be submitted to the Sovereign.[62] But the Tsar looked upon him as merely a convenient instrument for getting rid of the Duma.

It is unpleasant [he wrote on December 4, 1916] to speak to a man one does not like and does not trust, such as Trepov. But first of all it is necessary to find a substitute for him, and then to kick him out—after he had done his dirty work. I mean to make him resign after he has closed the Duma. Let all the responsibility and all the difficulties fall upon his shoulders, and upon the shoulders of his successor.[63]

[58] *Ibid.*, p. 409.
[59] Evidence of Sturmer in *Padenie Tsarskago Rezhima*, I, 226.
[60] *The Letters of the Tsar to the Tsaritsa*, p. 133.
[61] *Letters of the Tsaritsa to the Tsar*, pp. 436, 438, 449, 450, 454.
[62] Evidence of Count Ignatiev, in *Padenie Tsarskago Rezhima*, VI, 23.
[63] *The Letters of the Tsar to the Tsaritsa*, p. 307.

Barely five weeks after his appointment Trepov was dismissed —on December 27, 1916—and he was succeeded by the venerable Prince N. D. Golitsin, a man of sixty-six, entirely without experience in statecraft. This appointment came as a surprise not only to the country, but to Prince Golitsin himself. A *grand seigneur* devoid of political ambition, he always kept scrupulously away from the crowd of office-seekers. He was well known personally to the Empress in his official capacity of chairman of a committee for the relief of Russian prisoners of war of which the Empress was the president. A man with a keen sense of honor, he would have nothing to do with Rasputin and his followers; but he was a very loyal subject of his Sovereign and this was what led him to the presidency of the Council of Ministers. He was sincerely distressed by the appointment, and begged the Emperor to relieve him of the burden of an office the duties of which he knew he could not fulfil.[64] He frankly confessed that he had no political program.[65] He was merely an obedient tool in the hands of the Emperor and the forces behind him. The Revolution found the helm of the ship of State in his weak and inexperienced hands.

Such were the leaders of the Imperial Government during the War if the word "leader" may be used at all under the conditions we have described. It would be idle to attempt here to give a complete picture of the changes in the holders of cabinet offices. They were frequent and present a bewildering gallery of occupants largely allured by the illusory glamor of power. Some of them succeeded in maintaining themselves in office for a few months, others—merely for a few weeks. Purishkevich, the arch-conservative member of the Duma who took a direct part in the murder of Rasputin, wittily described the changes in the Government as "ministerial leap-frog." Even the Emperor was forced to recognize the danger of the situation. "All these changes make my head go round," he wrote on September 9, 1916,[66] "in my opinion they are too frequent. In any case, they are not good for the internal situation of the country, as each new man brings with him alterations in the administration." Nevertheless events pursued their former course. It was a grotesque and sinister procession of nonentities and adventurers who did nothing to prevent the drifting of the dynasty to its doom, and who prepared for the country a protracted period of unrest, dismemberment, civil war, and suffering.

---

[64] Evidence of Prince Golitsin in *Padenie Tsarskago Rezhima*, II, 250–251; also Rodzianko, *Gosudarstvennaya Duma i Fevralskaya 1917 Goda Revolutsya*, p. 37.
[65] Evidence of Prince Golitsin in *Padenie Tsarskago Rezhima*, II, 256.
[66] *The Letters of the Tsar to the Tsaritsa*, p. 257.

A. D. Protopopov

We have said above that no attempt would here be made to discuss in detail the shadowy human combinations who constituted the Russian war-time government. An exception, however, may be made in the case of A. D. Protopopov, the last Minister of the Interior of Imperial Russia. Protopopov was an outsider in the bureaucratic circles of the capital. He was connected for a long time with the zemstvos and then served as a member of the Duma, of which he had been vice-president since 1914. He belonged to the left wing of the moderately liberal party called the Octobrists. In 1916 he headed the Russian parliamentary delegation to the Allied countries. One might well imagine that the appointment of a man of this type to a high cabinet office would meet with the whole-hearted approval of liberal circles. The reverse proved to be true. Obsessed by an immense desire for power which was stimulated by predictions of fortune-tellers, in whom he appeared to have had unlimited confidence, Protopopov seemed to believe that he was called to save Russia from ruin.[67] He was clearly an appointee of Rasputin,[68] and he succeeded in inspiring a very sincere confidence in the Emperor and the Empress, especially the latter. There is no question that he himself was devoted to the Imperial family, but his physical strength, his mental equipment, and his nerves proved unequal to the strain. His acceptance of the office of the Minister of the Interior under Sturmer was interpreted as an insult by his colleagues of the Duma, although Rodzianko recommended him to the Emperor as a candidate for the portfolio of commerce and industry in another ministerial combination.[69] It would seem that Protopopov was suffering from the effects of a disease contracted by him in his early days. The bitter campaign which the Duma and the press directed against him following the scandalous revelations of his political association with Rasputin and Madame Vyrubov, a campaign which virtually ruled out even the possibility of his making an appearance in the legislative chamber over which he so recently presided, and his tenacious will to remain in office, greatly aggravated his mental condition. The Emperor soon realized that his new minister was not exactly a man to rely upon. Bowing before the storm of protests against Protopopov which broke out in the Duma, the Emperor decided to dismiss him. "I am

[67] Evidence of Protopopov in *Padenie Tsarskago Rezhima*, II, 2–7, 149–151.
[68] *Letters of the Tsaritsa to the Tsar*, p. 394.
[69] *The Letters of the Tsar to the Tsaritsa*, p. 219; also Rodzianko, *The Reign of Rasputin: an Empire's Collapse*, p. 213.

sorry for Protopopov," he wrote on November 10, 1916,[70] "he is a good honest man, but he jumps from one idea to another and cannot make up his mind on anything. I noticed that from the very beginning. They say that a few years ago he was not quite normal after a certain illness." But the Empress took at once the defense of the man whose presence in the government was obviously an immediate danger to the dynasty.[71] As usual she won and Protopopov continued in office until the Revolution of February–March, 1917. In the meantime his mental condition was growing rapidly worse. By the end of February, we are told by one of Protopopov's colleagues in the Cabinet, it was clear to the other ministers that they had to deal with a man who was no longer fully responsible for his actions. His speeches in the Council of Ministers were incoherent and did not make sense.[72] This opinion is amply confirmed by the evidence given by Protopopov before the Committee of Inquiry. It fills many pages and leaves no doubt that the former Vice-President of the Duma and Minister of the Interior was on the way to insanity.[73] This was the man to whom the Sovereign and the Empress looked for the restoration of order and the winning of the War.

The unfortunate story of Protopopov's rise to power is instructive for more than one reason. It was the last drop which filled to overflowing the cup of discredit of the Imperial Government. On the other hand, the fact that a man of Protopopov's character could be elected Vice-President of the Duma cast no little reflection on the whole of Russia's public life. And Rodzianko singularly failed in his attempt to clear himself and the assembly over which he presided of their share of responsibility.[74]

"The Dictatorship"

An abortive attempt to consolidate the whole power in the hands of one man was made toward the end of 1916. This attempt, which was inspired by considerations not entirely unlike

[70] *The Letters of the Tsar to the Tsaritsa*, p. 297.
[71] *Letters of the Tsaritsa to the Tsar*, pp. 439, 441, 446.
[72] Evidence of Pokrovsky in *Padenie Tsarskago Rezhima*, V, 356–357.
[73] See *Padenie Tsarskago Rezhima*, Vols. I, II, IV, V.
[74] Rodzianko's explanation (*Gosudarstvennaya Duma i Fevralskaya 1917 Goda Revolutsya*, pp. 50–51) that Protopopov's appointment to the Ministry of the Interior was devised by Sturmer in order to bring discredit upon the Duma must be rejected as contrary to all available evidence. It seems that Rodzianko himself did not insist on his theory. He did not revive it in his later writings. On the other hand it constitutes a considerable reflection upon the soundness of judgment of the former President of the Duma. A detailed discussion of Protopopov's career and rise to power is given in the evidence of Rodzianko in *Padenie Tsarskago Rezhima*, VII, 139–146.

those which brought about the formation of a War Cabinet in Great Britain, was officially laid before the Tsar in a report presented to him on June 15, 1916, by his chief of staff, General Alexeev. This report contained a very thorough survey of the situation with reference to the production of munitions and supplies for the army and pointed to the disorganization and lack of coördination between the work of the various departments and its disastrous results. Alexeev suggested the creation of a minister of national defense with very wide powers who would have the task of coördinating all work for the army.[75] This plan, however, met with little approval on the part of Sturmer, then President of the Council of Ministers. He drew the attention of the Tsar to the fact that the proposal would necessitate the practical absorption by the new department of the functions of the Ministries of War, Transport, Agriculture, and Commerce and Industry, and that it would demand the abolition of the four Special Councils[76] created in 1915 and to which the Duma and the nonofficial organizations working for national defense attached an immense importance.[77] The plan was also opposed by Rodzianko, who believed that it would only add to the confusion.[78] It practically came to nothing and resulted in the conferring upon the President of the Council of Ministers of undetermined power "for the coördination of measures directed to the supply of the army and of the navy and for the organization of the rear."[79] It seems that Sturmer himself had little idea what he was expected to do. The only thing he could remember about it ten months later was the term "dictatorship" which rather frightened than pleased him.[80] He certainly had little of the making of a dictator. It is not apparent that the "dictatorial" powers were ever used. But exaggerated rumors about them spread throughout the country and added to the suspicion with which the Government was already regarded. Thus the fundamentally sound idea of the necessity of a concentrated organ of power in time of war which proved so fruitful in Great Britain degenerated under Russian conditions into a mere useless gesture.

The Bureaucracy and the War

The decay of the bureaucratic system we have described was not limited to the upper levels of officialdom. To use an expres-

[75] *Monarkhya Pered Krusheniem*, pp. 259–266.
[76] *See below*, p. 102.
[77] *Monarkhya Pered Krusheniem*, pp. 256–257.
[78] Evidence of Rodzianko in *Padenie Tsarskago Rezhima*, VII, 138–139.
[79] *Monarkhya Pered Krusheniem*, p. 258.
[80] Evidence of Sturmer in *Padenie Tsarskago Rezhima*, I, 224, 240–242.

sion of the Emperor already quoted, "each new man brings with him alterations in the administration." With the appointment of new ministers the administration of their departments was submitted sometimes to very thorough remodeling and reorganization. New men, often entirely unfamiliar with the work entrusted to them, were called to subordinate but still very important offices and did not contribute to the strengthening of the system. Just as a stone thrown into a pond creates a disturbance which is felt, with decreasing force, in the remotest back waters, so the appointment of every new minister created repercussions all along the line.

The degeneration of the Petrograd bureaucracy had reached, by 1916, a degree which it would be difficult to believe if our information was not based on first-hand evidence. The written "confession"[81] made to the Committee of Inquiry by Beletsky, a former Director of the Police Department, member of the State Council, and Governor-General of Siberia (an appointment which was canceled before he started for his destination), is among the most amazing and the most damning documents any *régime* could possibly produce. The wildest melodrama of sensational story-writers seems tame when compared with the account of the conditions prevailing in Petrograd as given by the Director of the Police. And if such were the conditions at the center, what could be expected from the province?

The disintegrating effect of the forces behind the throne were felt not only in the civilian administration but with perhaps even greater force in the organization of the Church. The harm worked was not limited to the appointment to the highest offices of individually servile prelates, friends of Rasputin, like Pitirim, Metropolitan of Petrograd, but led to the creation of an obedient Synod, presided over by a no less obedient procurator (minister of religion), who offered no opposition to the "man of God." An illustration will suffice. In the second half of 1916, when the evil influence of the Empress was at its height, the Synod presented her with a holy image as a testimonial, a manifestation of servility which delighted Rasputin, but less so the Empress herself.[82] She notes nevertheless that it was the first time since the days of Catherine II that an Empress alone found herself receiving all the members of the Synod. This

[81] *Padenie Tsarskago Rezhima*, Vol. IV. The "excessive" frankness of Beletsky's statement has sometimes led to suspicion (*see* S. A. Korenev in *Arkhiv Russkoi Revolutsii*, VII, 20). His evidence, however, is fully corroborated by information obtained by the Committee from other sources, although minor mistakes have probably crept in. It must be remembered that the "confession" was written in prison and that Beletsky had no access to documents.

[82] *Letters of the Tsaritsa to the Tsar*, p. 406.

flattering demonstration of loyalty aroused her surprise as she had little admiration for the higher prelates and made no secret of it.

The decline of the bureaucratic system was due, on the one hand, to the direct interference of the military with the work of the civilian government, and on the other, to the decay from within which can be traced to the weakness of the Emperor and to the powers behind him. But in addition to these purely negative forces there were others which were brought into play by the War and gradually invaded the sphere reserved in the past to the bureaucracy. The prestige of the Duma was, temporarily, greatly increased by its courageous stand against abuses and its determination to help the army in its endeavor to repulse the enemy. The so-called nonofficial organizations—the Union of Zemstvos and the Union of Towns, the war industries committees—were rapidly growing in importance, and were assuming a part in national life which was entirely out of keeping with the bureaucratic tradition. The creation of the Special Councils by the Acts of August 17 and August 20, 1915, sanctioned the participation of the community at large, through its elected representatives, in the work of State institutions. All these, no doubt, were intrusions by the outside world upon the former prerogatives of the bureaucracy. But they were also the manifestations of that initiative and interest in national problems which form the very foundation of a modern democracy. Under a system different from the one which existed in Russia such manifestations would be welcome. In Russia they were accepted after a stubborn struggle as a necessary evil.

Chapter 5

The Rise and Fall of the Duma

The Weakness of the Duma

THE HISTORY of the vicissitudes of the Duma during the War presents a subject of unusual interest. From the subordinate position of a quasi parliament in a State that in its legal structure was not too remote from an absolute monarchy, the Duma rose in the course of the War to a height of national leadership and prestige which would have appeared unthinkable a few months before. It will be no exaggeration to say that throughout the years 1915 and 1916 and the first two months of 1917 the Duma was regarded by that relatively small group—but the only articulate group—of men and women who constituted public opinion, as the standard bearer of the ideas of statesmanship and the champion of the national cause against the forces of reaction. Nevertheless at the very moment when these forces were defeated and disappeared from the stage the Duma lost ground almost at once. In the great upheaval that followed the downfall of the monarchy new social forces, new ideas were flung to the surface by the mighty waves of the revolutionary storm, and they made a clear sweep of the institution which for a few months was undoubtedly the moral leader of the nation. An illegitimate child of western democratic ideas and of the Russian autocracy, the Duma suffered from that debility which was a natural consequence of the half-hearted legislation which brought it into being. Like the rest of the constitutional and social structure of the State it bore in itself the germs of its own destruction. The most important of them was the Election Act of June 3, 1907.

We know that the Emperor, faithful to the ideas of Alexander III and Pobedonostsev, was inveterately hostile to any constitutional *régime*.[1] The concessions embodied in the manifesto of October 17, 1905, which called the Duma into existence, were given in "a moment of fever."[2] And after the First and Second Dumas displayed a spirit of independence and radicalism which met with no approval in official circles, a revolutionary measure was taken to bring the lower chamber into obedience. This measure was the Election Law of June 3, 1907, which was enacted by Imperial decree in flagrant violation of the Fundamental Laws and which hopelessly distorted and mutilated the relatively broad and liberal franchise of 1905.[3] The suffrage introduced by the Act of June 3 was neither universal, nor direct, nor equal. It was, we are assured by Professor Gronsky, "the most complicated suffrage system that ever existed." Devised for the protection of the interests of the large landowners, it gave them in most of the provinces an overwhelming majority of votes. The part played by the peasantry and the small farmers in elections was purely nominal.

[1] *See above*, pp. 54–56.
[2] Evidence of Miliukov in *Padenie Tsarskago Rezhima*, VI, 294–295.
[3] P. P. Gronsky, "The Central Government," in the volume *The War and the Russian Government* (Yale University Press, 1929), pp. 12 *sqq.*, in this series of the "Economic and Social History of the World War" also evidence of Golovin in *Padenie Tsarskago Rezhima*, I, 365 *sqq.*; also evidence of Krishanovsky in *ibid.*, V, 417 *sqq.*

The new election law contained moreover one remarkable provision which deserves special attention.

The Act of 3rd June 1907 [writes Professor Gronsky] provided that the voters of various groups might be subdivided into several still smaller groups, for which different qualifications were assigned. By an order of the Minister of the Interior the voters might be split into smaller groups by reason of their residing in different sections of the district, or according to the kind or extent of their property qualifications, or according to racial groups. This disposition, enabling the Minister of the Interior to create smaller units and electoral districts which would vote separately for their own electors, placed in his hands one of the most powerful means of influencing the results of elections. In this manner the boundaries of the original electoral districts were not fixed by law, but might arbitrarily be shifted by the higher administration of the country for the purpose of obtaining results advantageous and convenient to the Government.[4]

These unusual powers were freely used by the Minister of the Interior in the elections to the Third Duma, and especially in 1912, in the elections to the Fourth Duma. A sad and humiliating part in the campaign of 1912 was played by the clergy. A number of their representatives, designated by the reactionary Procurator of the Holy Synod, Sabler, were elected as a result of the unceremonious rearrangement of the electoral districts by the Minister of the Interior. These abuses, scarcely disguised by the provision of the Act of June 3, were widely denounced in the press and from the tribune of the Duma itself.[5] They naturally added little to the prestige of the lower chamber, the standing of which was already compromised by the odium resulting from the very nature of the unconstitutional Act of June 3, 1907. The immense increase in its popularity during the War came therefore as a distinct surprise.

The Immediate Effects of the War

With the outbreak of the War the Duma was called for a short session which lasted only one day, July 26, 1914, and which turned into a patriotic demonstration. The deputies forgot or at least for a time postponed giving expression to their grievances against the Government, and promised it their unconditional support.[6] It was an outburst of patriotic enthusiasm

Gronsky, *op. cit.*, p. 16.
Evidence of Miliukov in *Padenie Tsarskago Rezhima*, VI, 302; also Rodzianko, *Gosudarstvennaya Duma i Fevralskaya 1917 Goda Revolutsya*, p. 13.
Rodzianko, *The Reign of Rasputin: an Empire's Collapse*, pp. 109–112; also evidence of Miliukov in *Padenie Tsarskago Rezhima*, VI, 307.

similar to those that took place in every belligerent country in the early days of the War. The session of June 26 was followed by an adjournment until the beginning of 1915.

The transition to war-time conditions brought two important changes in the work of the Duma which, logically, should have tended further to undermine its position in the country. These two changes were the curtailment of its financial authority and legislation under Article 87.[7] Let us examine them in turn.

Even in time of peace the financial prerogatives of the Duma were extremely limited, thus depriving the legislative chambers of the most effective method of control over the executive. A. J. Shingarev, for many years rapporteur of the budget committee of the Duma, said that the budget provisions of the Russian law were "an example of the most incomplete, muddled, and imperfect budget legislation" existing in any country he knew of.[8] A very important group of expenditures was entirely free from the control of the Duma. With the outbreak of the War the situation was at once changed for the worse. The budget, as we know, was split in two: there was the "peace budget" which did not include war expenditure, was voted by the legislature and made public, and there was the "war budget" which was not subject to the control of the legislative chambers and was not made public. The actual expenditure under the "war budget" was considerably greater than that under the "peace budget."[9] While the former was about 3,500 million rubles, war expenditure amounted to as much as 20,000 and 25,000 million rubles. And not only did it comprise the whole of the real "war" expenditure, but often included such unexpected items as construction of railroads, afforestation and hydrotechnical works, irrigation of steppes in Russian Asia, and other expenditure equally removed from the immediate problems raised by the War. The natural result of this situation was that the Duma and the State Council practically lost even that slight degree of control over State expenditure which they possessed before the War.

Another perhaps still more important change in the routine work of the Duma was due to the practice of legislating to an excessive degree under the authority of Article 87 of the Fundamental Laws. This article empowered the Emperor to issue during the recess between the sessions of the legislative chambers, decrees which had temporarily the force of laws, but were

[7] See below, pp. 98–99.
[8] Evidence of Shingarev in *Padenie Tsarskago Rezhima*, VII, 8.
[9] See Michelson, *op. cit.*, pp. 74–79; also Gronsky, *op. cit.*, p. 22; also evidence of Shingarev in *Padenie Tsarskago Rezhima*, VII, 12, 15 sqq.

to be submitted to the legislature within two months after the beginning of the next session. Before the War this provision was resorted to with a certain circumspection, especially since some of its more notorious applications were clearly used as a method of overriding the resistance of the legislature and of confronting it with a *fait accompli*.[10] The outbreak of hostilities accompanied by the prorogation of the Duma for six months made it imperative for the Government to make extensive use of the exceptional powers vested in the Crown, and legislation under Article 87 became the normal procedure. It covered a very wide field, including such important matters as State finance and money circulation, relief of soldiers' families, changes and amendments in the conscription law, changes in rates of taxation, the imposition of new taxes or tariffs, customs duties, the regulation of imports and exports, measures affecting trade and industry, measures of coöperation with the organs of zemstvo and municipal government, the limitation of the rights of nationals of countries with which Russia was at war and of settlers from such countries, etc.[11] The legality of some of these measures, especially of the right of the Crown to impose new taxes without the consent of the Duma, was sometimes questioned.[12] But war does not make for days fitted for legal discussion, and the point was not pressed. How large was the output of legislation under Article 87 may appear from the fact that during the premiership of Goremykin, between January 30, 1914, and January 20, 1916, no less than 384 measures were enacted in this manner.[13] And the practice continued to grow in following years. It is only fair to say that similar developments—legislation by some kind of administrative decrees such as the Orders in Council in Great Britain—took place in practically every belligerent country.

It might be expected that with the two principal branches of its work, the control of State revenue and expenditure and general legislation, gravely impaired by the War, the Duma would sink more than ever into popular indifference and disregard. Events, however, took a very different course.

The Growing Influence of the Duma

The recess of about six months which followed the short session of June 26, 1914, did not bring the work of the Duma to a complete standstill, and although the new activities were

[*] Gronsky, *op. cit.*, pp. 9–10.
Gronsky, *op. cit.*, pp. 26–27.
Evidence of Shingarev in *Padenie Tsarskago Rezhima*, VII, 19.
Evidence of Goremykin in *Padenie Tsarskago Rezhima*, III, 311–313.

not exactly of the regular kind they proved nevertheless to b
of considerable importance. The day following the session o
June 26, the members of the Duma met privately and decide
to constitute a provisional committee for the relief of wounde
soldiers and war sufferers. It was presided over by the Presiden
of the Duma and included all the members who happened t
be in Petrograd. The immediate purpose of the committee, i
is clear from its name, was the alleviation of the fate of th
victims of the War. But it also gradually developed that it ha
a different and far more important function to perform. Meetin
regularly twice a week and sometimes more frequently, th
provisional committee became the central organization to whic
the deputies reported on their war work and to which the
looked for inspiration and guidance. The military reverses suf
fered by the army in 1914 and in the spring of 1915 raised
number of problems which were, strictly speaking, outside th
field of relief work, but which were nevertheless closely con
nected with the conduct of the War. General political question
such as the shortage of war supplies, the policy of the Govern
ment, the conduct of the War, began to crop up in discussions
and the President of the Duma was occasionally instructed b
the committee to use his right of personal audience with th
Emperor to bring the attention of His Majesty to particula
problems. With the disasters of the Russian retreat from Galici
in the spring of 1915 the attendance of the committee wa
greatly increased and the purely political question of callin
the legislature for a protracted session at an early date cam
into particular prominence.[14]

The information obtained by the members of this relief com
mittee of the Duma was naturally haphazard, and could no
give a comprehensive picture of the situation as a whole. Th
first serious alarm was sounded at a private meeting of th
Duma's budget committee attended by the members of th
Cabinet, which took place a few days before the formal openin
of the Duma on January 27, 1915. The chief speakers for th
Government were Goremykin, the President of the Counc
of Ministers, Sukhomlinov, the Minister of War, and Maklakov
the Minister of the Interior. Sukhomlinov gave the assembl
an extremely optimistic outline of the general military situatio
and the question of army supplies, one in flagrant contradictio
with the information which was pouring into the Duma fron
all sides. The general spirit displayed by the ministers was any
thing but conciliatory. Goremykin limited himself to a fev

14 Gronsky, *op. cit.*, pp. 28–29.

general remarks which obviously could not satisfy anyone. Maklakov was aggressive, provocative, rude. The impression this meeting produced upon the deputies was most distressing. "It became clear," wrote Professor Miliukov, "that the Government is either concealing the actual condition of the army and the country, and is therefore deceiving the Duma, or that it does not understand the seriousness of the situation and is therefore constitutionally incapable of improving it."[15]

This meeting proved to be a turning point in the relations between the Government and the Duma. The promise of unconditional support given to the Government at the session of June 26 was not withdrawn at once. It was still believed necessary to maintain an appearance of national unity. Indeed at the three-day session which followed the private meeting of the budget committee with the ministers, the deputies officially renewed the pledge to "safeguard the moral unity of the nation, which itself would be a guarantee of victory." But behind this official optimism the cleavage between officialdom and the Duma was rapidly growing. It took the form of a stubborn struggle for the immediate convocation of the Duma not merely for a few days to transact formal business and assure the Government of its support, but for a protracted session, and for the purpose of taking an effective part in the conduct of public affairs. At the same time strong pressure was brought upon the Emperor to remove from office the most objectionable and unpopular ministers.[16] As we know, this action was not without effect. Sukhomlinov, Shcheglovitov, Maklakov, and Sabler resigned and were replaced by men more acceptable to public opinion. And then came the formula that called for a "government enjoying the confidence of the nation" which simply meant a Government constituted of men popular with the community at large, but not responsible to parliament. In their campaign for these changes the Duma and its President were working hand in hand with the representatives of the municipalities, zemstvos, and war industries committees.[17] And behind them stood a large and influential section of the public which lent its support of the Duma on a scale seldom experienced before.

[15] P. N. Miliukov, *Istorya Vtoroi Russkoi Revolutsii* (*History of the Second Russian Revolution*) (Sofia, 1921), I, Part I, 24; also evidence of Miliukov in *Padenie Tsarskago Rezhima*, VI, 309–311; evidence of Shingarev in *ibid.*, VII, 21–23. Shingarev speaks in his evidence of the meeting of the budget committee which took place in March, 1915. It would seem, however, that he is referring to the meeting of January 25.

[16] Evidence of Rodzianko in *Padenie Tsarskago Rezhima*, VII, 126 *sqq.;* evidence of Miliukov in *ibid.*, VI, 312–314.

[17] *See below,* pp. 128–129.

The Organization of Supplies

Parallel with their political struggle, the Duma and the forces behind it were waging a battle for the reorganization of supplies. The appalling conditions in which the army found itself in 1914 and during the retreat from Galicia in the spring of 1915, when the troops were short of everything, especially munitions of war and rifles, clearly pointed to the necessity of immediate measures. On the other hand, the Ministry of War, still headed by General Sukhomlinov, limited itself to the issue of optimistic official statements like the one made by him at the meeting of the budget committee on January 25. It became obvious that the truce of June 26 was not bringing the results hoped for, and that fundamental changes in the organization of supplies must be introduced at once if Russia was to continue the struggle. The scheme proposed by Rodzianko provided for the setting up of a special council to take charge of all matters connected with national defense.[18] He advocated it with considerable energy and the idea was finally embodied in the four Special Councils—for national defense, transport, fuel, and food supplies—which were created by the Law of August 17, 1915. A fifth Special Council—on refugees—was added on August 30. The important feature of these councils was the inclusion in their membership of representatives of the Duma, the State Council, the Unions of Zemstvos and of Towns, and the Central War Industries Committee.[19] This was an entirely new departure from Russia's constitutional practice, and represented a distinct victory for the more liberal elements. The hopes attached to the work of the new Councils were not all fulfilled and their organization was by no means free from defects. Nevertheless they were generally recognized as an important step in the right direction, and the part played in their creation by the Duma and Rodzianko himself greatly added to the popularity of the lower chamber.

The Progressive Bloc

The summer of 1915 witnessed another new and important departure in the political situation, the formation of the so-called Progressive Bloc.[20] The attitude of unconditional support of the

[18] Rodzianko, *The Reign of Rasputin: an Empire's Collapse*, pp. 129–135.

[19] Gronsky, *op. cit.*, pp. 32–42; Zagorsky, *op. cit.*, pp. 82–86, 97–102.

[20] Evidence of Miliukov in *Padenie Tsarskago Rezhima*, VI, 314–318; Rodzianko, *The Reign of Rasputin: an Empire's Collapse*, pp. 145, 151; Gronsky, *op. cit.*, pp. 43–45; Miliukov, *Istorya Vtoroi Russkoi Revolutsii*, I, Part I, 26; Yakhontov, *op. cit.*, pp. 106–126; *Monarkhya Pered Krusheniem*, pp. 123–124.

Government assumed by the Duma at the outbreak of the War and which survived throughout the session of January, 1915, was now abandoned, and a coalition of political parties came into being. It included about two-thirds of the members of the Duma, the extreme Right and the extreme Left not joining it, and also an influential group of the members of the State Council led by Count Kokovzov and Count Olsufiev. The program of the Progressive Bloc was indeed very moderate. In addition to the already familiar demand for a "government enjoying the confidence of the nation," it included such very reasonable demands as a more tolerant policy in the matter of racial questions, especially with reference to the Jews and the Poles, a religious and political amnesty, the return of all persons deported without trial, freedom for the trade unions and labor organizations. None of these demands were revolutionary in the least, and when they came under discussion in the Council of Ministers the majority of the ministers declared themselves entirely in their favor. But Goremykin, the President of the Council, was reluctant even to discuss the program of the Bloc because, in his opinion, an organization including members of the two chambers was illegal. "Its scarcely disguised purpose," he said, "is the limitation of the powers of the Sovereign." And he promised to "fight it to the last."[21] In spite of that, negotiations of a semiofficial nature took place between the representatives of the Duma and Kharitonov, the State Controller, who reported favorably on the general attitude of the members of the new coalition.[22] Nothing however came of it. Goremykin's only desire was to get rid of the Duma for as long a period as could be conveniently arranged for. The objections of his colleagues that a prorogation of the Duma at a moment when it was making a constructive effort to collaborate with the Government would produce a most unfavorable impression, and would be likely to create grave disturbances in the country were met by Goremykin with complete indifference: "That does not matter at all. It is a mere trifle," he remarked. "No one takes any interest in the Duma except the newspapers, and everybody is tired of its idle talk."[23] We know the situation which developed in the Council of Ministers in the summer of 1915. It resulted in the ministers' collective *démarche* before the Emperor which amounted to a resignation. We know also that the Emperor refused to yield and ordered the ministers to continue

[21] Yakhontov, *op. cit.*, p. 107.
[22] *Ibid.*, pp. 119 *sqq.*
[23] *Ibid.*, p. 120.

in office with Goremykin as their leader, in spite of the fact that the latter was equally unacceptable to his colleagues and to the Duma.

It seems little wonder that the session of the Duma which opened on June 19 and lasted until September 3, 1915, was very different in tone from the two preceding short sessions. Even the representatives of the Right, such as Count V. A. Bobrinsky, declared that "the policy of the Government should be accepted in a spirit of patriotic scepticism." And the Progressive Group now asked not merely for a "government enjoying the confidence of the country," but for a government responsible to the Duma. The influential liberal Constitutional Democratic Party, while not supporting the latter demand, insisted on a program of immediate reforms, and thus opposed the policy of Goremykin who maintained that only questions dealing with the War should be discussed by the legislature.[24] The session devoted much of its time to the passing of the act establishing the four Special Councils. It was brought to an abrupt end when Goremykin, disregarding the opinion of his colleagues in the Government, went to the Imperial Headquarters with the army and obtained the signature of the Emperor to a decree proroguing the Duma until "a date not later than November 15." This meant a final and formal breach of the coöperation between the Government and the Duma. All methods of bringing about a compromise were exhausted and the contest became an open struggle. Discussing the attitude of the deputies in September, 1915, Rodzianko writes that "feelings ran very high and some of the speeches were of an almost revolutionary character. Some of the deputies went so far as to refuse to submit to the prorogation and demanded that the Duma should proclaim itself a constituent assembly."[25] A more moderate opinion however prevailed.

In this struggle against the Government the Progressive Bloc proved a most important factor. Not only did it assure the collaboration of a very wide cross section of public opinion, but it also provided a foundation for a strong agitation in favor of a government responsible to parliament instead of making the familiar demand for a "government enjoying the confidence of the nation" but responsible to the Sovereign. One of the most important objections to a parliamentary government advanced in liberal circles was the non-existence in the legislative chambers of a stable majority. The formation of a coalition government under Russian conditions, in the absence of an established

[24] Miliukov, *Istorya Vtoroi Russkoi Revolutsii*, I, Part I, 25–26.
[25] Rodzianko, *The Reign of Rasputin: an Empire's Collapse*, p. 154.

parliamentary tradition, lack of experience, and low educational and cultural standards, would be a matter of extreme difficulty. This was fully recognized by the Constitutional Democratic Party led by Miliukov, which included the most brilliant representatives of the intellectual classes. With the formation of the Progressive Bloc this formal objection lost a great deal of its validity, and this was one of the reasons why in the second half of 1915 and in 1916 the movement for a government responsible to the Duma greatly gained in strength.[26]

The other and probably more important reason was the rapidly growing mistrust of the Government which followed the departure of the Emperor for the army and the immense increase in the influence of the Empress and Rasputin in the conduct of public affairs. The eclipse of the sovereign and the disintegration of the bureaucratic system could not escape the attention of the nation. The rule of a vulgar adventurer over an Empire of some 160 million people could obviously not be tolerated forever. "Ministerial leap-frog" and the type of men who made their way to power by unsavory means was not only revolting to the nation's dignity and sense of decency but was also an immense national danger. It was obvious that a change could not be delayed much longer. It could be effected in one of two ways: by the limitation of the powers of the Sovereign and with that the elimination of the irresponsible influences behind the throne from the conduct of public affairs, or by a revolution. The sympathies of the Duma and of liberal circles were divided between the two. It must be said however that the Progressive Bloc, in spite of the insistence of some of its members, refused to accept as a part of its program the demand for a government responsible to parliament. As late as October, 1916, almost on the eve of the Revolution, the counsels of Miliukov, which favored the more moderate and vague formula, "government enjoying the confidence of the nation," won the day.[27]

The Year 1916

The dismissal of Goremykin and the appointment of Sturmer to the presidency of the Council of Ministers, which, as we know, took place in January, 1916, did nothing to improve the relations between the Duma and the Government. Enough has been said about Sturmer to make it clear that he had no chance of commanding either fear or respect in the legislature. His desire to bring about an improvement in the relations between

[26] Evidence of Miliukov in *Padenie Tsarskago Rezhima*, VI 334–335.
[27] Rodzianko, *The Reign of Rasputin: an Empire's Collapse*, pp. 221–222.

the Cabinet and the lower house took the unexpected and rath
curious form of proposing a reception at his residence for th
deputies. The idea was probably suggested to him by forme
experiences as master of ceremonies of the Imperial court.
is hardly necessary to say that it proved a complete failure. H
was informed that the deputies would decline his invitations.
As a condition to the convocation of the Duma, Sturmer de
manded the assurance that Rasputin would not be mentione
in the debates. No such assurance was given him.[29] But the con
vocation of the Duma took place, on February 9, 1916, an
was accompanied by an event which, if brought to its logica
conclusions, might have proved a turning point in the relatior
between Duma and autocracy. For the first time in the life o
the Russian parliament the Tsar in person visited it. We kno
today that this visit was encouraged by Rasputin and the Em
press.[30] It seems to have been inspired by that mystical belie
in the miracle-working powers of the Tsar's personality whic
was an accepted dogma in inner court circles. It cannot b
denied that the appearance of the Tsar in the Duma produce
a strong impression upon a section of the deputies. Sturme
seemed to believe that it achieved much.[31] And Rodziank
described it in glowing terms.[32] But the practical results wer
nil. The remarks of the Sovereign were entirely noncommitta
The speech of Sturmer which followed the departure of th
Tsar was sufficient to kill any enthusiasm. The President of th
Council left the platform amid a chilly silence broken only b
the applause of a few members of the extreme Right.[33]

The months that followed witnessed a further development i
the struggle between Duma and Government. Exasperated b
the attitude adopted toward him by the legislature, Sturme
employed such unusual methods as threats to dissolve it, 1
send the deputies to serve with the army, and to suspend th
paying of their salaries.[34] Such attempts at compulsion natural
had effects exactly the opposite of those intended. The atmos
phere was so charged with electricity that an explosion seeme
unavoidable.

Although the policy of the Government offered ample groun

[28] Evidence of Miliukov in *Padenie Tsarskago Rezhima*, VI, 328.
[29] *Ibid.*, p. 327; Miliukov, *Istorya Vtoroi Russkoi Revolutsii*, I, Part I, 29.
[30] Evidence of A. N. Kvostov in *Padenie Tsarskago Rezhima*, I, 34–35; *Letters the Tsaritsa to the Tsar*, pp. 219, 225.
[31] Report of Sturmer to the Emperor in *Monarkhya Pered Krusheniem*, pp. 117–11
[32] Rodzianko, *The Reign of Rasputin: an Empire's Collapse*, pp. 173 sqq.
[33] *Ibid.*, pp. 177–178; evidence of Miliukov in *Padenie Tsarskago Rezhima*, VI, 32
[34] Report of Sturmer to the Emperor in *Monarkhya Pered Krusheniem*, p. 131.

for criticism of the severest kind, the accusations brought against it in the Duma were often of a nature that has been proved since to be entirely false. The most outstanding was the charge that the Empress and the ministers favored the enemy and were even guilty of high treason. We have said that the Empress was often referred to in the army and in the country at large as "the German." Similar accusations were advanced against Sturmer, but no evidence has been produced so far to support them, and all available information tends to show that they were entirely without foundation. Still more unhappy was the case of the members of the Baltic nobility, men bearing German and Swedish names, who belonged to families that have been in the service of the Russian Crown for generations, and who had suffered heavy losses during the War. Hunting for Germans and German spies became a sport in which even members of the Duma allowed themselves to indulge.[35] Rodzianko was much under such influences, and he was probably right when he said that his office became "the centre of all such talk," and that the Duma received "all the news and also all the gossip."[36] Even the enlightened and acknowledged representative of western ideas in Russian parliamentary circles, Miliukov, did not escape the general taint.

It was on this very ground that his celebrated attack, which played the important part of striking one of the final blows at the Imperial *régime*, was launched in the Duma on November 1, 1916. In his speech Miliukov enumerated the many failings and errors of the Government. He spoke of the dark forces behind the throne. And he ended every peroration with the question: "Is this stupidity or is it treason?" He declared afterward that he himself was inclined to take the former view, but his audience seemed to believe the latter.[37] His list included the names not only of Sturmer but also that of the Empress Alexandra Feodorovna. Openly denouncing Sturmer as a traitor, he quoted a statement printed in *Neue Freie Presse* describing Sturmer's appointment as "a victory for the court party grouped around the young Tsaritsa."[38] This speech, without precedent in the annals of the Duma, was followed by highly patriotic but no less violent attacks on the Government by the conservative deputy Shulgin and the leader of the extreme Right, Purishkevich. The latter, an orator of unusual power, exclaimed: "You

[5] *See* for instance evidence of Khvostov in *Padenie Tsarskago Rezhima*, I, 5 *sqq*.
[6] Evidence of Rodzianko in *Padenie Tsarskago Rezhima*, VII, 152.
[7] Miliukov, *Istorya Vtoroi Russkoi Revolutsii*, I, Part I, 33.
[8] Rodzianko, *The Reign of Rasputin: an Empire's Collapse*, pp. 225–226.

must all go to Headquarters, throw yourself at the feet of the Emperor, beg him to believe in all the horror of the influence of Rasputin, the terrible consequences of such conditions, and implore him to change his policy."[39] This appeal, however, remained without effect; and, a few weeks later, realizing the futility of words, Purishkevich became one of the organizers of the murder of Rasputin.

The attack by Miliukov was, no doubt, inspired by the highest motives and by what he understood at the time to be the interests of the country. The fact nevertheless remains that it was entirely without grounds, or merely based on hearsay, gossip and secondhand newspaper information. He practically admitted this himself before the Committee of Inquiry.[40] However great might have been the faults of the Empress—and no attempt has been made in these pages to conceal or minimize them—one cannot help but be sorry for a woman who had to experience the inexpressible outrage of seeing her attitude toward her country's enemies so grievously distorted and misrepresented.

It was probably at this time that the popularity of the Duma reached its highest point. In spite of the heroic measures of the censor, who not only deleted entire speeches like those of Miliukov and Purishkevich but even substituted, for speeches of some of the deputies, for instance for one by the socialist Chkheidze, pronouncements of his own composition which a socialist deputy would never have dreamed of delivering, the publicity received by the debates of the Duma was immense, and entirely without parallel in the history of the country.[41] The appearance of newspapers with whole columns blank merely excited public curiosity, and intensified the interest in the speeches prohibited. They were multiplied by all possible methods and were circulated in millions of mimeographed and typewritten copies, often with amplifications and additions which might have surprised their authors.[42] They could be found in the remotest corner of the country, in the trenches, and in peasant cottages. The Duma had gained a hold on the imagination of the nation which seemed to prepare the way for its future leadership. But its star was already nearing its eclipse. And this came as unexpectedly as its time of popular admiration and enthusiasm.

[39] Quoted in Rodzianko, *Gosudarstvennaya Duma i Fevralskaya 1917 Goda Revolutesya*, pp. 52–53.
[40] Evidence of Miliukov in *Padenie Tsarskago Rezhima*, VI, 369–371.
[41] Evidence of Rodzianko in *Padenie Tsarskago Rezhima*, VII, 172.
[42] Miliukov, *Istorya Vtoroi Russkoi Revolutsii*, I, Part I, 34.

The Last Stage

The trend of the session of November 1, 1916, produced in official circles that impression which one might well imagine it would. It was realized in high places that the position of Sturmer was no longer tenable, and he had to go, giving place to the relatively inoffensive Trepov. But the change was obviously short of the most moderate demands of the Duma. The presence of Protopopov in the Cabinet—he was retained, it will be remembered, against the better judgment of the Emperor, as the result of the insistence of the Empress and Rasputin—had all the effect of the red flag upon the bull in a Spanish arena. When Trepov appeared before the Duma to read the declaration of his Cabinet he was not permitted to speak. Three times he mounted the platform but was shouted down by the deputies of the Left. The more conservative parties did not approve of this method of protest but were unable to prevent the demonstration.[43] The weeks that followed brought no improvement in the situation. Trepov was followed by Golitsin, a man entirely incapable of filling the position of President of the Council. The Duma was prorogued until February, 1917, and rumors, not devoid of foundation, were in circulation that it would be dissolved. The murder of Rasputin which took place in December, 1916, did nothing to clear the atmosphere. Everyone was living in apprehension of the coming changes which, nevertheless, found the country entirely unprepared for them.

It must be said to the credit of Rodzianko that in his relations with the Emperor he was not lacking in courage and did not hesitate to use plain and even strong language when he felt this was required by the situation. His last written report submitted to the Tsar in February, 1917, a bare few weeks before the Revolution, gives a striking and vivid picture of the catastrophic condition of the country. It points out with remarkable clarity and power of expression that the terrible predicament of the country was due not to its inborn weakness or lack of resources, but to a deplorable absence of organization and leadership which threatened to make all past sacrifices useless and give victory to the enemy. The report, after a detailed analysis of the situation accompanied by suggestions for remedies, ended with the following moving appeal:

Only a government that enjoys the confidence of the country could induce it to accept further privations; only if this condition be ful-

[43] *Ibid.;* evidence of Miliukov in *Padenie Tsarskago Rezhima*, VI, 348–349.

filled will the slogan "war to a victorious end" acquire a real meaning Sire, in a moment of terrible national emergency, when the country was in mortal danger, your ancestor did not hesitate to entrust the conduct of public affairs to a man enjoying the confidence of the nation—and the country was saved and the name of Alexander I was written in golden characters on the pages of not only Russian, but world history. With all the power of which we are capable, fully conscious of the patriotic duty which rests upon us,—we implore you Sire, to follow the example of your noble ancestor. The final hour is striking, and the time is only too near when all appeals to the reason of the people will be futile and useless.[44]

This warning, which embodied the conviction of the Duma and the forces behind it, was of no avail. The monarchy blindly drifted toward its end.

The Sovereign, the Government, and the Duma

Enough has been said of the general outlook of the Emperor and the Tsaritsa to make it clear that their attitude toward the legislature could only be purely negative. The idea of a government responsible to parliament was particularly repulsive to the Empress, a point of view scarcely to have been looked for in a royal princess brought up in the shadow of the Palace of Westminster. One of her chief preoccupations during the War, it seems, was to keep the sessions of the Duma as brief as they could be made. It is true that this desire was in part stimulated by the fear that a question concerning which "the Duma had no concern," that is, the question of Rasputin, might be raised by the deputies.[45] But even the Empress was occasionally forced to admit that a short session of the Duma should be convoked in order not to make matters worse.[46] This however was merely a concession to external pressure. Her general attitude toward a parliamentary *régime* was stated in no uncertain words. "We are not ready for it [a constitutional government]," she wrote on September 7, 1915, "and it would be Russia's ruin, we are not a constitutional country and dare not be it, our people are not educated for it and, thank God, our Emperor is an autocrat and must stick to it."[47] "It will be a rotten Duma," she wrote on October 30, 1916, "but one must not fear; if too vile, one closes it."[48] This attitude toward the lower chamber was strengthened by her personal dislike of the President of the

[44] Report of Rodzianko to the Emperor in *Krasni Arkhiv*, X, 69–86; Rodzianko, *The Reign of Rasputin: an Empire's Collapse*, pp. 259–261.
[45] *Letters of the Tsaritsa to the Tsar*, pp. 100, 110, 130–131, 135.
[46] *Ibid.*, p. 225.
[47] *Ibid.*, p. 145.
[48] *Ibid.*, p. 429.

Duma. "How I wish one could hang Rodzianko," the Empress wrote on September 17, "awful man and such an insolent fellow."[49] This opinion, it seems, was shared by the Emperor himself. "It goes without saying," he wrote on June 26, 1916, "that Rodzianko has talked a lot of nonsense."[50] But it appears from the narrative of the President of the Duma himself that on a number of occasions the Sovereign sought his advice and sometimes followed it.

As to the attitude of the Cabinet toward the Duma, it must be clearly understood that this Russian Cabinet was not a cabinet in the sense in which the term is used in western Europe. There was no joint responsibility, and the appointment and dismissal of this or that minister were solely matters for the Emperor to decide. Even the appointment of a new President of the Council did not mean a change in the membership or policy of the cabinet. This is why the reactionary and antiparliamentary policies of Goremykin, Sturmer, and in a lesser degree, Trepov and Golitsin, did not mean that the Presidents of the Council were acting in concert with their colleagues. We have seen that the reverse was true. A number of ministers such as Krivoshein, who was even credited with taking a hand in the organization of the Progressive Bloc,[51] Samarin, Prince Shcherbatov, Count Ignatiev, Naumov,[52] Sazonov ("such a coward towards Europe and parliamentarists" the Empress called him),[53] and Polivanov were only too anxious to work with the Duma. We have seen that they displayed a good deal of courage in laying their views before the Council of Ministers and the Emperor himself. But under the Russian system their good intentions and efforts were doomed to failure. Important questions of policy were decided by the Emperor himself, with the assistance of a small circle of advisers who, not infrequently, had no connection with the Cabinet. The dissenting ministers were left without any recourse. As the crisis of the summer of 1915 has shown, they were not even permitted to resign. It was indeed a tragic situation, and the claim of Prince Shcherbatov above[54] that the future historian will absolve him and his colleagues "from the charges which are being heaped upon them to-day" deserves serious consideration. There is no doubt that the attitude of the Cabinet toward the Duma, as expressed in its official pronouncements and actions, was reactionary and

[49] *Ibid.*, p. 401.
[50] *The Letters of the Tsar to the Tsaritsa*, p. 219.
[51] Evidence of Miliukov in *Padenie Tsarskago Rezhima*, VI, 316.
[52] Evidence of Naumov in *Padenie Tsarskago Rezhima*, I, 332, 337.
[53] *Letters of the Tsaritsa to the Tsar*, p. 305.
[54] *See above*, p. 83.

unfriendly in the extreme. But it is also true that the Cabinet which adopted such a policy included a number of men who sincerely deplored it, and fought against it with all the weapons at their disposal.

The Duma and the Revolution

The events of February–March, 1917, which resulted in the overthrow of the monarchy and the establishment of the Provisional Government took place at the climax of the popularity of the Duma. The social forces behind the Revolution will be discussed elsewhere in this volume but it may be convenient to point out here that, in spite of the conspicuous part taken by the Duma in the abdication of the Emperor and the appointment of the Provisional Government, it had no real control over the course of the events. Although the Duma and the liberal groups which supported it constantly discussed the imminence of a forcible change in the existing *régime,* the revolt which started in the streets of Petrograd on February 23, 1917, and brought about the downfall of the monarchy, took them entirely by surprise. The revolutionary movement was spontaneous, and in its first days was given no guidance by the Duma. It was only on February 27, that it elected a Provisional Committee and attempted to assume the leadership of the movement. It succeeded in part in so far as it concerned the external history of these troubled days. The abdication of the Emperor at Pskov was secured by two emissaries of the Duma, the deputies Guchkov and Shulgin. The Provisional Government, which succeeded to the power of the Tsar pending the Constituent Assembly, was appointed by the Provisional Committee of the Duma. It included among its members some of the most prominent deputies. It might have appeared to a superficial observer that the leadership of the Duma was as strong as ever.[55] In fact, however, this was the beginning of its downfall.

The revolutionary upheaval brought to the surface new social forces which had been long ignored in the political life of Russia. They found their organized expression in the Soviet of Soldiers' and Workmen's Deputies which came into being simultaneously with the Provisional Government and became the leader of the more radical elements.[56] To them the Duma was nothing but an instrument of class domination and the survival of a hated *régime.* And, as the influence of these radical forces increased,

[55] Gronsky, *op. cit.,* pp. 43–55; Miliukov, *Istorya Vtoroi Russkoi Revolutsii,* I, Part I, 41 *sqq.;* evidence of Miliukov in *Padenie Tsarskago Rezhima,* VI, 351 *sqq.;* evidence of Guchkov in *ibid.,* VI, 262.
[56] *See below,* Chapter X.

the prestige of the Duma declined. It still continued to meet for some time in private sessions, and the members of the Provisional Government felt it their duty to keep in touch with the body which officially called them to power. But the Provisional Government itself suffered considerable changes in its membership, the new ministers coming from circles hostile to the Duma. The prestige of the latter suffered a further decline.

A certain revival of interest in the Duma was experienced in April, 1917, when the Provisional Government, fearful of the growing influence of the Soviet and looking for some kind of support, called a joint session of the members of the four Dumas. The political consequences of the experiment, however, proved negligible.[57] The Special Councils, those offsprings of the Duma, were subjected to a process of democratization which entirely altered their character.[58] The members of the four Dumas were still invited to participate in the work of the so-called Moscow State Conference, a kind of substitute for parliament which met in Moscow in August, 1917. This was their swan song. On September 1, 1917, Russia was proclaimed a republic, a step which necessitated the formal abolition of all institutions connected with the central machinery of the Imperial *régime*. No decree dissolving the Duma was published because the five-year term for which the deputies were elected expired, in any case, in October. The Duma which a year before was the recognized leader of the nation was simply allowed to lapse into oblivion.

The complete eclipse of the Duma and the disappearance from the political stage of its president, Rodzianko, whose massive figure had been for years the center of the struggle for liberal reforms was, of course, natural and even inevitable. The Duma was not only part of the machinery of Imperial Russia, but it also bore on its brow the stigma of the Election Law of June 3, 1907. It was based on class representation, and it voiced the views of a social group, the landed proprietors, whose death sentence was signed at the same time as the abdication of Nicholas II. Its presence in the new and rapidly changing world which was emerging from the revolutionary upheaval was an obvious anachronism, which could not have been tolerated much longer.

Among those who proved incapable of understanding the situation was Rodzianko, himself. Sincerely devoted to the welfare and happiness of his country, he was not lacking in courage, honesty, and loyalty to the cause of Russia's progress along the lines of constitutional government. A former officer in one of the smartest regiments of the guards, an aristocrat, a wealthy

[57] Gronsky, *op. cit.*, p. 67.
[58] *Ibid.*, pp. 74–75; Zagorsky, *op. cit.*, pp. 181 *sqq.*

landowner, and an official of the Imperial court, he was deficient in those qualities of vision and insight which are essential to real statesmanship. Sir Alfred Knox was probably right when, referring to the large build of the President of the Duma, he said, "Rodzianko is only big in physical bulk."[59] The immense social landslide which took place in 1917 was beyond his grasp. Writing several years after the Revolution, an exile in Yugoslavia, the former President of the Duma still maintained that the "fatal mistake" of the Provisional Government was its refusal to convoke the Duma and thus create an effective counterpoise to the influence of the Soviets.[60] He invariably referred to his colleagues of the Duma as the "chosen representatives of the people," a description which could hardly be applied to the members of a legislature elected under the Law of June 3, 1907. He could not see that the landed nobility he represented—and it had been for centuries the social group on which largely depended the functioning of the machinery of State—had now been replaced by new social formations. To the post-revolutionary Russia both he and the Duma were merely shadows of the past.

Chapter 6

The Plight of the Middle Class

The Middle Class

ONE OF THE MOST unfortunate consequences of Russia's historical development was the almost complete nonexistence of a middle class in the sense in which this term is used in western Europe. The extreme backwardness of the country's economic position, which was largely due to the fact that until 1861 the immense majority of the population were still living under the yoke of serfdom, was undoubtedly one of the chief causes which prevented the growth of that important social group. But even after the emancipation of the serfs the whole system of legal relationship created by the Emancipation Act, in accordance with which the ownership of the so-called allotment land was vested in the house elder as representative of the peasant family, established a purely artificial link between the younger members

[59] Knox, *op. cit.*, p. 531.
[60] Rodzianko, *Gosudarstvennaya Duma i Fevralskaya 1917 Goda Revolutsya*, p. 70.

of the peasant household and their native villages.[1] The rather undetermined and vague right of the junior members to a portion of the land held by the family had much to do in keeping the younger men from seeking permanent employment in trade or industry. It will be remembered that this link survived until the land reforms of Stolypin, which were introduced on the very eve of the War. Then, of course, the prevalence of communal land tenure, with all the evils which are inseparable from it, greatly hindered the growth of a class of independent peasant farmers. The extreme youth of Russia's industry, on the other hand, coupled with a chronic shortage of capital, offered little opportunity for the formation of a reasonably prosperous group of wage earners, artisans, and merchants such as played so important a part in the economic and political development of western European countries. Various obsolete legal restrictions dating back to the time of Catherine II further hampered the formation of a middle class.

Even the Russian language, oddly enough, has no appropriate term to express the concept of the middle class. Such a thing seems to embody an idea essentially democratic in its nature and the bureaucratic State had little use for it. There were nevertheless certain social groups in the former Russian Empire which should be treated as groups standing apart, alike from bureaucracy, manual laborers, and peasants. They included the so-called intelligentsia, that is, professional men and women, such as lawyers, doctors, journalists, college professors, teachers in elementary and secondary schools, representatives of trade, industry, and banks, employees of the various institutions of the zemstvos and municipalities, and of the coöperative societies, and, finally, landed gentry living upon incomes from their estates and investments. It might be even fair to include in this group a section of the government employees. No hard and fast line could be drawn which would separate this class from other social groups in which it was gradually merging. In spite, however, of the variety of the elements which composed it, this group, which we shall call the middle class, possessed two characteristics in common. One was its independence of the Government, which put it into a favorable position for the criticising of the policy of St. Petersburg without having to fear immediate inconveniences. This, of course, did not apply to all government employees. The other, a characteristic perhaps even more important, was its relatively high average education, coupled with a varying degree of interest in public affairs. These two char-

See below, pp. 178 sqq.

acteristics—independence of government and an interest in public affairs that was based on general education—gave the group we are now discussing a very important place in the community and in the State. In spite of its numerical weakness—in number the middle class was insignificant as compared with the masses of the peasantry—it was the only element capable of expressing an articulate and independent opinion upon the conduct of public affairs and of either criticizing or supporting the Government.

The notable progress made in the development of industry in the period following the 'nineties of the last century, the reforms by Stolypin, which brought to an end the bondage of the peasants to the commune and the disabilities of joint family ownership, the slow but steady spread of education, the reforms of October 17, 1905, which introduced freedom of speech and assembly—greatly curtailed, it is true, by the interference of the police—all these beginnings seemed to indicate that a new field of progress and influence was opening to the middle class. Unfortunately, these changes were far too short-lived to bear their fruit before the outbreak of the War. In spite of the potential forces behind such a class, it was not yet in a position successfully to defend its claims against bureaucracy and the conservative landed aristocracy, in which the tradition of absolute monarchy found some of its staunch supporters. But the Great War with its unlimited demands upon national resources offered the middle class an extraordinary opportunity, chiefly through the institutions of local government with which it had always been identified, to expand the domain of its activities. We have already seen the remarkable growth of the prestige of the Duma during the War. The same thing was true of the zemstvos and municipalities: the two unions they organized in August, 1914, for the relief of wounded soldiers developed into institutions of national importance working on a national scale. The movement for the mobilization of industry, which started in the spring of 1915 and found its expression in the creation of the war industries committees, was a purely unofficial movement which originated with the public-minded leaders of industry and won the whole-hearted support of the intelligentsia. In wartime history the middle class, in fact, played a marked part.

Until the establishment of the Duma the institutions of local government, especially the zemstvos, were the chief organs for the expression of liberal opinions. After 1906 this rôle naturally passed to the Duma. This body, even after the enactment of the Law of June 3, 1907, included many representatives of the middle class, among them some of its outstanding leaders, who naturally looked for support and inspiration to the social elements to which they belonged. With the outbreak of the War and the Duma's successive and lengthy prorogations, the organizations of the middle class, the most important of which came into existence during the War itself, gradually acquired a place in the political and economic life of the nation which was no less surprising than the rise of the Duma.

It may be fitting here to note that while the general trend of opinion in the middle class was of a distinctly liberal cast, it also counted among its members a small but rather active group of very conservative, not to say reactionary, men and women who received the special protection of the Government, and succeeded in exercising a considerable influence upon the conduct of public affairs, above all since they possessed the confidence of the Emperor.

The war activities of the middle class were affected in no small degree by the economic privations and hardships they had to endure. First among them was the rise in the cost of living.

The Rise in the Cost of Living

It was pointed out in an earlier chapter that that general impoverishment of the masses which was looked for at the beginning of the War failed to materialize.[2] On the other hand, the disparity between agricultural and industrial production, especially upon the diversion of the latter into war channels, resulted in an extreme unwillingness on the part of the peasants to sell their produce for paper money, with which they could buy none of the goods they wanted. This unforeseen development, coupled with the inadequacy of the railroads to perform the double task of providing for the army and the civilian population, soon led to a considerable reduction in the supply of foodstuffs for the cities and towns, which was aggravated by a general dearth of all articles of prime necessity. The unavoidable consequences of this situation was a rapid rise in the cost of living. The chief sufferer from both the shortage of foodstuffs and commodities, and from high prices, was the urban population, especially that part of it which depended for its living on fixed incomes of moderate size. And this applied to the bulk of the middle class.

The shortage of foodstuffs and the rise in the cost of living were further aggravated by the rapid growth of the urban population during the war years. The population of Petrograd, for instance, increased from 2,100,000 in 1914 to 2,465,000 in January, 1917; the population of Moscow increased from 1,600,000 in 1912 to over 2,000,000 in January, 1917. A similar process

[2] See above, pp. 47 sqq.

of urbanization took place all over the country. The total urban population of Russia before the War was estimated at 22,000,-000; in 1916 it had risen to 28,000,000.[3] The explanation of this phenomenon must be sought in the mobilization of large numbers of men who had been moved from the country into city barracks; in the development of war industries which required vast labor forces, in the return of sick and wounded soldiers from the army; and, finally, in the arrival of refugees from the areas occupied by the enemy, refugees whose numbers ran into millions.

One of the immediate effects of this unforeseen growth of the urban population was an acute shortage of living accommodations. An illustration of the conditions which prevailed in Moscow at the beginning of the second year of the War is given by Professor Novgorotsev. "When in September 1915 the constant flow of refugees was augmented by all the students who had returned to Moscow after their vacations," he writes,[4] "many searched in vain for lodgings." And he quotes the following illuminating statement from an appeal issued by the Mayor of Moscow:[5] "Students are vainly looking for accommodations regardless of distance or of sanitary conditions; being unable to find any, they spend hours at the railway stations, in tea rooms, and in the streets. Finally, in despair they leave Moscow, with heavy hearts and with their last pennies in their pockets, thus abandoning all hope of continuing their education." The attempts to remedy this situation had little effect, and an official statement issued a year later, in August, 1916, was forced to admit that "this year there is a still more acute and hopeless shortage of accommodations, especially for women students. . . . The houseless condition of the Moscow student is now a fact beyond question and it is daily becoming worse."[6] Similar information was forthcoming from other university cities, even from those relatively remote from the front such as Odessa.

No less acute than the housing crisis was the shortage of foodstuffs and fuel. The situation, of course, was not uniform all over the country and depended a great deal on local conditions, especially on the geographical factor. Nevertheless a general trend toward the disruption of the balance of demand and supply was observed everywhere, and the difference was merely one of time and degree. The larger cities were the first to suffer,

[3] Astrov, *op. cit.*, pp. 272–273.
[4] P. J. Novgorotsev, "Universities and Higher Technical Schools," in the volume *Russian Schools and Universities in the World War* (Yale University Press, 1929), p. 205, in this series of the "Economic and Social History of the World War."
[5] *Ibid.*, p. 206.
[6] *Ibid.*, p. 207.

and among them Petrograd was in a particularly unfavorable position.

In Petrograd the rise in prices had become alarming within six months after the outbreak of the War [writes M. Astrov]. . . . The supplies of coal and firewood were the first to be affected. Before the War Petrograd obtained a large part of its coal supply from abroad, mainly from England via the Baltic Sea; in 1913, 125,000,000 puds (about 2,000,000 tons) were so imported. . . . But in 1915 such imports were entirely suspended. Everything had to come from the Donets Valley. . . . The transport of coal from the Donets Valley, however, met with enormous difficulties. Of the 11,625 coal cars required only 5,185 were actually supplied. Under the system as planned, the municipality of Petrograd was to receive 250 carloads a month. But as a matter of fact in September it received only 41 carloads; in October, eight; in November, none; in December, 50. Of the 140,000 cubic sachines[7] of firewood for which contracts were entered into by the executive board of the municipality, only about 60,000 cubic sachines were actually delivered. The firewood bought by the municipality—and it had paid 70 per cent of the price in advance—was requisitioned by the railway.[8]

The same shortage of the necessaries of life gradually developed in practically all the cities of Russia. The rise in prices began within the first six months of the War. And by October, 1915, most alarming news as to the condition of supplies was arriving from everywhere.

In their replies to the inquiries made by the Government and the Central Committee of the Union of Towns [writes M. Astrov] almost all municipalities stated that their towns were suffering from the shortage of the necessaries of life. By 1916 life in towns and cities had become a virtual ordeal, so great was the inadequacy of the food supply. The most essential commodities disappeared from the market one after another. The newspapers were filled with reports from all parts of Russia, all alike dealing with the crisis of foodstuffs. Large cities and small towns, the north and the south, the central districts, the regions of the Volga and the Caucasus—all were passing through a violent crisis. . . . Even in the wheat-growing provinces, such as the provinces of Simbirsk, Samara, and Saratov, the work of the flour mills had to be periodically suspended for lack of grain.[9]

The growing disparity between demand and supply naturally resulted in a rapid increase in the cost of living.[10] According to

---

[7] One cubic sachine = 343 cubic feet. Wood, it will be remembered, was the fuel generally used in Russia for household purposes.

[8] Astrov, *op. cit.*, pp. 281–282.

[9] *Ibid.*, p. 270.

[10] See Demosthenov, *op. cit.*, especially Chapters III and IV.

M. Demosthenov the general index number of thirteen principal foodstuffs (1913 = 100) for July–December, 1914, was 110.1; for January–June, 1915, 141.9; for July–December, 1915, 155.5; for January–June, 1916, 195.6. In August, 1916, the latest date for which the information on which M. Demosthenov's computation was based was available, it reached 221.6.[11] This computation includes a number of markets, and seems to be the most careful and thorough estimate in existence of price movements in Russia during the War. The rise of prices in the large cities, especially in the latter part of the War, was probably considerably more rapid than appears from the figures quoted above. The increase in the price of separate commodities had been particularly striking. Taking, for instance, the average price in the chief cities in 1913–1914 = 100, the price of meat in July, 1916, was estimated as 332; flax, 265; and salt, 583.[12] The increase of prices in Moscow in June, 1916, compared with their level at the outbreak of the War, will appear from the following figures: butter, 220; animal fat, 273; sugar, 153; coffee, 271; eggs, 193; milk, 171; beef, 371; mutton, 381; potatoes, 144; rice, 243; fuel (coal and firewood), 224; petroleum and candles, 210; matches, 500; textiles, 262; footwear, 334.[13] No reliable data for the movement of the prices in the second half of 1916 and in 1917 are available. It has nevertheless been computed that, on the 1913 base, the general index number of prices in 1916 was 203, and in 1917, 673, an increase of 470 points in one year.[14] While the accuracy of this figure may be questioned, the fact itself, the increase in the cost of living by leaps and bounds in 1917, seems well established.

The Impoverishment of the Middle Class

Let us now attempt to determine how the position of the middle class was affected by these immense economic changes. The question is not quite so simple as may appear at first sight. As a matter of fact it has been argued by well-informed writers that the purchasing power of the urban population as a whole was increased rather than decreased during the War. This opin-

[11] Demosthenov, *op. cit.*, pp. 257–258.

[12] Zagorsky, *op. cit.*, pp. 60–61.

[13] Data of the publication of the Union of Towns, *Dvizhenie Tsen za Dva Goda Voini (The Movement of Prices during the Two Years of the War)* (Petrograd, 1916), quoted in Astrov, *op. cit.*, pp. 271–272.

[14] S. G. Strumilin, *Zarabotnaya Plata Russkoi Promishlennosti za 1913–1922 (Wages in Russian Industry in 1913–1922)* in *Na Novikh Putyakh (On the New Road)* published by *Soviet Truda i Oboroni (The Council of Labor and Defense)* (Moscow, 1923), III, 90.

on is based on the examination of the deposits and current accounts in the savings banks and joint stock banks, which indicate a distinct growth between 1914 and 1917. The cash deposits in the state savings banks, for instance, increased from ,685,000,000 rubles on January 1, 1914, to 4,915,000,000 rubles on October 1, 1917.[15] There is little doubt that a section of the urban population succeeded in realizing handsome profits during the War. First among them were manufacturers engaged in the industries working for national defense. The earnings of the executive staffs of such enterprises, of the directors, managers, and engineers, also greatly increased. Another group whose financial position was strengthened rather than weakened during the War were the families of army officers, who were now in receipt of salaries which exceeded by a wide margin their peacetime earnings. The same applied to a certain extent to the rather numerous personnel of the semiofficial war organizations such as the Unions of Zemstvos and of Towns. These groups, however, formed a very slight percentage of the total urban population, even if we admit that the extra earnings they received were sufficient to counterbalance the rise in the cost of living, which is by no means proved. Nor, of course, would the extra earnings in rapidly depreciating paper rubles compensate them for the terrible overcrowding of the cities and the shortage of fuel, foodstuffs, and other bare necessaries of life.

Most of the circumstantial and some direct evidence seems to point to the rapid decline of the economic standards of the middle class, which were never too high. An increase in salaries, no doubt, had taken place in every branch, but it seems extremely doubtful whether in the majority of cases it could keep pace with the increase in the cost of living, as has been claimed in the case of industries working for national defense. The computation of the changes in real wages of employees who were "white-collar" workers (as distinct from workmen) for all industries is shown in Table 1, gives a much more real picture of the situation.

This table indicates a steady decline in real earnings of such employees, a decline which continued in spite of the rise in their nominal earnings. It was greatly accentuated in 1916, and became catastrophic in 1917. That this was the general trend followed by the incomes of the bulk of the middle class is supported by evidence from other sources.

Demosthenov, *op. cit.*, p. 336.

TABLE 1

Average Monthly Earnings of Employees in All Industries in 1913–1917.[16]

(Data of the Census of 1918)

Year	Nominal (in paper rubles)	Real[17] (in gold rubles)
1913	85.5	85.5
1914	85.5	84.6
1915	103.0	79.2
1916	142.0	69.8
1917	255.6	38.0

Discussing the position of university undergraduates, who were drawn mostly from the social group we are now discussing, Professor Novgorotsev speaks of their "general impoverishment due to the high cost of living and lack of resources." And he notes that the majority of them were unable to pay their tuition fees. The situation was still worse in 1916. "High cost of living, profiteering, lack of food products, these were the standing topics of the day." Many of the undergraduates were compelled to abandon their studies and either to return home or to seek some employment.[18]

The statement of M. Astrov quoted above[19] that "by 1916 life in towns and cities had become a virtual ordeal" was by no means an exaggeration. What it was like by the end of the same year will appear from the following facts taken at random from the reports received by the Union of Towns. In Odessa one had to spend two days in line to buy a little oil. Thousands of people were waiting in line for oil in Aleksandrovsk. In Odessa the lack of fuel necessitated the closing down of the electric power station, the shutting off of the water supply, the suspension of the street car service, and the closing down of municipal bathhouses. Cases of permanent injuries received by those compelled to stand in meat and fuel lines, in the bitter cold, were reported from Kiev. In Tambov the daily ration of bread was reduced to half a pound. Municipal stores of grain were completely exhausted in Kazan.[20] Of the suffering that resulted the middle class had its full share.

[16] Strumilin, op. cit., Appendixes III and IV, pp. 122–123.
[17] See below, p. 149.
[18] Novgorotsev, op. cit., pp. 208–209.
[19] See above, p. 119.
[20] Quoted in Rabochee Dvizhenie v Godi Voini (The Labor Movement during the War), edited by M. G. Fleer (Moscow, 1925), pp. 8–9.

The Revolution of February–March, 1917, brought no relief to the urban population. The belated attempts of the Provisional Government to take over the whole work of the collection and distribution of fuel, foodstuffs, and other necessaries of life had little chance of success in the midst of the revolutionary turmoil. For instance, out of the monthly quota of 2,100 car-loads of grain and flour allotted to Moscow, only 863 were received in March, and 679 in April. A considerable improvement took place in May when 2,019 carloads were received. In June, however, the number dropped to 1,052; in July, to 383; and in August, to 785. The result was that in Moscow also the daily ration of bread was reduced to half a pound.[21]

The fuel situation was just as bad.

It led [writes M. Astrov] to the closing down of gas-works in many towns for an indefinite period, and to a considerable reduction in the supply of electric power. In many towns it was no longer possible to carry on even the street railway service. And the whole urban population had to live in houses no longer heated.[22]

The fate of the Russian universities, of which the educated classes were so justly proud, may serve as a last illustration of the hardships which they had to endure. In June, 1917, the principals of the universities were summoned to Petrograd by the Minister of Education.

The account they gave of the material conditions of life in the universities at the end of the third year of the War [writes Professor Novgorotsev] furnished a striking picture of genuine financial distress. . . It was shown that the old budgetary grants covered but a small portion of the total requirement. The special resources of the universities derived from tuition fees were now insignificant in relation to the increased expenditure. The professors' salaries were obviously insufficient.[23]

This account, even if obviously incomplete, of the economic plight of the middle class may be useful, it is hoped, in providing the necessary background for an added understanding of the political activities of its organizations such as the Unions of Zemstvos and of Towns, and the war industries committees. The personal privations endured by the rank and file of the middle class, as well as their apprehension for the future of the cultural institutions in the creation of which they took such

Astrov, *op. cit.*, p. 295.
Ibid, p. 296.
Novgorotsev, *op. cit.*, p. 204.

a leading part, were undoubtedly an important factor in determining the character of their political activities.

The Union of Zemstvos and the Union of Towns[24]

Attention has been already drawn to the public spirit which invariably animated the zemstvos and which became particularly active in times of national emergency. It will not be a surprise therefore to find the zemstvos in the forefront of the nonofficial organizations which lent their whole-hearted support to the Government from the very outbreak of the War. The relations between the central government and the institutions of local government, it will be remembered, were not altogether happy ones, the Ministry of the Interior using every conceivable means to curtail their work. The zemstvos naturally resented this interference and waged a stubborn struggle for greater freedom from administrative tutelage. This traditional antagonism between the bureaucracy and the liberal-minded men and women gathered under the banners of the zemstvos was brought to an end, at least for a time, with the declaration of war. The wave of patriotic feeling which swept the Duma in the sitting of July 26, 1914, in its train of confused but stirring emotions, carried the zemstvo assemblies away. Former grievances, offenses, humiliations, and disappointments were forgotten and the country offered a united front to the enemy. It must be said that, in lending their unconditional support to the Imperial Government, liberal-minded Russians were guided not merely by nationalistic motives. There was a vague but strong feeling that Russia was entering upon a struggle on the issue of which much depended, and that not merely from the point of view of imperialistic expansion and national grandeur. To the mind of Russian liberals the Entente Powers—Great Britain and France—represented the embodiment of those essential conceptions of democracy for which they were struggling at home. The winning of the War against the Central Powers, which were pictured as the stronghold of imperialism and reaction, side by side with the great European democracies would immensely facilitate, it was hoped, the realization of their most cherished dreams. This attitude toward the War was consistently adhered to, and its abandonment by liberal circles proved psychologically impossible even in the face of the complete breakdown of the country and the disintegration of the army, which reached its culmination in 1917. In 1914 it offered

[24] For a detailed discussion of the work of the zemstvos and municipalities during the War, and of their unions, see Polner, *op. cit.*, and Astrov, *op. cit.*

124

good reason for a state of national exaltation the importance of which should not be minimized.

The patriotic sentiments of the zemstvos were characteristically expressed in a report adopted by the zemstvo assembly in Moscow on July 25, 1914. "Gone are now," declared the report, "the barriers which have divided our citizens; all are united in one common effort." And it outlined the immediate task confronting the zemstvos: "Who, if not the members of public institutions whose business it is to provide for the needs of the people, who have had many years of practical experience in caring for the sick, and who have organized forces at their command, should undertake the task of uniting isolated efforts in this great work, which demands so immense an organization?"[25]

The sentiments expressed in Moscow were fully shared by the zemstvo institutions all over the country. It must be remembered that an inter-zemstvo organization for the relief of sick and wounded soldiers came into being during the Russo-Japanese War, and succeeded in rendering most valuable services to the army in spite of the stubborn opposition of von Pleve, then Minister of the Interior. It continued to exist after the Japanese War as a central organ of zemstvo relief work in cases of famine, epidemics, and other national emergencies. It was only natural therefore that the desire of the zemstvos to come to the assistance of the army should take the same form as in 1904. The representatives of thirty-five provincial zemstvos met at Moscow on July 30, 1914, and decided on the organization of the "All-Russian Union of Zemstvos for the Relief of Sick and Wounded Soldiers." All other zemstvos, with the notorious exception of the reactionary zemstvo of Kursk, joined the organization. It was headed by Prince George E. Lvov, later on head of the Provisional Government, who was also the leader of the inter-zemstvo organization in the Russo-Japanese War. The Government on this occasion abandoned its hostile attitude of 1904. Prince Lvov was received by the Emperor, and the loyal coöperation of the central administration was promised him. This promise, unfortunately, was not fulfilled.[26]

The Union of Towns, the great war association of the municipalities, came into existence immediately after the creation of the Union of Zemstvos. It was inspired by similar motives. The conference of mayors which met in Moscow on August 8–9, 1914, and decided to proceed with the establishment of a union,

[25] Polner, *op. cit.*, p. 55.
[26] Polner, *op. cit.*, pp. 53–58.

fully agreed with the statement of one of its speakers who declared that "the success of the War would not depend on the strength and organization of the army alone; it would depend directly upon the efficient organization of public forces, on the organization of the community."[27] The Imperial sanction was received on August 16, but it characteristically limited the Union's existence to the duration of the War.

The organization of the unions was free from formalism and bureaucratic rigidity, and tried to adapt itself to the needs and requirements of war-time conditions. During the first six months of the War the unions devoted most of their energy to the relief of the sick and wounded, the purpose for which they were created. But the news from the army which began to penetrate to the rear was anything but satisfactory. The shocking unpreparedness of the Ministry of War, the lack of equipment, guns, rifles, and munitions, coupled with the unskilful conduct of military operations, resulted in the heavy reverses of the spring of 1915. The turn of military events seemed to indicate that the War was not being conducted by the Government as it should be, and that the truce to which the opposition had become a party was not bringing the results anticipated. The meeting of the budget committee of the Duma and the Cabinet in January, 1915, had, as we have seen, been a stormy one. The nature of the discussion was, of course, an open secret. It was becoming clear that if the War was to be brought to a successful conclusion certain drastic steps for the reorganization of the country must be taken without delay. In their attempt to bring about these changes the two unions found themselves coöperating with the Duma and with other organized liberal forces.

To gain a better understanding of the attitude of public opinion during the first six or eight months of the War it is important to keep in mind that the immensity of the economic changes wrought by the outbreak of hostilities was not yet generally realized. There was a widespread and rather naïve belief, which was shared even by some of the most eminent economists and scientific societies, that the public at large should not concern itself with the War. This was the real meaning of the formula "business as usual" which was accepted as the concise expression of both patriotic duty and the last word in economic theory. The aim of a war economic policy, as understood during this period, was to leave everything unchanged and as it was before the War.[28]

[27] Astrov, op. cit., p. 171.
[28] Zagorsky, op. cit., pp. 75–76; see above, pp. 47 sqq.

The military reverses and the rapidly growing economic disorganization at the end of 1914 and in the spring of 1915 came as a rude awakening.

The Effects of the Military Reverses of 1915

The necessity of a fundamental change in the general attitude, and in that of the Government, was realized by individuals in responsible positions almost at the very beginning of hostilities. Guchkov, President of the Russian Red Cross and later Chairman of the Central War Industries Committee, has stated that as early as August, 1914, after a visit to the Russian army in East Prussia, he came definitely to the conclusion that the War was lost unless there was immediate betterment in the organization of supplies. His efforts, however, to break through the wall of official indifference and patriotic optimism did not succeed at once.[29] And it was not until the beginning of the retreat from Galicia, in April, 1915, a retreat which was rendered infinitely more tragic by the almost complete absence of rifles and general munitions of war, that public opinion became so seriously alarmed as to gather the necessary energy to overcome both its own apathy and the resistance of official circles. The recent creed of "business as usual" was contemptuously rejected as outworn and misleading, and its place was taken by a new watchword—"the mobilization of industry," a principle which gained almost immediate recognition among the most diverse social groups and was accepted even by the Government. Professor Zagorsky points out that there was an essential difference between the Russian movement and the analogous movement in the countries of western Europe in that in Russia "it was primarily a political movement confined to unofficial circles."[30]

One of the immediate results of this new attitude was a feverish activity on the part of the Unions of Zemstvos and of Towns, institutions of local government, and political parties. At a conference of the Union of Zemstvos in the spring of 1915 Prince Lvov declared:

The duty of supplying the army with munitions, the organization of its transport, and the problem of supplying food in the interior are tasks in which unofficial forces are not allowed to have any part. But they have proved to be beyond the unaided strength of the government officials. We must mobilize our forces, and all Russia must be welded into one military organization.[31]

[29] Evidence of Guchkov in *Padenie Tsarskago Rezhima,* VI, 256.
[30] Zagorsky, *op. cit.,* p. 82.
[31] *Ibid.,* p. 84.

It was clear, however, that no time could be lost, especiall
since even the Government was giving evidence of a desire t
meet some of the wishes of liberal opinion. It was about thi
time that four of the more undesirable members of the Cabine
were withdrawn and replaced by men acceptable to the Dum
and the country at large. Then came the establishment of th
four Special Councils.[32] But no real improvement could b
expected until the whole organization of the country for wa
was put on a broader basis. An important step in this directio
was the organization of the war industries committees.

The War Industries Committees

The idea of such an organization had its birth among th
leaders of industry and was advanced with particular vigor i
Moscow.

Without losing a moment [wrote the *Utro Rossii,* a paper which e
pressed the views of the Moscow industrialists] we must set to wor
mobilize all industry, and adapt all mills and factories to the requir
ments of war. The demands of the market and the needs of privat
life must be sacrificed. Every factory that is wanted for the War mu
be enlarged and thoroughly equipped with machinery and appliance
All workers must be mobilized, placed on a military footing, and a
signed to the factories where they are needed; for at a time like th
present, work in a factory is just as responsible and as necessary fc
victory as sentry duty on an outpost.[33]

At the end of May, 1915, a conference of the representatives c
commerce and industry passed a resolution in favor of th
formation of district committees which would undertake bot
the adaptation of the existing factories and works to the manu
facture of articles required for the army, and the coördinatio
of all commerce and industry, with this purpose in view. Th
organization was headed by the Central War Industries Com
mittee with headquarters in Petrograd. By the end of 191
twenty-eight provincial war industries committees were orgar
ized. They consisted of representatives of industry, commerc
the Government, the Unions of Zemstvos and of Towns, an
those of labor. The inclusion of the latter constituted an almo
revolutionary departure from the practice of the past. We sha
see in Chapter 7 that the attitude of the workers themselve
was by no means unanimously in favor of their participatio
in the labor of the committees. It will suffice to observe her
that in spite of this opposition labor was represented in th

[32] *See above,* p. 102.
[33] Quoted in Zagorsky, *op. cit.,* pp. 86–87.

entral War Industries Committee and in the majority of the
istrict committees.[34]

The war industries committees were based on the idea of the
oluntary organization of industry, carried out with the consent
f the Government, but not under its control or by its order.
'hat compulsory mobilization which would have been more
>gical, and which had been advocated by the zemstvo of Mos-
>w, was rejected on the ground that what was needed was the
'ithdrawal from the Government of the handling of the prob-
'm of army supplies, and not any increase of its powers in this
irection. This decision, which was open to criticism from the
oint of view of theory, was amply justified by the experience
f the first year of the War, and found further confirmation in
ie degeneration of the bureaucratic system in 1915 and 1916.

'he Zemgor

That anxiety for the fate of the army which brought into
fe the war industries committees called for an action on the
art of the Unions of Zemstvos and Towns. We have already
>en that they were fully conscious of the danger of the situa-
on. They did not limit their support to a mere encouragement
f the important steps taken by the industrialists in organizing
ie war industries committees, but decided to take an immediate
art in the work of supply. Their well-established position,
iorough knowledge of local conditions, and wide experience
>emed to offer a sufficient guarantee that their work in this
eld would prove exceptionally fruitful. The new organization
>ok the shape of a joint committee of the unions "for the supply
f the army," usually described by the abbreviated name of
emgor, which came into being in July, 1915, almost simulta-
eously with the war industries committees. Its work consisted
f the placing of the orders of the Ministry of War and assist-
nce in their execution; the evacuation of industrial establish-
ients from the area threatened by the enemy; the organization
f factories and other industrial enterprises; and the direct
ipply of the needs of the front. The work of the Zemgor,
ndoubtedly, duplicated to a certain extent that of the war
idustries committees, and the distinguished historian of the
emstvos, M. Polner, admits that it was not an unqualified
iccess.[35] It would seem, nevertheless, that the efforts of the
nofficial organizations brought their fruit, and it is generally
greed that by the end of 1916 the Russian army was provided
vith war supplies as it had never been before.

Ibid., pp. 88–90, 93; *see below,* pp. 163 *sqq.*
Polner, *op. cit.*, pp. 270–286.

The Awakening of Public Opinion

What we are interested in at the present moment are not so much the actual achievements of the war industries committees and the Unions of Zemstvos and Towns as the immense change in the attitude of the liberal section of public opinion represented by them; a change since July, 1914. The military reverses of 1915 made plain the futility of the formula "business as usual." But they also made it clear that the bureaucratic government was hopelessly inadequate to face the task before it. It came to be felt that to bring the War to a successful end the mobilization of industry alone was not sufficient. It must be accompanied by important changes in the government of the country; and the liberal circles were among the first to advocate the speedy bringing about of such changes.

The spring and summer of 1915 were, for these liberal elements, a period of feverish activity. Their political demands were still quite moderate, and were chiefly embodied in the formula, a "government enjoying the confidence of the country" which, to repeat, did not mean a government responsible to parliament. From the beginning of 1915, an important group of members of the influential Constitutional Democratic Party had already turned to a more radical solution.[36] But the more moderate demand still seemed wisest to the majority, and it was invariably advanced in the resolutions passed by the zemstvos, municipalities, and their unions. It was endorsed by a private meeting of liberal leaders, who met in Moscow at the house of M. Konovalov, a wealthy Moscow manufacturer and later on a member of the Provisional Government. This private meeting, which gave no little trouble to the Cabinet, decided that the "government enjoying the confidence of the country" should be their goal, and that they would organize a campaign for it. The first step should be the passing of a resolution by the Moscow municipal council, and the same step was to be taken by other municipalities and by the zemstvos.[37] It will be remembered, too, that this plan was actually carried out.[38] Then followed conferences of the Unions of Zemstvos and of Towns which showed themselves to be of the same opinion, and appointed a joint deputation to wait on the Emperor. But by that time the transient era in which the Tsar manifested a more friendly attitude toward liberals was already approaching its end. His departure for the army in August meant the rapid

[36] Evidence of Miliukov in *Padenie Tsarskago Rezhima*, VI, 334.
[37] Yakhontov, *op. cit.*, pp. 77, 82.
[38] *See above*, pp. 80 *sqq.*

growth of reactionary influences. In spite of the support of the project of a government that should enjoy the confidence of the country by the majority of the Council of Ministers, it was rejected by the Tsar. The audience asked for by the deputation of the Unions was refused.[39]

The Attitude of the Sovereign and the Government

As in the case of the Duma, the summer of 1915 proved a turning point in the relations between Government and liberals. It was due to the same causes, and took a similar direction. Those ministers who were in favor of closer collaboration with the Duma were also ready to encourage the work of the unofficial organizations. General Polivanov, Minister of War, was an intimate friend of Guchkov, chairman of the Central War Industries Committee, and even procured the latter an opportunity to address the Council of Ministers in the summer of 1915, an event which, since the days of Count Witte, was unexampled.[40] The parting of the ways which followed the departure of the Emperor for the army, the prorogation of the Duma on September 3, 1915, the rejection of the plea of the ten ministers for a reorganization of the Government or their dismissal, and the refusal of the Emperor to receive the deputation of the Unions of Towns and of Zemstvos also meant a new era of repressions against unofficial organizations. Their activities were treated by the Empress as an attempt to undermine the very foundation of that autocracy to which she was so devoted. The refusal of the Emperor to see the delegation of the unions met with her full approval, and was probably inspired by her.[41] Her personal dislike of Guchkov amounted to hatred. "Guchkov ought to be got rid of," she wrote to the Emperor on August 30, 1915,[42] "only how is the question . . . is there nothing one could hook on to have him shut up?" And she returns to the same idea in December when she writes that "a clever minister of finance could easily catch Guchkov a trap and make him harmless."[43] And she suggests a few weeks later that "people of the Duma, such as Guchkov, should no more be allowed to go to the front and speak to the troops."[44]

The Empress' dislike of the chairman of the Central War Industries Committee extended to the organization over which he presided. "I wish you could shut up that rotten war industries

[39] Astrov, *op. cit.*, p. 178.
[40] Yakhontov, *op. cit.*, p. 36.
[41] *Letters of the Tsaritsa to the Tsar*, p. 159.
[42] *Ibid.*, p. 130.
[43] *Ibid.*, p. 241.
[44] *Ibid.*, p. 257.

committee," she wrote to the Tsar in March, 1916,[45] "as they prepare simply antidynastic questions for their meetings." And she naturally approached the Unions of Towns and of Zemstvos in the same spirit. She suggested—using her own words—that the authorities should make "counter propaganda against the Union of Cities [Towns] out in the army—to have them watched and those that one catches at cleared out; the Ministry of the Interior must get nice, honest people to be 'his eyes' out there and with military help see what they can do—we have no right allowing them to continue filling their ears (the soldiers') with bad ideas—their doctors (Jews) and sisters [nurses] are awful."[46] The Empress was particularly alarmed by the thought that the Union of Towns might become a permanent organization, and also by the fact that the work of the unions was carried on with the help of funds provided by the Treasury.[47] On her special instigation an official statement was issued giving the amount of these appropriations.[48] But the way in which this was done did not please her. She wrote:

He [Protopopov] got the thing at once printed about the millions the Union got and which the other [ministers] were dawdling over ... but it was to be cleverly written—this is too naked for my taste. One can cry to think of half a milliard has been thrown to the Union, when existing organizations could have done marvels with a quarter of the sum.[49]

We have seen that the Empress became practically a decisive factor in the political situation after the Tsar assumed the command of the army. Her attitude toward the offending unofficial organizations therefore determined the policy of such colorless ministers of the interior as followed each other in rapid succession. The war industries committees and the two unions did not merely come under suspicion; they were also submitted to direct persecution. Police officers were ordered by Protopopov to attend even their private meetings.[50] The conferences of the unions were prohibited and when they attempted to disregard the ban imposed upon them by the Ministry of the Interior, the assembled delegates were dispersed by force. Then came the arrest of the labor group of the Central War Industries Committee. No wonder that by that time little survived of the

[45] Ibid., p. 301.
[46] Ibid., p. 404.
[47] Ibid., p. 304.
[48] Monarkhya Pered Krusheniem, pp. 158, 170.
[49] Letters of the Tsaritsa to the Tsar, p. 415.
[50] Evidence of Miliukov in Padenie Tsarskago Rezhima, VI, 342.

nthusiastic support given the Government by the middle classes
i the early months of the War, and that the general trend of
ublic opinion was decidedly toward the Left.

The Trend of Public Opinion at the End of 1916

An interesting and surprisingly detailed picture of the general
ttitude of the country on the eve of the Revolution has been
reserved in the reports of the Police Department. At the end
f 1915 the Minister of the Interior sent a circular order to the
ocal police demanding monthly information upon the political
ituation. The report from Petrograd for October, 1916, is a
locument of unusual skill, and gives a picture of the situation
vhich deserves attention.[51] Whatever we may think of the meth-
ds of the Ministry of the Interior, there can be no doubt that
t had among its police officers men of very considerable ability.
Ve quote the report at some length.

It opens with a general statement of the political situation.

The exceptional importance of the present historical moment . . .
lictates the necessity of urgent and exhaustive measures for the elimi-
iation of the prevailing disorder and the clearing up of the atmos-
>here of public discontent. Lack of determination in decisions and
asual half-measures, as has been proved by recent experiences, are
nadmissible. They do not solve the problem. They merely add further
lifficulties to the already strained relations between the Government
ind the people; and by fostering the general feelings of hostility and
liscontent, they pave the way for the wildest outbursts at the first op-
>ortunity. . . . The summer campaign of 1915 ended the noisy and
onstant manifestations of chauvinist enthusiasm seen in the first days
>f the War, and brought to light the hopeless inadequacy of theo-
etical peace-time calculations when applied to the immensities of
ictual modern war. Military reverses brought the masses to a clearer
inderstanding of the problems of war and of the danger there may be
n a disorganization of the rear. But here, again, the officially pro-
laimed and generally accepted watchword "all for victory" forced
he country to seek a way out of its difficulties in new, energetic and
irgent measures for the welfare of the army, measures that were not
nfrequently taken without absolute necessity, and were even harm-
ul to that stability in the rear upon which, in the last resort, depends
he issue of the War. . . .

The brilliant success of the offensive of General Brusilov in the
pring of the present year [1916] and the current solution of the prob-
em of supplying the army proved convincingly that the task under-
aken by the Government and the community has been fulfilled more
han successfully. The question of the organization of the army sup-

i *Politicheskoe Polozhenie Rossii Nakanune Fevralskoi Revolutsii v Zhandarm-
kom Osvyashchenii (The Political Situation in Russia on the Eve of the Revolution
>f February as Viewed by the Police)*, in Krasni Arkhiv, XVII, 3–35.

ply may be held to have been satisfactorily settled. . . . But, on the other hand, the disintegration of the rear, that is of the whole country, which is now steadily increasing has to-day reached such monstrous and extreme form that it has begun decidedly to be a menace to the success obtained at the front, and in the very near future promises to throw the country into chaotic, spontaneous, and catastrophic anarchy.

The rapidly increasing disorganization of transport, the unchecked orgy of abuses by unscrupulous men in every branch of commerce and industry, and in public and political life as well; the incoherent and mutually-exclusive policies of the central and local authorities, the dishonesty of minor government officials in the provinces—all these things have led to an unfair distribution of foodstuffs and articles of prime necessity, an immense and rapid increase in the cost of living, and to inadequacy in sources of supply and means of existence. The population of the capital and large cities are in fact already suffering from hunger. These factors which show that the neglect of the rear is the prime cause of the disorganization of the huge machinery of the State also contain categorical evidence that a terrible crisis is already on the way and that it must be met in either one way or the other.

The above analysis is entirely confirmed by the extreme anxiety which may be observed everywhere. At the beginning of this present month, September, exceptionally strong feelings of opposition and hostility to the Government were in evidence in every section of the capital's population. Complaints against the administration were growing more and more frequent, and the policy of the Government was being severely criticized. Now, by the end of the month, these hostile feelings, according to reliable information, have attained a power among the masses which was without precedent even in 1905–1906. Openly and without restraint there are complaints of the "dishonesty of the administration," the unbearable burden of the War, the impossible conditions of everyday life. The inflammable statements of the radicals, and other elements of the Left to the effect that one must "first get rid of the Germans at home, and then proceed against those abroad" are meeting with more and more approval. . . .

There is little doubt that rumors [that Russia is on the eve of a revolution] are exaggerated as compared with the actual conditions, but nevertheless the situation is serious enough to deserve immediate attention. The members of the Constitutional Democratic Party residing in the capital, who are familiar with the economic situation, have already long been predicting that Russia is nearing—if not exactly a revolution—then, at least, that wholesale disturbances may arise anywhere unless immediate measures are taken.

The various committees taking care of the refugees, the food supply committees, the municipal committees for the relief of the poor and other institutions which have opportunities to keep in close touch with the average citizen, his needs and feelings—all of them without exception have recently expressed their belief that we are on the eve

134

f important events "compared to which those of 1905 are a mere
ifle," that the Government's policy of keeping the people in the
ark has proved a complete failure: the citizen is now awake, and
istead of the expected "Hurrah" is is crying "Help!"

Considering that similar statements are to-day coming from virtu-
lly everywhere, including circles which in former days never voiced
iscontent (for instance even certain groups of officers in the Guards),
ne is forced to admit that there is a great deal of truth in the pro-
ouncements of the leaders of the Constitutional Democratic Party
vho maintain, to use the expression of Shingarev, "that events of pri-
ary importance are approaching, events which are entirely unfore-
een by the Government, which are bewildering and terrible, and at
ie same time unavoidable. . . ."

After this preliminary survey of the general situation the
eport proceeds to discuss the attitude of separate social groups.
rominent among them was the Constitutional Democratic
arty.

The Constitutional Democratic Party, which keeps in particularly
lose touch with all popular movements, has been for some time col-
ecting a large amount of information and it gives a very dark picture
f Russian conditions. This information is used by the members of
ie party in their reports to party organizations and also to unofficial
odies, where they expect to find a large number of supporters (to
emstvos, conferences of the Unions of Zemstvos and of Towns, com-
iittees of the Duma, and the like). The views expressed by Shingarev
t a conference with provincial leaders who met in the capital at the
nd of August deserve special attention. "The Government continues
► make mistakes and plays a double game which is often described by
ie members of the Constitutional Democratic Party as criminal. By
ostponing the convocation of the Duma the Government has derived itself of the support of the moderate parties. . . . It has im-
gined that the country consists of little children who would not guess
vhy there was such a postponement. It has imagined that it could do
vithout the Duma, and it has failed. . . . All the measures enacted
nder Article 87 clearly prove the lack of confidence in the Duma,
ie fear of just criticism, the desire to avoid the disclosure of abuses,
. . The result is apparent. The whole nation, almost, distrusts the
iovernment, and, unfortunately, is beginning to lose confidence even
a the Duma, for deputies have been involved in questionable trans-
ctions. . . . The above constant postponement of the convocation of
ie Duma, the uncovering of abuses, the stupidity of the measures
.ken to deal with the high cost of living, the inadequacy of supplies,
–have all contributed to a sudden awakening of political opposition.
. . I am afraid that the policy of the Government will lead to a situ-
tion in which the Duma will be powerless to do anything for the
acification of the masses. The Constitutional Democratic Party real-
:es that under the existing conditions peace negotiations are absurd
nd inadmissible; but what will it do if from all sides comes the stern

135

call: Down with the War or down with the Government! The Le⁻ demands that we should openly proclaim our lack of confidence in th Government; but will it not be ridiculous if we, who more than an other party understand the necessity of unity and of the coördinatio of all efforts in the present emergency, bring discord into the force of the nation? I do not believe that any responsible party would at th present time dare to withdraw its support from the Governmen whose position is more than precarious. Only an important event suc as the dissolution of the Duma, or the introduction of new taxe could force our party to make an open protest."

The report stresses the fact that the importance attached b Shingarev and his colleagues of the Duma to the convocatio of the legislature was not shared by those members of the Con stitutional Democratic Party who were working with the Union of Zemstvos and of Towns, the war industries committees, an other unofficial organizations. The information supplied b them gives a devastating picture of the complete disorganizatio of the army and the country, a disorganization which the Dum would probably be incapable of remedying. In the words of th men who had returned from the provinces,

the same thing may be observed all over Russia: it is understoo everywhere that a victory over the Germans is out of the questio under the old *régime*, that the liquidation of German land tenure⁻ alone can achieve nothing, that the nation itself must intervene in th war.... This movement, of course, is not uniform: in the north it i mostly carried on by the democratic coöperative societies...; in cer tral Russia the zemstvos are very active; in the south it is rather matter for individual leaders. But it is a movement which, purel economic at the beginning, is now decidedly political, and may in th future gain much force and acquire a definite program.

The report is interesting as to the attitude of the rank an file of the Constitutional Democrats toward the War. It point out that they were never very enthusiastic about it even at th beginning and that they have now been frightened by the ris in the cost of living and the disorganization of the country. "I spite, therefore, of the support by the proponents of the formul 'War with the victory,' the majority of the party is in favor o that immediate peace which would make possible the settlemen of home problems." And in support of this assertion the repo quotes the views expressed at a conference of professors belong ing to the Constitutional Democratic Party which met in Aug

⁵² During the War the Russian Government enacted a number of measures for th expropriation of the land held by German nationals and by settlers of Germa descent. *See* Nolde, *Russia in the Economic War*, pp. 103–115.

136

ust, 1916. At this conference the opinion was advanced that "Russia has reached complete bankruptcy—financial, political, and moral. The continuation of the War therefore endangers the very existence of the State, and of the nation." But this view, as we know, was never accepted by the responsible leaders of the party.

In summing up the discussion of the attitude of the Constitutional Democratic Party the report states that it believes in the outbreak of a revolution in the very near future. "Anticipating the approach of important events," says the report, "the Constitutional Democrats seem to overestimate their forces and their influence in the country—a reproach which had already been made against them by other political parties." The developments which followed the downfall of the monarchy have proved that this forecast was only too true.

The moderately liberal party of the Octobrists, which included the well-to-do classes, also took a very gloomy view of the situation.

The nobility [one of its representatives is reported to have said] has lost all influence during the War. We are on the verge of complete ruin. The peasants lease no more land because they feel sure that after the War land will be distributed to them free of charge. The increase in the cost of living is so immense that the nobility now finds itself in an impossible position financially.... At the beginning of the War the very idea of revolution seemed preposterous, but now everyone is sure it is inevitable. Of course we, the Octobrist Party, will stand to the end by the Government and the order established by law, but what can we do if the Government itself is largely responsible for what is happening? . . . The Octobrists have always been and will always be for the prosecution of the War to a victorious end; but what can we do if the whole country demands either the end of the disorders and a change in the Government, or the termination of the War?[53]

Such was the frame of mind of the two leading liberal parties on the eve of the Revolution. There is no reason to doubt the accuracy of the opinions expressed in the report of the Petrograd police, which are moreover confirmed by information from other sources. The Government was losing ground and had nothing to rely upon except, perhaps, the parties of the extreme Right. But before we go on to this phase of the question, a few words more may be said of the liberals. Two rather important groups which should be included with them have not been men-

[53] *Politicheskoe Polozhenie Rossii Nakanune Fevralskoi Revolutsii v Zhandarmskom Osvyashchenii* in *Krasni Arkhiv*, XVII, 23.

tioned so far: the group identified with the coöperative movement and students. We have omitted them because neither played an independent political rôle during the War. The coöperative societies, indeed, went through a period of extraordinary if not very healthy growth, and performed rather important functions in connection with the mobilization of industry and various sorts of war work. Their support was enlisted by the Unions of Zemstvos and of Towns and by war industries committees. They shared their political aspirations and supported them in their struggle against the Government by all the means at their disposal, but they seldom took any independent political action.[54] As to the students who used to play if not a really important at least a rather spectacular part in the political life of the country, their participation in politics after the outbreak of the War was reduced almost to nothing. To begin with, their ranks were greatly depleted by the calling of new classes and the cancellation of exemptions. The majority even of those who remained at the universities became associated with one or the other of the organizations working for the army and shared in its activities.[55]

One more word may be added as to the general remedy for the evils from which Russia was suffering, the remedy advocated by the liberal circles. This remedy was by no means new nor was it even a radical one. It varied from the vague formula of a government enjoying the confidence of the nation (but not responsible to parliament) to the demand for a parliamentary *régime*. It would seem extremely doubtful if in a country with low educational standards, an exceptionally large percentage of illiterates, no tradition of self-government, and no popular press, a really democratic system of government could have been introduced, unless gradually and by slow stages. This, as it appeared in 1917, was not the Russian conception of reform. It seems fairly clear that the country was not ready for self-government. On the other hand it was also clear that the existing system of conducting public affairs could not be tolerated any longer. Russia was in a dilemma. Its solution proved a surprise to liberals and reactionaries alike.

The Parties of the Extreme Right

The liberals who grouped themselves around the Duma and the institutions of local government had their counterpart in the

[54] See E. M. Kayden and A. N. Antsiferov, *The Coöperative Movement in Russia during the War* (Yale University Press, 1929) in this series of the "Economic and Social History of the World War."

[55] The decline of university life during the War is dealt with elsewhere in this series; see Novgorotsev, *op. cit.*

reactionary Union of the Russian People (*Soyuz Russkago Naroda*) and affiliated organizations which came into being during the troubled period of 1905–1906. The roots of the movement may be traced back to the year 1900 when the conservative groups began to feel the necessity of organizing themselves to offer a resistance to the rising movement of liberalism. Complying with the police regulations then in force which prohibited political parties, the new organization at first took the form of an association for cultural purposes and became known as the "Russian Assembly" (*Russkoe Sobranie*). It consisted mostly of the upper classes of the nobility and the higher bureaucracy and clergy. Its activities were limited to the publication of penny pamphlets and were rather narrow in scope. The revolutionary outbursts of 1904–1905 led the conservative groups to take measures to make their organization more democratic and put it on a broader basis. Thus the Union of the Russian People, headed by the notorious Dr. A. J. Dubrovin, came into being.[56]

The fundamental demands in the program of the Union of the Russian People were anything but new. It borrowed from the days of Nicholas I the venerable formula of "orthodoxy, autocracy, and nationality" which was so dear to the heart of Nicholas II. At the same time it advanced a principle which was intended to weaken the rule of the bureaucracy and was devised by the Slavophils: "To the Tsar—the power of decision, to the people—the power of opinion." Translated into more intelligible language, this meant the rule of the absolute monarch with the assistance of an advisory assembly known as *zemsky sobor*. The Union's economic and social program was extremely vague. It contained references to the maintenance of communal tenure, the increase of the peasants' allotments, the assistance to settlers, and the betterment of economic standards. But there was no doubt as to their attitude toward the question of nationalities, and especially toward the Jews. Antisemitism in its most vulgar and aggressive form was one of the fundamentals of their creed.[57]

The Union of the Russian People and other organizations of a similar type such as the "Union of Archangel Michael" headed by Purishkevich were under the effective leadership of the "Council of the United Nobility" (*Soviet Obedinennago Dvoryanstva*), an association of the reactionary landowners

[56] *Soyuz Russkago Naroda* (*The Union of the Russian People*), documents of the Committee of Inquiry of the Provisional Government. With an introduction by V. P. Viktorov (Moscow-Leningrad, 1929), p. 4. Also evidence of E. N. Markov in *Padenie Tsarskago Rezhima*, VI, 176 *sqq.*
[57] *Soyuz Russkago Naroda*, pp. 5–6.

which had among its members the most prominent leaders of the other reactionary bodies such as Purishkevich and Markov. While the Union of the Russian People consisted mostly of the lower middle class, the Council of the United Nobility counted among its members men prominent in social and bureaucratic circles, members of the Duma and of the State Council, and therefore was in a particularly favorable position to assume the leadership of the reactionary forces. The policies of these organizations were directed toward the preservation of the principle of autocracy, and they were in arms against anything that could suggest a constitutional *régime*. They were strongly opposed to the Duma, and successfully used their influence with the Sovereign to obtain the dissolution of the First and Second Dumas. To impress their wishes upon the Tsar, who saw in the activities of the Union of the Russian People a genuine expression of the devotion of the nation to its anointed head, the local departments of the Union, acting under orders from their central office, sent telegrams to the Tsar imploring him to take reactionary measures. A notable instance was the demand for the dissolution of the Second Duma. It would appear that the order for each new flow of telegrams took the form of a black cross published on the front page of the reactionary paper *Russkoe Znamya* (*The Russian Flag*).[58]

The membership of the Union of the Russian People was mostly drawn from the lower middle class. The exact number of members was never known, as no real lists of members were available, and the official figures issued from time to time were admittedly fictitious.[59] Among the more prominent members and local leaders were a number of lower government officials and representatives of the clergy. Certain ministers, such as Shcheglovitov, Rukhlov, and N. A. Maklakov, were ardent supporters of the Union, and this naturally acted as a strong inducement to the employees of their departments to join the organization. One of the worst features of the situation was the close affiliation of the reactionary parties with the Ministry of the Interior and the Police Department. It was an open secret that they regularly received large sums from a fund at the disposal of the Minister of the Interior, and that they used the money so obtained not only for the spreading of their ideas but also for the arrangement of political murders. Their participation, with the connivance of the Police Department, in the

---

[58] Evidence of Miliukov in *Padenie Tsarskago Rezhima*, VI, 299–300; evidence of Beletsky in *ibid.*, IV, 128; *Soyuz Russkago Naroda*, pp. 7–8.
[59] Evidence of Markov in *Padenie Tsarskago Rezhima*, VI, 197–198.

murders of two deputies of the First Duma, Iollos and Hertsenstein, both of them members of the Constitutional Democratic Party, are well-established facts. They were also responsible for two unsuccessful attempts against the life of Count Witte. In each case the prosecution of the criminals was extraordinarily lax, and all but one, who was convicted by a Finnish court, escaped the hands of justice. Count Witte himself was firmly convinced that the attempts against his life were organized with the full knowledge of the police, if not of the Cabinet.[60]

The activities of the reactionary parties were of a sporadic kind, and were in the nature of that reflex movement which usually followed an awakening among the liberals. They made themselves conspicuous during the revolutionary period of 1905–1906. Then, with the pacification of the country, relatively little was heard of them until the summer of 1915 when the organization of the war industries committees, the immense popularity of the Unions of Zemstvos and of Towns, the growing influence of the Duma and the general trend of public opinion toward a government enjoying the confidence of the country called them again to life. In their newspapers, subsidized by the Government, at their conferences, and in their telegrams and memoranda to the Tsar and the ministers, they stubbornly fought against any concessions to the demands of liberal opinion. The Duma, the Unions of Zemstvos and of Towns, and the war industries committees, they believed, were, more than anything else, responsible for the turmoil that prevailed in the country. The Progressive Bloc, this unheard of innovation in Russian politics, became the object of their bitter attacks. The "Jews and the free-masons" (!) were as usual proclaimed the real enemies of the Russian people.[61]

These unintelligent and ridiculous accusations would hardly be worth mentioning if they had not borne their evil fruit. For they confirmed the Sovereign in the illusion that he was beloved by real Russia as distinct from the perverted educated classes. They also had immediate political consequences. The reactionary Shcheglovitov, a patron of the Union of the Russian People, was appointed President of the State Council on January 1, 1917, a nomination which was accompanied by the strengthening of the extreme Right wing of the upper chamber in violation

[60] Witte, *Vospominanya*, II, 363–386; *see also* his letter to Stolypin in *Soyuz Russkago Naroda*, pp. 107–130.
[61] *See* for instance the circular letter issued by the Union of the Russian People in October, 1915, *Soyuz Russkago Naroda*, pp. 99–102. Also Evidence of Miliukov in *Padenie Tsarskago Rezhima*, VI, 318–319.

of the spirit of the Fundamental Laws.[62] The activities of reactionary members of the State Council such as Rimsky-Korsakov and Govorukha-Otrukh did not pass unnoticed in high places. The Tsar lent a willing ear to counsels which flattered his personal inclinations. In the middle of January, 1917, five weeks before the outbreak of the Revolution, he examined, apparently with considerable interest, a memorandum submitted to him by the "Russian orthodox circles of Kiev."[63] This characteristic and pretentiously written document began with the assurance that "all the orthodox residents of Kiev categorically declared that the immense majority of the laboring population of villages and townships—peasants, commoners, village clergy, farmers, government officials, and Russian landlords—that is, all who in the southwestern region represented the Russian people—in spite of the strenuous putting forth of radical views by the local liberal press, still remained deeply conservative in all that concerned their political, social, public, and religious life; they still retained their traditional view that the autocracy of the Russian Tsars was the sole fountain of power in the Russian State." This ominous beginning was followed by a most violent denunciation of the Duma, the Unions of Zemstvos and of Towns, etc., by the usual accusations against the Jews, the liberal press, and so on. Several passages in this document were carefully underlined by the Tsar, and he left on it the following comment: "A memorandum which deserves attention." The Prime Minister, Prince Golitsin, hastened to assure his Imperial master that at least one of the many suggestions incorporated in the memorandum—that chairmen of zemstvo assemblies and municipal councils who allowed the discussion of political matters should be prosecuted—had already been favorably acted upon by the Council of Ministers.[64]

[62] Half the members of the State Council were elected by certain social groups and bodies, and the other half were appointed for life by the Emperor. Of the members appointed by the Emperor, only those whose names appeared on a special list issued on January 1 of every year actually took part in the work of the Council. The members not included in the list were merely holders of honorary titles. This category was originally created for those members whose advanced age, health, or residence abroad made it impossible for them to carry on their duties. It was eventually used as a method of removing the members of the upper chamber who proved recalcitrant, and replacing them by men whose views were more in line with the policies of the day. This practice, which was often denounced as unconstitutional, allowed the Cabinet to exercise a certain pressure upon the vote of the appointed members. The changes in the membership of the Council announced in the list of January 1, 1917, were unusually many and clearly punitive in their nature. See Gronsky, *op. cit.*, pp. 17–19; evidence of Protopopov in *Padenie Tsarskago Rezhima*, II, 284–285; evidence of Shcheglovitov in *ibid.*, II, 434–435.
[63] *Monarkhya Pered Krusheniem*, pp. 285–293.
[64] *Ibid.*, p. 293.

142

We know that one reason for the whole-hearted support given to the Government by the liberals was their belief that Russia's participation in the struggle side by side with the great European democracies would lead to important changes in the government of the country. It would seem only natural that the conservatives should have been hostile to war for the same reason. This is also the opinion of the Petrograd police, as stated in their report.

The parties of the Right [says the report] also consider the present moment as menacing, and anticipate the possibility of important disturbances. In their opinion the War has grown unpopular with the masses because autocratic Russia is fighting for the preservation of a republic and a constitutional monarchy, against Germany whose government is similar to the Russian. At the beginning there was enthusiasm for the cause of Serbia, but now, when the chief burden of the struggle is on Russian shoulders, and "victory will go to England," the majority have come to understand the disadvantages of an alliance between Russia and Great Britain. A great many pamphlets directed against Great Britain, and demanding the termination of the War and a lasting peace with the Central Powers are in circulation everywhere. Still more, discontent among the conservatives is provoked by the freedom which the Jews have acquired during the War. . . . The masses, in the opinion of the conservatives, believe that the high cost of living and the lack of supplies are due to profiteering, but do not know what to do about it. This situation cannot last long: "The people will finally organize a pogram for which the Government that has permitted the establishment of the Jewish rule, will itself be responsible. In any case this pogrom will show that the people are tired of bearing a foreign yoke, that they are willing to fight for their own interests, but not for those of others. If the Government wants to see order restored in Russia it must get rid of the Jewish crowd, conclude an honorable peace with Germany, and break off all relations with Great Britain. Otherwise disturbances infinitely worse than those of 1905 seem extremely likely." To this we may add that the negative attitude of the conservatives towards the War has recently become more pronounced, while disturbances have broken out everywhere, and strikes of town and agricultural laborers have assumed a more intensive character.[65]

The pogrom which the conservatives were so confidently expecting did actually occur in 1917. This time, however, it was directed not against the Jews, but against all the elements which supported the monarchy. The organizations of the extreme Right were among the first to be swept away by the mighty waves of the revolutionary tide.

[65] *Politicheskoe Polozhenie Rossii Nakanune Fevralskoi Revolutsii v Zhandarmskom Osvyashchenii*, in *Krasni Arkhiv*, XVII, 23–24.

The Middle Class and the Revolution

The downfall of the monarchy in March, 1917, was received among the educated classes, with the exception of the extreme Right, with a feeling of satisfaction or even enthusiasm, mingled not infrequently with apprehension and fear. The composition of the Provisional Government headed by Prince Lvov seemed to open unlimited possibilities for those democratic reforms which were so dear to hearts of liberal-minded Russians, and in the realization of which they always saw the real purpose of the War Russia was fighting side by side with the great democracies of Europe—democracies soon to be joined by the United States. The landslide of official oratory and of innumerable declarations and resolutions which poured from everywhere in the first days of the Revolution gave full expression to this official optimism. But behind the outward manifestations of joy and the constantly renewed promises of defending the Revolution and its "conquests" there was a distinct and rapidly growing feeling that events were taking a turn which no one had fully foreseen. The "great unknown" of the illiterate mass of the peasantry, which soon began to give signs of life, introduced a new factor in the political situation; and it gave cause for the gravest anxiety. The Soviet of Soldiers' and Workmen's Deputies freely interfered with the Provisional Government. The masses of revolutionary workmen and disorderly soldiery, instead of returning to their workshops and barracks after the *coup d'état* of February–March and leaving to the educated classes the arrangement of the new State, made themselves every day more conspicuous and more objectionable. Economic disorganization proceeded at an unexampled pace. The army was obviously unwilling to fight the Germans, but openly discussed the necessity of a class war. Everyday life was growing more and more difficult.

It was, indeed, a time of terrible trial for those men and women who, all their lives, had cherished the hope of seeing Russia a truly democratic country, and had often made heavy sacrifices for the cause they had at heart. Now that the long-coveted prize was at last within their reach they suddenly saw it slipping from their hands. The complete divorce between the educated classes and the masses now brought its evil fruit.[66] The liberals, who so stubbornly defended what they believed to be the true interests of the people against the Imperial *régime*, appeared to the revolutionary masses headed by the Soviets as nothing but the representatives of the same hated class of op-

[66] *See below,* Chapter X.

144

pressors. With the rapid rise of the revolutionary tide between the downfall of the monarchy and the Bolshevik Revolution of October the position of the educated classes was becoming more and more precarious. With the exception of the extreme radicals, who joined the Bolsheviks or were always in sympathy with Bolshevik doctrine, the intelligentsia came gradually to recognize the unpleasant fact that even the very modest place they held in Imperial Russia was denied to them in the new State which emerged from the Revolution. Some accepted the inevitable, and with characteristic pliability submitted to the heavy yoke of the Communist rule. Others fought against the Bolsheviks a desperate, cruel, and futile civil war, which merely added to the sufferings and impoverishment of the country. Many took the road to exile. The middle class of Imperial Russia, as a social group, ceased to exist.

Chapter 7

The Awakening of Labor

The Working Classes

ALL THE ELEMENTS of the Russian State we have examined so far, in spite of their marked differences, suffered a not unsimilar fate at the hands of the War and the Revolution. The decay of the monarchical form of government led to the collapse of the rule of the Tsar. This was inevitably followed by the breakdown of the bureaucratic system and the eclipse of the Duma, that quasi parliament of the old *régime*. Their fate was shared, after a brief delay, by the educated middle class, who joined the banners of the organizations of local government, and by the liberal intelligentsia in general. In striking contrast with this process of destruction stands the remarkable change that took place in the political fortunes of labor. From utter political and social insignificance which, indeed, bordered upon outlawry and put them at the mercy of their employer as well as of every police officer, Russia's workingmen rose in the course of a few months to a position of national leadership, and became the torchbearers of a new world to which post-war mankind looks, not without hope, for the solution of innumerable social and economic riddles.

Although the organization of Russia's industry on a large

145

scale goes back to the days of Peter the Great, it is impossible to speak of an industrial proletariat in the modern sense of the word before the emancipation of the peasants. The year of the abolition of serfdom, 1861, was indeed a milestone in the economic history of the country. The immense economic and social readjustment which followed the Emancipation was not favorable, at the beginning, to the development of industry. The mining and metal industries were particularly affected and their output was considerably reduced.[1] This depression, however, was purely temporary. The introduction of free labor was an element essential to the industrial development of the country; and the ensuing increase in output, and in the number of men and women employed was particularly rapid in the course of the last twenty-five years preceding the War.

TABLE 2
Progress of Industry in 1890–1913.[2]

Year	Number of establishments	Number of hands employed	Value of output in thousands of rubles
1890	32,254	1,424,800	1,502,600
1900	38,141	2,373,400	---------------
1913	29,965	2,931,300	5,738,100

The decrease in the number of industrial establishments, it will be noticed, was accompanied by an increase in both the number of workers employed and in the value of the output. This would appear to indicate that Russia was moving toward the concentration of industry, following the general trend of development of all capitalistic countries. This statement is fully borne out by Table 3 which summarizes the 1913 data for 17,877 enterprises belonging to differing branches of industry and employing 2,319,577 workers.

TABLE 3
Distribution of Industrial Enterprises in 1913.[3]

Enterprises employing hands	Number of enterprises	Percentage of total	Number of hands	Percentage of total
From 1 to 10	2,366	13.2	17,314	0.7
From 11 to 100	11,900	66.5	432,430	18.3
From 101 to 500	2,717	15.3	616,594	26.6
Over 500	894	5.0	1,253,139	54.4
Total	17,877	100	2,319,477	100

[1] M. J. Tugan-Baranovsky, *Russkaya Fabrika v Proshlom i Nastoyashchem (The Russian Factory, Its Past and Present)* (St. Petersburg, 1907), pp. 307 *sqq.*
[2] Zagorsky, *op. cit.*, p. 5.
[3] *Ibid.*, p. 10.

At the outbreak of the War the number of men and women employed in industry was about 3,000,000. And the number of wage earners in industry, commerce, transport, and various urban professions connected with industries was estimated at about 9,000,000, or about one-seventeenth of the total population of the country.[4] In spite of the progress of industry Russia was still primarily an agricultural country.

The predominance of agriculture had an immediate and far-reaching effect upon the organization of industry and the position of labor. If industrial labor represented a very small percentage of the total population, the proportion of the urban proletariat in the narrow sense of the word, that is, of wage earners who had entirely severed connections with their native villages, was still smaller. The very existence of such a social group in Russia has occasionally been denied. But the interesting investigation carried out by M. Dementev in 1884–1885 shows that even at that time an industrial proletarian class was in process of formation. "This class," M. Dementev writes, "already has its 'factory genealogy' which in a large number of cases goes back to the third generation."[5] Professor Tugan-Baranovsky, discussing the conditions of Russian labor at the end of the last century, rightly pointed out that, although the formation of an industrial proletariat was an undeniable fact, the ties which united the men and women working in factories and workshops with their villages, while growing more and more loose, were nevertheless numerous and strong. Industrial workers may no longer be actively engaged in farming and may not even return home for the harvest season, as was often the practice with the industrial labor of the "first generation." But they may still continue to send their earnings or savings to the relatives who remained behind, their families not infrequently continued to live in the village, and it was to it, too, that they returned when faced with unemployment, sickness, disability, or old age. The reasons for the maintenance of the close ties between the industrial worker and the farming peasant must be sought, on the one hand, in the peculiar organization of land tenure and the legal disabilities of the peasant family,[6] and on the other hand, in the rapid growth of industry which constantly called for new recruits from the countryside.[7]

This close link between the farmer and industrial labor must

Ibid., p. 13.

E. Dementev, *Fabrika, Chto Ona Daet Naselenyu i Chto Ona u Nego Beret (The Factory, What It Gives to the Population and What It Takes from Them)* (Moscow, 1897), 2d ed., p. 46.

See below, pp. 176–181.

Tugan-Baranovsky, *op. cit.*, pp. 446–449.

be constantly kept in mind if we are to understand the position and psychology of the working classes and the extraordinarily low wages they were forced to accept. The steady increase in *real* wages which was in evidence from the beginning of the century to the Emancipation suffered a definite setback after 1861, and a continuously reverse movement then set in. Real wages in the 'eighties and the 'nineties, we are assured by competent observers, were decidedly lower than they were before the Emancipation Act.[8] But by the end of the century, the curve of wages began to rise again. In spite of this improvement, it remained remarkably low, far below the level of industrial earnings in western Europe, not to speak of the United States. The explanation of this phenomenon will be found in the close link between industrial labor and the countryside.

So long as the wages of our industrial workers are so insignificant [writes Professor Tugan-Baranovsky] that the maintenance of his family near the factory is out of the question, so long will the link with the village be preserved. On the other hand, there is not the slightest doubt that this link, in its turn, is one of the causes of the low wages of our industrial workers. In western Europe the employer provides for the maintenance of the whole family of his employees, while with us, as a result of the close connection between industrial labor and peasants, the employer provides only a portion of the family's expenses, the other part being supplied by the worker's family in its agricultural establishment. The "link with land" therefore is at once the cause and the effect of low wages. The lack of differentiation between agricultural and industrial labor is, furthermore, one of the powerful reasons of the low efficiency of the Russian workman which, again, prevents the increase in his earnings. The necessity of maintaining two separate households, one in the village, and the other near his place of employment, is in itself a grave economic disadvantage and the source of extra expenditure which burdens the worker's already meager budget.[9]

To these economic hardships must be added the social and moral inconveniences resulting from this highly abnormal state of affairs.

Only the extremely low general standards of the Russian working man and his habit of accepting everything patiently [says Tugan-Baranovsky] make it possible for him to tolerate a situation in which family ties are almost completely divested of their moral content and are reduced to something approaching a purely economic relationship.

[8] Tugan-Baranovsky, *op. cit.*, pp. 433–441.
[9] *Ibid.*, p. 450.

148

t would seem as if the whole problem were moving in a vicious
circle: There could be no increase in wages so long as the
"link with land" was not destroyed, but the latter was to survive
so long as wages were low! The solution of the puzzle was to
be found, in the opinion of Tugan-Baranovsky, in the general
economic progress of the country.

Wages and the Standard of Living

The fundamental difficulty in dealing with wages and the
standard of living of the working classes lies in the absence of
adequate, comprehensive, and reliable statistics. Nevertheless
the data collected by the Factory Inspectors and those of the
Census of 1918, as well as the investigations carried out by such
organizations as the Union of Zemstvos and the Union of
Towns, throw a great deal of light upon the problem in which
we are now interested. Unfortunately, comparison between them
is not always possible. Another complication arises from the
fact that the expression of wages merely in rapidly depreciating
paper rubles means little or nothing, and it is essential to express
industrial earnings in terms of commodities. For this purpose it
became necessary to compute general index numbers of prices,
a formidable task, especially under the conditions which prevailed in Russia during the War when, as a result of the breakdown of the railways, the country became divided into a number of virtually independent economic areas having their own
sets of prices. With commendable courage some of the Russian
economists attacked the problem, and the result of their investigations will be briefly summarized below. Although extreme
caution is recommended in accepting these figures at their face
value, they may prove useful as a foundation for determining
the trend of the general evolution in the economic position of
labor.

Table 4 gives an idea of the general movement in the average
monthly wages of all industrial workers as it appears from the
data of Factory Inspectors and of the Census of 1918. Real
wages are obtained by dividing the nominal wages by the general index number of prices for the respective year and multiply-
ing the result by one hundred. Nominal wages are given in
paper rubles.

The difference between the two sets of figures is explained in
part by the fact that the Census of 1918 covered only thirty-
one provinces, while the data of the Factory Inspectors referred
to the whole of Russia. There is, however, another even more
important distinction between the two sources. The data of the
Factory Inspectors do not include the large State-owned estab-

149

TABLE 4

Average Monthly Wages in Russian Industry, 1913–1917.[10]

Year	General Index numbers of prices	Data of the factory inspectors		Data of the Census of 1918	
		Nominal	Real	Nominal	Real
1913	100	22.0	22.0	21.7	21.7
1914	101	22.6	22.4	22.9	22.7
1915	130	26.8	20.6	31.6	24.3
1916	203	(43.9)	(21.6)[11]	50.0	24.6
1917	673	142.8	21.2	143.0	21.2

lishments, such as shipbuilding yards, munition factories er gaged in work for national defense, and so on. All suc enterprises, on the contrary, were covered by the Census c 1918. As we shall see in a moment, enterprises working fo the army found themselves, from the point of view of wage in a more favorable position than those producing for the ma ket. In 1917, after the Revolution, production for the arm declined, establishments working for national defense lost the privileged position, and in our table the two sets of figures fe that year are almost identical.

The general impression which one obtains from the examina tion of Table 4 is that real wages suffered no appreciable declin and the data of the Census of 1918 seem even to indicate th a steady improvement in the economic position of labor too place during the War, until the Revolution of March, 191

TABLE 5

Average Monthly Wages in the Textile and Metal Industries in 1913–1916.[12]

(Data of the Factory Inspectors)

Year	Textile Industry		Metal Industry	
	Nominal	Real	Nominal	Real
		(in rubles)		
1913	17.9	17.9	33.5	33.5
1914	17.6	17.4	38.0	37.6
1915	19.5	15.0	46.4	35.7
1916	(28.3)[13]	(13.9)	(78.6)	(38.7)
Wages in 1916 as compared with 1913 (in percentage)	158	78	234	115

[10] Strumilin, *op. cit.*, pp. 90, 120, 121, 124.
[11] Figures given in parentheses indicate incomplete data.
[12] Strumilin, *op. cit.*, p. 90.
[13] Figures given in parentheses indicate incomplete data.

150

which was followed by a very slight decline. This picture, however, is far too favorable and is completely at variance with information obtained from other sources.

To begin with, there was a marked difference in the trend of wages in industries working for national defense and those producing for the market. How important was this difference will appear from Table 5.

It will be seen from this table that real earnings in the textile industry, which was producing for the market, declined steadily throughout the War, while real earnings in the metal industry were growing. In 1916 the former lost about 22 per cent of their pre-war pay, while the latter gained some 15 per cent.

The same phenomenon will appear even more strikingly if we examine more detailed data for smaller regions and for shorter periods. M. Mindlin arranged data relating to 94 industrial establishments employing 95,000 men and women in the Moscow industrial region. Table 6 summarizes some of his findings.[14]

TABLE 6

Average Monthly Wages in the Textile and Metal Industries in the Moscow Region, 1914–1917.

Period	All industries		Textile industry		Metal industry		Ratio column 6 to 4	General index numbers of prices
	Nominal	Real	Nominal	Real	Nominal	Real		
	1	2	3	4	5	6	7	8
			(in rubles)					
1914								
First half	22.53	22.5	14.47	14.5	31.21	31.2	2.15	100
Second half	21.18	20.8	14.25	14.0	32.40	31.8	2.27	102
1915								
First half	23.35	19.5	15.31	12.8	34.95	29.1	2.27	120
Second half	30.07	21.5	17.14	12.2	46.59	33.3	2.71	140
1916								
First half	36.76	22.1	20.17	12.1	59.38	35.8	2.95	166
Second half	46.42	19.4	27.29	11.4	71.39	29.8	2.62	240
1917								
First half	70.45	19.3	46.05	12.6	103.03	28.3	2.24	365
Second half	135.00	13.8	115.78	11.8	171.84	17.5	1.48	982

It appears from Table 6 that the War resulted in an all-round reduction in real wages. Only at the end of 1915 and at the beginning of 1916 can a certain increase in real wages be observed in industries working for national defense; but this im-

14. Mindlin in *Statistika Truda* (*Labor Statistics*), Nos. 8–10 (1918), pp. 8–14.

provement was a purely temporary one, and as early as in the second half of 1916 and in 1917 this group suffered even more than the textile workers from the decline in their real earnings.

An important factor in the situation was the decline in the efficiency of the worker due to the mobilization of a large number of skilled men. It has been computed that between 1914 and 1916 the output of a spinner and weaver declined by an average of 21 per cent; in the textile industry the average decline was 27 per cent; in the brickmaking industry, 40 per cent, and so on.[15] The decline in the output per worker was bound to have an adverse effect upon the general level of wages. The increase in the employment of female and juvenile labor, and of such substitutes as Chinese labor, refugees, and prisoners of war, also tended to decrease efficiency.[16]

The low productivity of Russian labor was always considered by the students of the labor problem as one of the fundamental reasons for its equally low remuneration. Schulze-Gaevernitz, for instance, estimated that one thousand spindles in England demanded the attention of only three men, while according to Mendeleev, in Russia the same number of spindles kept busy 16.6. Therefore an English spinner who received a wage four times as high as a Russian spinner actually cost the employer less. The low educational and cultural standards of the population were undoubtedly among the chief causes which prevented the development of the country's resources.[17]

That the wages of Russian labor even before the War were so shockingly low that any substantial decrease in them appeared almost out of the question is apparent from Tables 4 and 5. The average monthly earnings of an industrial worker was computed at something like 22 rubles, or about $11. Even making full allowance for the very great difference between the cost of living in Russia and in western Europe, or in the United States, it must be admitted that a man burdened with a family could hardly maintain reasonable standards on $11 a month. It will also be remembered that in certain industries, as in textiles, monthly earnings were still lower, and averaged only about 18 rubles, or $9. Out of such an income, a worker had to spend for lodgings about two rubles or even more. For instance, the average monthly rent paid by a workingman was estimated at 3.15 rubles in St. Petersburg in 1908, at 2.24 rubles in Baku,

[15] N. Volens, *Izmenenie Zarabotnoi Plati i Rabochee Vremya za Dva Goda Voiny* (*Changes in Wages and the Length of the Labor Day during Two Years of the War*) in *Materyali po Statistike Truda* (*Materials on Labor Statistics*), II, 1918. Strumilin, *op. cit.*, pp. 96–97.
[16] *See above*, pp. 34–35.
[17] Tugan-Baranovsky, *op. cit.*, pp. 383–384.

in 1909, and even in the small provincial town of Sereda, in the province of Kostroma, it amounted in 1911 to 1.80 rubles.[18] The kind of lodgings that could be obtained for such sums the reader may easily imagine. No wonder that the outlay of a workingman on "recreation and cultural needs"—one feels rather ashamed to use the high-sounding phrase—was negligible. In St. Petersburg in 1908, according to the data collected by M. Davidovich, such monthly expenditures as might be classified under this heading were: bathhouses, 28 copecks (14 cents); postage, 18 copecks (9 cents); street cars, 14 copecks (7 cents); theaters and movies, 10 copecks (5 cents); a total of 70 copecks (35 cents), some 2.6 per cent of the monthly wages. And this in St. Petersburg, the capital of the Empire! That bathhouses, postage, and street cars can rightly be listed as luxuries is something one finds difficult to admit. Nevertheless, outside the capital, expenditures under this heading were still smaller. In a remote provincial town like Sereda there was no bathhouse, and the expenditure on recreation and movies was estimated at 3 copecks (1½ cents) a month! The average expenditure of that nature for the whole country was put at something like 50 copecks (25 cents) a month.[19]

In spite of the low level of wages, which hardly seemed to offer a margin for further reduction, we are forced to admit that a deterioration of the economic position of the working class took place during the War, with the exception, perhaps, of certain groups employed in enterprises working for the army. This conclusion is unanimously supported by all students of the subject. The value of their evidence is enhanced by the fact that it is based on information drawn from independent sources. In addition to the data presented in the preceding pages we may quote here the authoritative statement of M. Prokopovich, one of Russia's leading authorities upon problems of the standard of living. M. Prokopovich expressed the firm belief that the rise in industrial wages during the War lagged behind the rise in the cost of living. He estimated that in 1914–1915 the cost of living increased by an average of 53 per cent, while the average rise in wages for the same period was only 19 per cent. The wages of men employed in cotton mills were in 1915 between 16 and 20 rubles a month, and were "obviously inadequate."[20] A Soviet economist, M. Arsky, arrives at a very similar conclusion, based on the data of the Association of Employers

[18] Strumilin, *op. cit.,* p. 104.
[19] Strumilin, *op. cit.,* p. 105.
[20] S. N. Prokopovich, *Voina i Narodnoe Khozyaistvo* (*War and National Economy*) (Moscow, 1917), p. 146.

(*Obshchestvo Zavodchikov i Fabrikantov*), which cannot be suspected of underestimating the amount of wages paid. He believes that by 1915 the prices of the articles of prime necessity increased by about 100 per cent. In May–June, 1916, the average increase in the price of foodstuffs was about 131 per cent for the country as a whole, and about 150 per cent for the city of Petrograd. During the same period rents in Petrograd increased by 200 or even 300 per cent. A similar rise occurred in the price of footwear, clothing, etc. The increase in industrial earnings was much slower. In 1915 earnings increased 41 per cent in Petrograd, and 36 per cent in Moscow. In 1916 the average increase in wages was 50 to 60 per cent over the 1915 figures. The situation was still worse in the provinces where wages showed an out-and-out tendency to fall—for instance in Siberia—or increased during the whole of the War by as little as 10 or 15 per cent, a mere trifle in comparison with the rise in the cost of living.[21] Although M. Arsky's estimate of actual rise in prices for different periods of the War is open to criticism, his conclusions as to the effect of the War upon the economic position of the working classes seem well justified.

The position of the families of workers who were called to the colors was still more desperate. Separation allowances paid by the Government were calculated merely to provide nutrition for the dependents of the enlisted men. Such provisions were sufficient in the case of peasants, who satisfied most of their needs from the products of their own establishments. But they were utterly inadequate to meet the expenditure of a workingman's family residing in a city. The dependents of a mobilized urban worker had to buy, in addition to food, fuel, clothing, etc., and to pay rent for lodgings. No such expenditure was included in the government allowance. Moreover, the *per capita* expenditure of a family grows less with its increase in size. The majority of families of industrial workers living in the cities and towns consisted, in the opinion of M. Prokopovich, of only one or two persons. And the government allowance, therefore, was not sufficient even for the purchase of foodstuffs.[22]

A certain relief to the working population was offered by the organized sale of foodstuffs at fixed prices, which were considerably below the market prices. The rationing of certain commodities dates back to 1916. For instance, sugar cards were introduced in Moscow in August, 1916. Bread cards became operative in Moscow on March 1, 1917. In June the system of

[21] R. Arsky, *Rabochi Klass vo Vremya Voini* (*The Working Class during the War*) in *Trud v Rossii* (*Labor in Russia*) (1925), I, 18–32.
[22] Prokopovich, *op. cit.*, p. 149.

rationing was extended to grits, in July to meat, in August to butter, in September to eggs, in October to vegetable oils, in November to sweetmeats, and in December to tea. Similar measures were introduced in Petrograd and in other cities. In May, 1917, food cards applied only to bread (1½ lb. per day), and to sugar (2½ lb. per month). In June, rationing was extended to grits, in July to fats, in August to meat and eggs, and so on.[23] The difference in prices paid on the market and at the stores where goods were issued to card holders was substantial, but the organization itself was by no means free from defects; and, not infrequently, goods which could easily be obtained on the market at exorbitant prices were entirely lacking in the stores where cards were accepted. This says nothing of the inconvenience and loss of time involved in waiting in endless lines in front of food shops. The importance of the relief obtained from this source, therefore, should not be exaggerated.

One unmistakable evidence of the plight of the working class will be found in the revival of the strike movement, especially in the immense increase in the number of strikes which had for their purpose the improvement of the economic position of labor.

Strikes

A study of the changes in the strike movement is made relatively easy by the detailed reports of the Factory Inspectors, reports which were elaborated by the Ministry of Commerce and Industry and were distributed to the members of the Government. Although the data of the Factory Inspectors did not include the enterprises owned by the State, they nevertheless give a very significant, if not exhaustive, picture of the trend of the strike movement.[24] In inspector's reports strikes were classified, in accordance with their purpose, either as economic or political. The latter group also included all strikes which had any but purely economic ends. For instance, several strikes directed against the employment of enemy labor at the beginning of the War were counted as political. Strikes demanding the

[23] Strumilin, *op. cit.*, p. 100; also R. Kabo, *Potreblenie Gorodskogo Naselenya Rossii* (*Consumption by the Urban Population of Russia*) (Moscow, 1918), pp. viii–ix; S. Strumilin, *Pitanie Petrogradskikh Rabochikh v 1918 Godu* (*Nutrition of the Petrograd Workers in 1918*), in *Novi Put* (*The New Path*) (Petrograd, 1919), No. 4, p. 19.

[24] At the beginning of 1917 the Factory Inspectors had under their jurisdiction 12,392 establishments employing 2,043,000 men and women, or about 40 per cent of the total number of industrial establishments, and about 70 per cent of the total number of workmen. *Materyali po Statistike Truda* (*Materials on Labor Statistics*), Vol. VIII (1920) quoted in *Rabochee Dvizhenie v 1917 Godu* (*Labor Movement in 1917*) edited by V. L. Meller and A. M. Pankratov, with an Introduction by Y. A. Yakovlev (Moscow-Leningrad, 1926), p. 13.

removal of an unpopular foreman, engineer, or director were also included in this group.

Table 7 will give an idea of the general trend of the strike movement.

TABLE 7
Strikes in 1910–1916.[25]

Year	Economic		Political		Total	
	Number of strikes	Number of strikers	Number of strikes	Number of strikers	Number of strikes	Number of strikers
1910	214	42,846	8	3,777	222	46,623
1911	442	96,730	24	8,380	466	105,110
1912	732	175,678	1,300	549,813	2,032	725,491
1913	1,370	384,654	1,034	502,442	2,404	887,096
1914 Jan.–July	1,560	413,972	2,538	1,035,312	4,098	1,449,284
Aug.–Dec.	61	31,907	7	2,845	68	34,752
1915	819	397,259	215	155,835	1,034	553,094
1916	1,167	776,064	243	310,300	1,410	1,086,364

It appears from this table that in the years immediately preceding the War the number of both strikes and strikers was rapidly increasing, reaching its highest point in the first seven months of 1914. The increase in the number of men engaged in noneconomic strikes was particularly great. On the eve of the War the industrial outlook was, indeed, alarming. The outbreak of hostilities brought a most spectacular change in the situation. While the number of political strikes in the first seven months of 1914 was over 2,500, and involved more than 1,000,000 men, in the later part of the year the number of such strikes had fallen to 7 in which less than 3,000 men took part. The only explanation we can give of this phenomenon is that Russian industrial workers, in common with their fellow workmen in other belligerent countries, were willing to forget for the time being their grievances, and lend the Government their unqualified support in its struggle with the enemy. In August, 1914, the number of strikes, as compared with July, was almost 40 times less and the number of strikers almost 13 times.[26] This downward trend continued throughout the autumn

[25] Data for the years 1910, 1911, 1912, and 1913 are taken from *Rabochee Dvizhenie v 1917 Godu*, p. 16. Data for the following years are taken from *Rabochee Dvizhenie v Godi Voini* (*The Labor Movement during the War*), edited by M. G. Fleer (Moscow, 1925), pp. 4, 6, and 7.
[26] *Rabochee Dvizhenie v Godi Voini*, p. 19.

nd winter of 1914. But, with the early spring of 1915, an upward movement set in, with a rather sharp increase in April, 1915, when the number of strikes reached 104 and the number of strikers 35,700, the highest figure since the outbreak of the War. This corresponded, one will remember, with the awakening of the general feeling of discontent with the way in which the War was being conducted, and with the rapid deterioration of the economic condition of the urban population. The upward trend in the strike movement continued until the Revolution of March, 1917. The character of strikes also changed during the War. In 1913 and the first half of 1914 the majority of men who went on strike were pursuing noneconomic aims. In 1915 and 1916 the economic strikes exceeded by a wide margin those of the other group. Demands of the strikers for an increase in wages which would allow them to face the rapid increase in the cost of living were the chief causes of the cessation of work.

An analysis of more detailed data than those quoted above discloses some interesting characteristics of the strike movement. The number of days lost per striker increased during the War. It was .50 in August–December, 1914, 1.41 in 1915, and 2.16 in 1916. In 1913 the average loss of labor days per striker was 1.40. This change indicates that the strike movement had gained in intensity. Another feature of the strike movement was the growth in the average number of men taking part in a strike, a development which points to the concentration of industry. Table 8 illustrates this process.

TABLE 8

Average Number of Strikers per Strike, 1913–1916.[37]

Year		Economic	Political
1913		280	485
1914	January–July	265	407
	August–December	523	406
1915		485	1,034
1916		665	1,410

The policy of the Government toward strikers was one of severe repression. This was especially true in the case of the establishments working for national defense. A method of breaking down the resistance of the workers was the mobilization of the age group which was liable to military service.

[37] *Ibid.*, p. 5.

Some of them were sent to the trenches, while others were re tained in their former jobs, no longer as "free" workmen, but a soldiers subject to military discipline.[28]

The beginning of 1917 saw a rapid growth in the number o strikes. In January and February, 1917, that is, in the tw months immediately preceding the Revolution, the number o strikes reported by the Factory Inspectors reached 1,330, in volving 676,286 strikers. Petrograd was leading in the politica strike movement which is explained by the concentration i the capital of the country's large engineering works. Men work ing in the metal industry, as we have seen, were better pai than other workers; they were not so hard pressed by economi necessity as their less fortunate fellow workmen in othe branches of industry. They always occupied a conspicuou position in the front rank of militant labor and retained i throughout the War. Indeed, theirs was the only group i 1914–1916 whose political strikes had a predominance ove their economic ones. January 9, the anniversary of the abortiv labor demonstration of 1905 led by Father Gapon, which re sulted in the death of over a hundred men and women ("th bloody Sunday"), was invariably used by the workers for po litical demonstrations. On January 9, 1916, these demonstra tions took place chiefly in Petrograd and were made by th men employed in the metal industry. Out of 53,000 striker 45,000 or 85 per cent belonged to this industry. The strike o some 181,000 workmen in October, 1916, was also chiefly strike in Petrograd which provided 139,000 strikers or abou 77 per cent. The beginning of 1917 witnessed an immens expansion of the strike movement. In January, 1917, the num ber of strikers reached 244,000, of whom 162,000 or 66 pe cent made purely political demands. Petrograd led the list wit 95,000. In February, 1917, the movement gained further forc The Factory Inspectors reported 432,000 strikers, 200,00 being in Petrograd and 161,000 in Moscow. It was estimated tha about 96 per cent of all strikers were out for political reason There is little doubt, however, that political and economi reasons were closely interwoven. The protest against politica conditions was also a protest against the deterioration of th economic position of the workers, which to a large extent, wa a result of the political situation.[29]

An interesting characteristic of the strike movement durin

[28] Letter of the Minister of the Interior to the President of the Council of Ministe of January 30, 1916, in *Rabochee Dvizhenie v Godi Voini*, p. 251; also Memora dum of the Police Department dealing with the disturbances at the Putilov Wor in February, 1916, in *ibid.*, pp. 252–254.

[29] *Rabochee Dvizhenie v 1917 Godu*, pp. 20–22.

he War is given in a Soviet publication which cannot be suspected of intentionally minimizing the part of organized labor
in the progress of events that led to the downfall of the monarchy. According to the Soviet writer, strikes during the War
presented the following important features: (1) they were spontaneous, and were almost completely free from leadership by
the trade unions which had had little influence since their annihilation following the labor disturbances of 1905–1906; (2)
they were very brief and centered around labor anniversaries
such as January 9 or May 1; (3) reoccurrence of strikes in the
same establishment was unusual; (4) strikes took place chiefly
in provinces and cities with strongly developed industries, among
which Petrograd had a leading place; (5) they were primarily
economic, with the exception of those of the metal workers;
(6) the intensity of the movement greatly increased in the second half of 1915.[30] Of these conclusions, which are substantially correct, the first which speaks of the absence of leadership
on the part of trade unions, and the spontaneous nature of their
movements, is of particular interest. It brings us to the important
question of labor organizations.

Labor Organizations

The amazingly rapid rise to power of Russian labor in the
course of 1917 may suggest to an observer unfamiliar with
Russian conditions that this remarkable change in the position
of industrial workers was the result of a carefully devised plan
put into effect by a powerful organization. Nothing could be
more remote from the truth. The trade unions and other organizations of the working classes which came into being during
the short-lived liberal era of 1905 were wiped out by the reactionary policy of the following years. Some of the smaller trade
unions, such as the printers' and the woodworkers' unions, which
managed to survive, enjoyed little influence and hardly counted
at all in the economic and political life of the labor masses. The
only labor organizations which succeeded in gaining a footing
were the sick benefit funds established under a law passed in
1912. The total number of such funds on June 1, 1914, was
2,826 with 2,049,104 members.[31] Their recent origin, however,
and the limited scope of their work kept such sick benefit fund
organizations from assuming a position of real leadership by the
time the War broke out. The sole representatives of the aspira-

[30] Ibid., p. 13.

[31] Statisticheski Ezhegodnik (Statistical Yearbook) published by the Permanent
Council of the Congress of Representatives of Commerce and Industry, edited by
V. E. Shary (St. Petersburg, 1914).

tions of the working class were the thirty socialist members of the Duma who, thanks to the hopeless minority in which they constantly found themselves, could do little except, from time to time, give voice to labor grievances from the tribune of the Duma.

The War naturally brought no improvement in the situation. Labor organizations, which had always been treated with suspicion by the Imperial Government, were put under a supervision by the police which was stricter than ever. An interesting light was thrown upon the attitude of the Government toward labor organizations by a discussion which took place in the Council of Ministers in August, 1915. The program of the Progressive Bloc[32] contained an article calling for the freedom of labor organizations. When the matter came under examination at the Council of Ministers, Prince Shakhovskoy, Minister of Commerce and Industry, thought it necessary to inform his colleagues that "trade unions are not forbidden by law. If they are not functioning for the present, that is because they have been closed 'under emergency powers' [powers conferred upon the military and civil administration on the declaration of a 'state of emergency']. In many instances, indeed, the liquidation of trade unions has been carried out without sufficient reason by unduly active generals, or by too energetic governors of provinces." And Prince Shcherbatov, Minister of the Interior, amplified the explanation of his colleague by confessing that "it must be admitted that abuses are frequent in dealing with trade unions in the provinces. The generals and the governors prefer to close down the organizations they dislike rather than to look after them and be responsible for them."[33]

The labor press, obviously an essential medium for the spreading of ideas of class solidarity among workers, was reduced to silence by prosecutions directed against it as a result of the strikes in the summer of 1914. It did not recover from this blow until after the Revolution of March, 1917. No attempts were made during the War to create a daily paper for the use of the working class except for the establishment of the short-lived *Narodnaya Gazeta* issued in Moscow by the Social-Revolutionary Party, and a few newspapers in Siberia which had an uncertain existence and a limited circulation. The chief reasons for the discontinuation of all socialist publications were the intolerable conditions of military censorship, to which we must add the generally unfavorable economic situation, the undoubted impoverishment of the laboring class, the rise in the

[32] *See above*, pp. 102–103.
[33] Yakhontov, *op. cit.*, p. 113.

cost of printing, etc. A number of periodicals, published by the various socialist parties, but dealing with such relatively inoffensive questions as the trade union movement, labor insurance, and coöperative societies, continued to appear, but they were careful to preserve the strictest neutrality in dealing with political problems.[34]

The Social-Democratic Party, with which labor organizations were closely associated and on which they largely depended for leadership, also suffered a heavy blow at the beginning of the War. Its five representatives in the Duma—Petrovsky, Muranov, Badaev, Samoilov, and Shagov—were arrested on November 4, 1914, in Petrograd, while attending the meeting of a secret organization. They were accused of subversive activities, tried in February, 1915, with several other persons, and were sentenced to deportation to Siberia.[35] It is characteristic of the state of political apathy in which labor had sunk since the outbreak of the War that their arrest was accepted with indifference by the masses and brought no protest. At no time was the strike movement so low as at the end of 1914 and early in 1915.

The underground or illicit activities of the revolutionary parties were also at low ebb. The crushing blow inflicted by the Government upon the Social-Democratic and the Social-Revolutionary Parties during the strikes of June and July, 1914, was further aggravated by the general disorganization brought about by the War, the mobilization of a large number of men, and the interruption of communications with revolutionary headquarters abroad. Even M. Fleer, the enthusiastic and not too discriminating historian of the Bolshevist movement in Russia during the War, is forced to admit that the work of the party in the second half of 1914 and the first half of 1915 was quite disorganized. Its activities at that time, he confesses, were limited to the publication of propaganda leaflets and attempts to reëstablish connections with party organizations in the provinces.[36] He also regretfully concedes that the arrest of the five Bolshevik members of the Duma failed to stir the masses.[37] He maintains, however, that by the end of 1915 the Petrograd Committee of the Bolshevik Party succeeded in establishing it-

[34] S. Levin, *Sotsialisticheskaya Pechat vo Vremya Imperialisticheskoi Voini* (*The Socialist Press during the Imperialistic War*), in *Krasni Arkhiv*, II, 200–225.
[35] *Vo Vremya Imperialisticheskoi Voini* (*During the Imperialistic War*) in *Krasnaya Letopis* (*The Red Chronicle*) (Leningrad, 1924), No. 10, pp. 86–201.
[36] M. G. Fleer, *Peterburgski Komitet Bolshevikov v Godi Voini* (*The Petrograd Committee of the Bolsheviks during the War*) in *Krasnaya Letopis*, No. 19, pp. 100–102.
[37] *Ibid.*, p. 107.

self and in exercising a real and effective control over the workers of Petrograd. He claims for the Committee the honor of organizing the strike in the Putilov Works, which took place in February, 1916.[38] This claim seems to be greatly exaggerated. The Police Department, which had an excellent knowledge of the activities of the revolutionary parties, rightly discounted their part in the labor troubles during the War.[39] Several attempts made in recent years by Bolshevik writers to glorify the rôle of their party in bringing about the downfall of the monarchy have succeeded only in demonstrating the groundlessness of their claim.[40] There is no doubt that attempts were made by the revolutionary organizations to agitate among the working population and to promote disaffection, but it is also clear that their equipment and means were hopelessly inadequate. One of the active members of the Bolshevik organization in Petrograd has stated that "at the outbreak of the War the proletariat was abandoned to its fate, because all its intellectual elements had joined the ranks of the Union of Towns; the number of those who remained with the party organization was very small."[41] He also states that the "labor movement in the middle of 1915 was practically non-existent."[42] The struggle of these men single-handed and without leaders against the immense machinery of the Russian Empire was pathetic and perhaps even heroic. But it certainly had little promise of success. The activities of the Bolshevik organization were almost entirely limited to the publications of leaflets in very small number which they distributed among the workers. The printers and even the authors were often almost illiterate.[43] They were lacking in everything, they had no money, no personal security, and were continually being hounded and arrested by the police. Even those who deplore the purpose to which their energies were directed, will find it difficult to deny them credit for perseverance and personal courage. On the other hand, it is just as difficult to admit, without going against common sense, that a few hand-printed proc-

[38] Fleer, *op. cit.*, in *Krasnaya Letopis*, No. 22, pp. 121–128.
[39] *Politicheskoe Polozhenie Rossii Nakanune Fevralskoi Revolutsii v Zhandarmskom Osvyashchenii* in *Krasni Arkhiv*, XVII, 28.
[40] *See*, for instance, A. Slavsky, *Peterburgskie Bolsheviki v Pervomaiskie Dni 1913-1916 (The Petrograd Bolsheviks and the Celebration of May 1 in 1913–1916)* in *Krasnaya Letopis*, No. 17, pp. 82–101; F. Lemeshov, *Na Putilovskom Zavode v God Voini (The Putilov Works during the War)* in *Krasnaya Letopis*, No. 23, pp. 5–38; N. Gavrilov, *Na Viborgskoi Storone v 1914–1917 (The Viborgski Section of Petrograd in 1914–1917)* in *Krasnaya Letopis*, No. 23, pp. 39–61.
[41] *Podpolnaya Rabota v Godi Imperialisticheskoi Voini v Petrograde (Underground Work in Petrograd during the Imperialistic War)* in *Krasnaya Letopis*, Nos. 2–3, p. 118.
[42] *Ibid.*, p. 123.
[43] *Ibid.*, p. 124.

lamations issued by a small group of enthusiasts, some of whom could hardly read and write, were sufficient to overthrow the century-old edifice of the Empire, however shattered may have been its foundations. Forces infinitely more powerful than the subversive activities of the revolutionaries were working toward this end. In the case of labor they were the immense economic hardships the working class had to endure and, with them, of course, the general weariness of the War.

That the Bolsheviks were far from having established a firm hold over the working class, as claimed today by some of their writers, will appear from the fact that at the end of 1915 their attitude toward the participation of labor in the war industries committees suffered a severe rebuke.

Labor and the War Industries Committees

The war industries committees came into being in the summer of 1915 as the first and most important step in the self-mobilization of industry.[44] The leaders of the new movement, who were drawn from the ranks of liberal-minded industrialists and business men, fully realized the necessity of a close collaboration with labor if the reorganization of national industry for the needs of the War was to be made a success. The Central War Industries Committee, at one of its first meetings, passed a resolution demanding the election of ten representatives of labor to take part in its work. This request, which marked a striking departure from the traditional policy, was nevertheless granted by the Government. But it met with a mixed reception in labor circles.

The Left wing of the Social-Democratic Party (the Bolsheviks) took an uncompromising attitude on the ground that the overthrow of the Imperial Government was the one and sole aim of Russian labor, by which the international proletariat would benefit. No workingman therefore should participate of his own free will in any organization which had for its purpose the assisting of the Government of the Tsar in its struggle against the enemy.

We are against participation in the war industries committees which are helping to carry on an imperialistic, reactionary war [wrote Lenin]. We are in favor of taking advantage of the electoral campaign, for instance by participating in its first stages, but only for purposes of propaganda and organization.[45]

[4] See above, pp. 128–129.
[5] N. Lenin, *Neskolko Tezisov* (*A Few General Principles*) in *Sobranie Sochineni* (*Collected Works*), III, 207.

163

The Menshevik wing of the Social-Democratic Party and the Social-Revolutionary Party held a different point of view. They agreed with the Bolsheviks that the overthrow of the Tsarist *régime* was the chief aim of labor, but they also maintained that the military defeat of Russia would bring only misery and sufferings to the country, including its working classes. They believed that the War would, better than anything else, demonstrate the faults and the inadequacy of the Imperial *régime* and lead to its downfall. They counted upon the War to make disaffection general and thus assure their final aim, that is, revolution. This attitude became known as "defensism," while the Bolshevik point of view received the name of "defeatism."[46]

The question of elections to the war industries committees aroused much interest and discussion in labor circles. The advantages organization offered the workers by the elections finally gained the upper hand. All factories employing 500 workmen or more were to take part in the elections. Every 1,000 workmen were to return one voter; factories employing less than 1,000 but more than 500 workmen were also to return one voter. The voters were to elect the actual delegates. In Petrograd the elections took place on September 21, 1915. They resulted in the election of 218 voters representing 101 establishments with 219,036 workmen. The meeting of the voters, however, had negative results, and decided by a small majority (90 against 81) to refrain from electing delegates to the Central War Industries Committee. This, no doubt, was a victory for the Bolsheviks. It was, however, short-lived. New elections were held on November 29 and ended, by a majority of 109 to 67, in a decision to elect the delegates. Among those elected was Abrosimov who eventually proved to be an agent of the secret police.[47] Elections of delegates to the local war industries committees also took place in Moscow and in the provinces. In May, 1916, labor representatives were duly elected to 20 regional and 98 district committees.[48] All this would seem to indicate that the hold of Lenin and his followers upon the working class was by no means as firm as some Bolshevik writers would like us to believe.[49]

The labor delegates in the Central War Industries Committee

[46] K. Kareev, *Rabochaya Pechat i Voenno-Promishlennie Komiteti* (*The Labor Press and the War Industries Committees*) in *Krasnaya Letopis*, No. 21, pp. 130–142; also Zagorsky, *op. cit.*, pp. 91–92.

[47] Kareev, *op. cit.*, pp. 142–152.

[48] Zagorsky, *op. cit.*, pp. 92–93.

[49] This is admitted by other Bolshevik writers. M. Yakovlev, discussing strikes in Petrograd in January–February, 1917, remarks: "The rôle of the party in the movement was still insignificant," *Rabochee Dvizhenie v 1917 Godu*, p. 3.

and in the local committees formed separate groups and kept in touch with the rank and file which elected them. It was the first instance in the history of Russia where the representatives of labor, as such, were called upon to take part in the settlement of national problems.

The appearance of labor groups in the war industries committees was a source of continuous annoyance and suspicion to the Police Department. It was kept well informed of the activities of the labor group in the Central War Industries Committee by Abrosimov who, as we have said, was an undercover agent of the police. With the swing of the Government toward the extreme Right which took place in the course of 1916, the position of the labor group became more and more precarious. Its members were finally arrested, early in 1917, by the orders of Protopopov, then Minister of the Interior.[50] Under the conditions then prevailing in Imperial Russia all attempts at national coöperation, such as the war industries committees, were doomed to failure.

The Attitude of Labor on the Eve of the Revolution

An interesting and instructive picture of the general condition and attitude of labor on the eve of the Revolution is given by the report of the Police Department for October, 1916, to which we have already referred.

In the opinion of the spokesmen of the labor group of the Central War Industries Committee [says the report], the industrial proletariat of the capital is on the verge of despair and it believes that the smallest outbreak, due to any pretext, will lead to uncontrollable riots, with thousands and tens of thousands of victims. Indeed, the stage for such outbreaks is more than set: the economic position of the masses, in spite of the immense increase in wages is distressing. . . . Even if we assume that wages have increased 100 per cent, the cost of living in the meantime has risen by an average of 300 per cent. The impossibility of obtaining, even for cash, many foodstuffs and articles of prime necessity, the waste of time involved in spending hours waiting in line in front of stores, the increasing morbidity due to inadequate diet and anti-sanitary lodgings (cold and dampness as a result of lack of coal and firewood), etc., all these conditions have created such a situation that the mass of industrial workers are quite ready to let themselves go to the wildest excesses of a hunger riot.

In addition to economic hardships the "legal disabilities" of the working class have of late become "intolerable and unbearable"; the denial of the mere right to move freely from one factory to another has reduced labor, in the opinion of the Social-Democrats, to the state

[50] Evidence of Protopopov in *Padenie Tsarskago Rezhima*, I, 142–143; IV, 87.

of mere cattle, good only for "slaughter in the war." The prohibition of all labor meetings, even those for the organization of coöperative stores and dining-rooms, the closing of trade unions, the prosecution of men taking an active part in the sick benefit funds, the suspension of labor newspapers, and so on, make the labor masses, led by the more advanced and already revolutionary-minded elements, assume an openly hostile attitude towards the Government and protest with all the means at their disposal against the continuation of the War.

In the opinion of some of the more thoughtful Social-Democrats, groups of responsible workers find it difficult to prevent the masses from bursting into demonstrations growing out of the lack of necessities and the rise in the cost of living. A saying by one of the speakers at a meeting of a sick benefit fund. . . . "You must end the War if you do not know how to fight" has become the war-cry of the Petrograd Social-Democrats.

The close relations between the workers of Petrograd and the army also indicate that the atmosphere at the front is disturbing, not to say revolutionary. The high cost of living and the shortage of foodstuffs from which soldiers' wives are the first to suffer have been made known to the army by the soldiers returning from furloughs. The rumors of famine in Petrograd which circulate at the front are perfectly monstrous and have already soared into the realm of pure imagination. According to statements by the soldiers themselves, the army believes that in the capital "a pound of bread is worth a ruble," that "meat is sold only to the nobles and the landlords," that "a new cemetery has been opened for those who have died of starvation," and so on. The anxiety of soldiers about their families is perfectly legitimate and understandable, but it is unfortunate that it grows from day to day and offers a fertile ground for the spreading of both German and revolutionary propaganda. The sick benefit funds are swamped with letters and communications from "comrades" and to "comrades" in the army. These letters are full of invectives against the authors of the rise in the cost of living, and speak of the "day of reckoning" when the War is over, or even before.

In the workshops one hears more often than ever the speeches of avowed "defeatists" who call for a policy of "sabotage" in munition works or spread false stories of a general strike which has finally been decided upon, by someone, for October. These speeches are not always believed but they are eagerly listened to. . . . The question of a lasting general strike has been frequently and repeatedly discussed in many factories and workshops; and if it has not met with unanimous support it is only because the workers are in favor of putting forward their economic grievances, while the Social-Democrats advocate a purely political platform. Nevertheless the Social-Democrats are firmly convinced that the general strike is bound to come in the very near future. Many of them believe that it will coincide with the prorogation of the Duma, which is expected to take place before long.

Revolutionary circles, then, have no doubts that a revolution will begin soon, that its unmistakable precursors are already here, and that the Government will prove incapable of fighting against the revolutionary masses, which are the more dangerous because they consist largely of soldiers or former soldiers.[51]

It will be conceded that the Police Department, with all its faults, was not lacking in information and displayed keen powers of analysis and foresight. It will be noted that the report laid particular stress upon the influence of the economic factor in that rapidly growing labor discontent which, by the end of 1916, bordered on despair and hunger riots. The evidence we have presented seems to indicate that here, too, the police used sound judgment.

After the Revolution of March, 1917

The Revolution of March, 1917, brought no economic relief to the proletariat. It appeared from our examination of the trend of wages that at no time during the War were real wages of industrial workmen so low as in 1917, and we may add that they continued to decline, even more rapidly than in 1917, in the following years, or until 1921 or 1922. It is still a matter of controversy whether even today, thirteen years after the overthrow of the Imperial Government, they have reached their pre-war level.[52] And we know how incredibly low this level was. This question, however, is beyond our scope. We are concerned only with the fact that the Revolution brought no immediate improvement in the economic position of labor. On the contrary, it even emphasized and accelerated the deterioration of the living conditions of the working class. The economic breakdown of Russia in the turmoil of the Revolution is a fact of general knowledge. The well-to-do classes, who were completely uprooted by the social upheaval, were indeed the heavy losers. But the poorer classes were not spared either. Those who have little have little to lose, but when a few rubles are dropped from a budget which allows 50 copecks (25 cents) a month for "recreation and cultural needs" the total of privations, undernourishment, and suffering which even this loss means, however trifling the sum involved may appear, is large indeed.

But if the Revolution imposed a new and heavy burden on the working class, it also brought it important compensations in the shape of a social and political status entirely new and without precedent in the annals of mankind. The rise of labor to political power began at the end of February, a few days before the abdication of the Emperor, with the formation of the Execu-

[51] *Politicheskoe Polozhenie Rossii Nakanune Fevralskoi Revolutsii v Zhandarmskom Osvyashchenii* in *Krasni Arkhiv*, XVII, 10–14.

[52] *See* for instance Panait Istrati, *La Russie nue* (Paris, 1929), and *Soviets 1929* (Paris, 1929), by the same author.

tive Committee of the Petrograd Soviet of Soldiers' and Workmen's Deputies. It continued throughout 1917 until the Bolshevik Revolution of October (November), 1917, which officially sanctioned the dictatorship of the proletariat. Labor's struggle was carried on through the following three channels: the Soviets, the trade unions, and the factory committees. Soviets of workers' and soldiers' deputies sprang up all over the country, and their activities were mainly political. They constituted the basis of the system of government which today rules the Union of Soviet Socialist Republics.

The growth of trade unions was no less spectacular. Industrial workers, whose legitimate desire for class representation had for so long been denied, now turned to trade unions with all the zeal of neophytes. The growth of trade unions in size and number increased by leaps and bounds. Unions with thousands of members were organized in the course of a few days. For instance, the union of metal workers in Petrograd had 16,432 members on March 29, 1917, the day when its organization meeting was called. Of the total number of trade unions which came into being in 1917, 51 per cent dated from April–March.[53] An interesting investigation into the growth of trade unions in 1917 was made by the first congress of Russian trade unions, held in January, 1918. It covered 158 unions and contains valuable information as to the number and size of such labor organizations.

TABLE 9

Trade Unions in 1917.[54]

Membership per union	Number of unions	Total membership
Under 3,000	21	37,300
From 3,000 to 5,000	41	160,300
From 5,000 to 10,000	47	356,500
From 10,000 to 20,000	32	441,300
Over 20,000	16	1,257,200
No information	1	....
Total	158	2,252,600

The average membership per union was thus 14,300. More than half the entire membership belonged to sixteen large unions; but the majority were much smaller, and were limited to the workers living in the same town or employed in the same factory. The bulk of the trade unions was drawn from the two large and

[53] *Rabochee Dvizhenie v 1917 Godu,* p. 83.
[54] *Ibid.,* p. 85.

elatively well-organized industries—manufactures of textiles
nd metals. The textile industry was responsible for 15 unions
vith 571,400 members, and the metal industry, for 35 with
25,900. The membership of trade unions in other industries
·as smaller, but they were found everywhere, even in the most
ackward industries and in the remotest parts of the country.[55]

The factory committees, like the trade unions and the Soviets,
ame into being in the process of the Revolution. They had for
heir purpose the regulating of the relations between employer
nd employee in factories and workshops. They soon became
he chief instruments for what was known as "workers' control,"
he movement which eventually led to the nationalization of
idustrial undertakings. There does not seem to be any precise
iformation on the number of factory committees, but it was
ndoubtedly very large. At the first conference which these new
gencies called, in May–June, 1917, they boldly declared them-
elves in favor of strict labor control, with the ultimate aim of
ssuming responsibility for the conduct of the country's gov-
rnment as the best method of bringing about the socialization
f industry.[56]

The Soviets, trade unions, and factory committees were all
roducts of the Revolution, and were not based on any legis-
ation. The attempts of the Provisional Government to clothe
ie trade unions and the factory committees with a semblance
f legality were belated, inadequate, and were generally
isregarded.

The appearance of organized militant labor naturally wrought
complete change in the relations between employees and em-
loyers. The latter attempted to protest, to make appeals to the
atriotism of the workers, and to speak of the necessity of a
nited national front at least until the end of the War, but with-
ut success. The fate of the old order of things was already
ealed. The result was endless conflict between factory owners
nd employees. As early as the middle of March the Petrograd
oviet was informed that a state of "constant conflict" between
.bor and employers was being reported from practically every-
here.[57] In September, 1917, *Torgovo Promishlennaya Gazeta*
Gazette of Trade and Industry), describing the industrial situ-
tion in July–August, stated that "the closing down of factories
nd the suspension of work are of everyday occurrence."[58] The
esult was unemployment and new hardships for both owners

Ibid., p. 86.
Rabochee Dvizhenie v 1917 Godu, pp. 75–81.
Ibid., p. 41.
Ibid., p. 153.

and workers. But the conflict between the social groups ha
reached a stage where compromises could no longer solve th
problem.

To the protests of the employers and their refusal to meet th
demands, often inacceptable, of labor, the organization of th
working class answered by strikes and the seizure of factorie
Important strikes took place in the textile, leather, printing, an
metal industries, and in the mining region of the Donets. Th
demands of the workers were still partly economic and include
such items as the eight-hour day, higher wages based on definit
agreements, and collective bargaining. But, in flagrant contra
with the prerevolutionary strikes, these demands no longe
headed the list. The political side of the struggle had now bee
brought to the forefront. The workers insisted on the intr
duction of labor control, the limitation of profits, the nationa
ization of industry, the transfer of land to the peasants, and th
ending of the War. To these no *bourgeois* government coul
possibly consent. And when the conflict broke out into ope
struggle, labor won the day, not so much because of its ow
strength as because of the extreme weakness of its opponent
The first Republic of Workers and Peasants came into bein;
For this victory, too, labor has paid, in common with all othe
classes, a heavy price.

Chapter 8

The Peasant Colossus

The Peasant State

IN OUR DISCUSSION of the effects of the War upon Russia w
have said very little so far about the social group which form
the bulk of her population and on which largely depends th
character of the nation's development. Russia has always bee
and still remains primarily a peasant State. The fragile grow
of European civilization which had been forcibly transplante
to the Russian soil by Peter the Great succeeded in taking fir
root only in the large cities. Even the provincial towns, especia
those remote from the railways, led a life of their own whic
often had little in common with the busy activities and the i
terests of St. Petersburg and Moscow. Completely cut off fro

e general business and cultural trends of the world were the
ussian villages, where millions of men and women still lived
nder conditions reminiscent of those which were common in
estern Europe in the Middle Ages. About the time when the
'ar broke out 85 per cent of the population of Russia were
ıral, and it was estimated that about 70 per cent derived their
ving from agriculture; in certain localities this percentage was
; high as 90 per cent.[1] In 1892 of the total number of owners
f agricultural land 98.1 per cent were peasants.[2] One might well
xpect that in a country so constituted the peasants' interests
ould be the leading concern of the Government. It was on their
elfare that depended, in the last resort, the progress and pros-
erity of the country as a whole. In spite of this simple and self-
vident truth the economic well-being of the peasants had been
onsistently neglected by the Imperial Government, and it was
ot until after the revolutionary outbursts and agrarian riots of
905–1906 that it embarked on a definite policy for the im-
rovement of peasant land tenure and farming. This does not
ıean, of course, that the "peasant question" did not attract a
reat deal of attention. On the contrary, it was continuously
iscussed in the columns of Russian periodicals, both liberal and
eactionary, in the second half of the nineteenth and the be-
nning of the twentieth centuries. But this discussion was often
ighly theoretical and was not infrequently based on premises
hich had nothing in common with the actual condition of the
easants. The idealizing of the peasants, as a separate "estate"
ıd the glorification of peasant institutions, such as the land
ommune, was one of the few points on which revolutionary
ıd reactionary elements found themselves in complete agree-
ent. We have seen that the Emperor had a profound belief
. the mystical union between the throne and the people, as rep-
sented by the illiterate masses of the peasants. And as late
, in 1913 a titled member of the Duma delivered in that high
ssembly an address in which he deplored the fact that serfdom
ıd been abolished too early and that it had had merely 300
ears in which to develop its beneficial effects, a period, in his
inion, utterly inadequate. His address, it is true, provoked
good deal of hilarity in the Duma; but it was nevertheless
tened to for over an hour, and was printed by its author and
stributed among the members of the two chambers.[3] In the
eantime, while a controversy was raging among Russian in-

ntsiferov and others, "Rural Economy," p. 45.
bid., p. 29.
Iaxime Kovalewsky, *La Russie Sociale* (Paris, 1914), pp. 5–6.

tellectuals about the value of communal land tenure and th
mission of the Russian people, the economic position of th
peasants was steadily growing worse. The roots of this proces
of deterioration must be sought in the defects of the measure
for the emancipation of the peasants in 1861.

The Emancipation

There is practically a general agreement among Russia
writers that the Emancipation Acts, which raised the forme
serfs to the dignity of free human beings, fell short of creatir
for the small peasant farmers conditions which would allo
them to support themselves and their families. We must mentio
however briefly, some of the more important features of th
situation created in 1861, without a knowledge of which th
position of the peasants in the first quarter of the twentie
century cannot be properly understood. The chief defects o
the Emancipation consisted in the inadequacy of peasant allo
ments, the excessive burden of "redemption payments," con
munal land tenure, and the legal disabilities from which th
peasants suffered. Let us examine each of them in turn.

Peasant Allotments

To begin with, the area of allotment land which the peasan
received on their emancipation fell, in many cases, below the
requirements. Under the *régime* of serfdom it was customa
for the members of a peasant family to work three days a wee
for the landlord and to devote the remaining three days to the
own plots. The area farmed by the peasants therefore, eve
before 1861, was sufficient merely to provide employment fe
half the peasant population. Nevertheless not only was that are

TABLE 10

Peasant Land Holdings before and after the Emancipation.[4]

Region	Before the emancipation	After the emancipation	Increase or decrease
	(in deciatines)		(percentage
Less fertile region (15 provinces)	13,944,000	13,390,000	−4.0
Black-soil and eastern provinces (21 provinces)	14,016,000	10,709,000	−23.6
Russian Poland (9 provinces)	7,737,000	10,901,000	+40.9

[4] S. N. Prokopovich, *Krestyanskoe Khozyaistvo (Peasant Farming)* (Berlin, 1924
pp. 47–48.

172

used as a point of departure for the calculation of the size of the average holding to which the former serfs should be entitled in the various parts of the country, but it even suffered further reduction in the course of the redistribution of land which accompanied the Great Reform. The importance of this reduction will appear from Table 10.

It appears from this table that, with the exception of Russian Poland, where the area held by the peasants increased as a result of the Emancipation, the peasants lost a considerable portion of the land they used to farm. The generous treatment accorded to the nine provinces of Russian Poland is explained by purely political considerations. After the Polish uprising of 1863 the Government attempted to win the support of the peasants in the Polish provinces by increasing their land holdings at the expense of the Polish landlords. In the Russian provinces, on the other hand, we observe a decrease in the area of peasant holdings which was particularly large in the black-soil and eastern provinces where the loss amounted to almost one-quarter of the area formerly held by the peasants. If we examine more detailed data, for separate localities and for separate classes of peasants, the decrease in the areas of their holdings will appear even more striking. In the province of Saratov, for instance, the former landlord peasants lost as much as 37.9 per cent and in the province of Samara even 41.8 per cent of the area they farmed before the Emancipation.[5] At the same time the peasants were deprived of their customary right of using the landlords' forests and meadows, and of grazing their cattle on the manorial commons.

On an average, for the whole of Russia, the former landlords' serfs obtained 3.2 deciatines (8.6 acres) per male adult, those on appanage estates 4.9 deciatines (13.2 acres), and State peasants, 6.7 deciatines (18.1 acres).[6] It has been computed that the total area transferred to the peasants was some 40,000,000 deciatines short of what was required to provide full-time employment for the peasant population.[7] The result was that the peasants, from the very beginning of their newly acquired freedom, found themselves in an extremely precarious economic position, and one which practically made it impossible for them to meet their obligations, or even to earn a living. This was forcibly brought out soon after the Emancipation by the well-

D. S. Rosenblum, *Zemelnoe Pravo R.S.F.S.R.* (*The Land Law of the U.S.S.R.*) Moscow-Leningrad, 1929), p. 17.
Bilimovich, *op. cit.*, p. 306.
Prokopovich, *Krestyanskoe Khozyaistvo*, p. 48.

173

known Russian economist, Yanson. Commenting on the situation in the less fertile regions he asserted in a book published in 1877, that

with rare exceptions the peasants' allotments, or rather the total area farmed by them, may provide them with the necessary foodstuffs and leave nothing with which to meet the other needs of the household; but in the majority of cases their holdings are incapable of accomplishing even so much. It could not be otherwise. On a poor soil one requiring generous fertilizers and, therefore, a sufficient area in meadows and grazing land, the allotment including the farmhouse must not be less than eight deciatines per male person if the family is to be provided for, and this on condition that the land is not of too poor a quality. And we have seen that the average allotment of the former State serfs does not reach this figure, while that of the landlords' serfs is only the half of it. But, in addition to foodstuffs the peasant must obtain the money with which to pay taxes and redemption payments.

The position of the peasants in the black-soil provinces was no better.

The needs of the peasants in the less fertile regions are facts of common knowledge [wrote Yanson] . . . but few are aware that similar if not worse is the fate of the peasants in the black-soil provinces . . . All the former landlords' serfs in 62 per cent of the districts of the black-soil belt where the three-field rotation of crops is prevalent can not produce on their allotments even their daily bread, while in the remaining 38 per cent of the districts a considerable section of the peasants are just as badly off.

And Yanson maintained that even in the western provinces, in spite of the specially favorable position created for the peasants by the legislation of 1863, "the farmers are not only incapable of paying taxes and other fiscal obligations, but even of providing sufficient food for their families."[8]

The pessimistic conclusions of Yanson should not be accepted too literally. The figures given above, while correct in themselves, do not give an exact picture of the distribution of land among the peasants. Like all generalizations they contain a part but not the whole truth. Certain groups of peasants, especially the former State peasants, received allotments large enough to provide them and their families with an income adequate to

[8] Y. E. Yanson, *Opit Statisticheskago Izsledovanya o Krestyanskikh Nadelakh i Platezhakh* (*Statistical Investigation of Peasant Allotments and Redemption Payments*) (St. Petersburg, 1877), pp. 25, 63, 64, 68, 69, 109, quoted in Prokopovich, *Krestyanskoe Khozyaistvo*, p. 46.

neet their needs and satisfy the requirements of their customary standard of living.

Many peasants, especially those who were formerly landlords' serfs [writes Professor Kaufman, an eminent student of the peasant question] were undoubtedly inadequately provided with land from the very beginning, but side by side with them we find a large group of peasants who received sufficient allotments or even allotments exceeding the area that can be farmed by a peasant family. Among the former State and appanage serfs about six-sevenths were adequately provided with land, and even among the lardlords' serfs almost three-fifths belonged to this class.[9]

Redemption Payments

The whole Reform of 1861 bears the earmarks of a compromise between the ideas of those who were satisfied with the granting of personal freedom to the former serfs and those who struggled to put them on a sound economic foundation. The redemption payments were, in theory, a compensation to the landlords for the land which was transferred to peasant ownership. No compensation was allowed for the loss of free labor resulting from the Emancipation. This principle, however, was not carried out in practice, although it was not openly violated. The redemption payments due from the peasants were graded in accordance with the number of deciatines they obtained; the heaviest burden was attached to the first deciatine, the payments due on each subsequent deciatine being considerably smaller. For instance, in the provinces outside the black-soil belt the payments were graded as follows. The first deciatine received by the peasant involved the payment of half the entire sum for which the allotment was assessed; the second deciatine, one-quarter of the assessment; and the remaining quarter was distributed equally over such additional deciatines as a peasant might be entitled to. Let us take an illustration. If the redemption payment was twelve rubles and the allotment for the district was five deciatines, the first deciatine was assessed at six rubles, the second at three rubles, and the remaining three deciatines at one ruble each. An allotment of one deciatine, therefore involved a payment of six rubles; an allotment of two deciatines, nine rubles; an allotment of three deciatines, ten rubles, an allotment of four deciatines, eleven rubles, and so on. It is clear that this method of assessment was based on a principle the very opposite of that of the modern income tax. The redemption

A. A. Kaufman, *Agrarni Vopros v Rossii* (*The Agrarian Problem in Russia*) Moscow, 1919), p. 42.

payments per deciatine decreased with the increase in the size of the allotment. The scale of payments moved in an inverse ratio to the ability to pay. The explanation of this paradoxical situation seems to be that the payment on the first deciatine included a premium on the freedom of the former serf.[10]

It was also submitted that the payments which the peasants were called to make were unduly high. M. Lositsky has calculated that they had to pay 876,000,000 rubles for the land ceded to them, while its market value in 1854–1858 was only 544,000,-000 rubles, and even at prices in 1863–1872 did not exceed 648,000,000 rubles. The difference between the market value of land and the price paid by the peasants, according to Lositsky was particularly striking in the provinces outside the black-soil belt where he put it at 90 per cent.[11] That these calculations contain an element of truth was admitted even by the defenders of the reform.

We consider as unjustified the charges brought against the framers of the Emancipation Acts [writes Professor Migulin], charges which accuse them of putting too high a valuation on the land transferred to the peasants in order to compensate the landlords for their loss of free labor as a result of the abolition of serfdom. The landlords undoubtedly suffered large financial losses, and a certain compensation from the State was a matter of mere justice.[12]

The history of the redemption payments indicates that they imposed upon the peasants a burden which they could not carry. The amount of arrears grew rapidly.[13] In November, 1905 redemption payments were reduced by one-half, and on January 1, 1907, they were finally canceled. There seems to be little doubt that they materially contributed to peasant impoverishment.

The Land Commune

Another weakness in the Reform of 1861 was the adoption of communal land tenure as the fundamental form of peasant ownership. Previous to the Emancipation communal tenure prevailed throughout European Russia except in the southern and western provinces. The Reform of 1861 not only sanctioned

---

[10] *Ibid.*, pp. 27–30.
[11] A. Lositsky, *Vikupnaya Operatsya (Redemption Payments)* (St. Petersburg, 1906) pp. 16–17.
[12] Migulin, *Gosudarstvenni Kredit (Public Finance)*, I, 249, quoted in Lositsky, *op. cit.*, p. 18.
[13] Kaufman, *op. cit.*, pp. 62–63.

communal tenure wherever it existed, but even introduced it in provinces where it was practically unknown before. In 1877, out of the total number of 25,000,000 peasants, 20,000,000 were members of communes. The reason for the adoption of communal ownership was primarily fiscal. The members of the commune were bound by joint responsibility for the payment of taxes and redemption payments which, as we have seen, were not easy to collect. The Government naturally found it simpler to deal with whole villages forming parts of a commune or *mir* than with individual peasants. This purely fiscal approach to the problem of communal tenure is evident from the fact that, by paying before the expiration of the term the whole amount of redemption charges assessed on his allotment, any member of the commune could obtain an individual title to it. Eventually, however, communal tenure became an object of passionate political discussion. It was extolled by conservatives of the Slavophil brand as an eminently national institution, which invoked to prevent the spreading in Russia of proletarianism and socialist ideas. On the other hand, the "populist" wing of the Russian Socialists saw in the communal arrangements a distinct step toward the accomplishment of their final aim, and hoped that it would allow Russia to make an immediate transition to socialism without passing through the capitalistic stage.[14]

The opponents of communal tenure pointed to its many drawbacks. Under this system the ownership of all land, not including the farmhouse and the garden plot in the village, was vested in the village commune, and occasionally even in several villages in common. A distribution of land among the members of the commune was carried out at more or less regular intervals, and was based either on the working power of a peasant household, as determined by the number of adult men in the family, or on consumption standards, that is, the aggregate membership of the household. The purpose of the redistributions was primarily to give equal shares. All the land of the commune, therefore, was divided into a number of fields in accordance with the nature of the soil; and each member received a plot, sometimes only a few yards wide, in each of these fields. The inevitable result was the intermixture of strips, with all the accompanying evils: the compulsory rotation of crops for all the members of the commune; the extreme difficulty in introducing improvements and more intensive methods of cultivation; the waste of time involved in cultivating a number of narrow strips frequently

Bilimovich, *op. cit.*, p. 312.

scattered over a wide area; the inadequate use of manure on land the tenure of which was uncertain, and the consequent exhaustion of the soil; the waste of much land on boundary furrows; and violent conflicts, sometimes accompanied by loss of life, which usually marked redistributions.[15]

It would seem, however, that by the end of the nineteenth century the practice of redistribution was much in abeyance. M. Kachorovsky, who collected data relating to 87,000 communes with some 25,000,000 inhabitants, reached the conclusion that about one-half of the former landlords' serfs who held their land in communal tenure had given up the practice of periodic redistribution.[16] According to the data of the Ministry of the Interior in 1904, about 50 per cent of the total number of communes had had no general or even partial redistribution of land in the last twenty-five years. And it was estimated that in the case of about 3,500,000 peasant farms which were held in communal tenure, or about one-third of the total number, there had been no redistribution of land since the Emancipation. "The dying commune," remarks Professor Bilimovich,[17] "still held its members in bondage and the adverse influence on farming progress of the living communes, in which redistributions of land still continued, was even stronger."

Legal Disabilities

Even more striking were the legal disabilities to which the peasants were subject. According to the Emancipation Acts the right to a share of the allotment land was vested not in the individual peasant, but in the peasant household (*dvor*), which consisted of one or more families. The term *dvor* was never strictly defined by law and was loosely used in the various legislative enactments, meaning sometimes the farm buildings, sometimes the peasant farm as an economic entity, sometimes the peasant household as an association of physical persons. In the latter sense the *dvor*, or peasant household, became the unit for the assessment of taxes, local government, and communal organization.[18]

The legal ideas embodied in the term *dvor* were just as loose and ill defined as the use of the term by the legislator. Certain characteristics, however, were common to the majority of households

[15] Bilimovich, *op. cit.*, pp. 311, 316.
[16] K. Kachorovsky, *Russkaya Obshchina (The Russian Commune)* (1900), quoted in Bilimovich, *op. cit.*, p. 313.
[17] Bilimovich, *op. cit.*, p. 313.
[18] Baron Alexander F. Meyendorff, *Krestyanski Dvor (The Peasant Household)* (St. Petersburg, 1909), p. 58.

holds. The *dvor* was uniformly headed by a house elder, who usually, but not necessarily, was one of the oldest male members of the family. Sometimes the house elder was one of the younger members recognized as more worthy of the position, or even a woman. The house elder was the head of the household, he was liable for its obligations, for taxes and redemption payments, and had wide powers, limited only by local customs, in the disposal of the property of the joint family, such as its share of allotment land, the harvest, the live stock, horses, farm buildings, and all money derived from the sale of the produce of the family farm or from the earnings of its male members. The members of the family owed him obedience; he decided the kind of work they were to perform on the farm, or hired them out. It is worth noting that while women were permitted to retain the proceeds of some of their earnings, trifling as these might be, this right was, in many localities, completely denied to men.

There are no goods and chattels, save his clothing, that a male member of the household can call his own. All the proceeds of his work on the family farm and all his earnings outside are the property of the household as a whole . . . and are put unconditionally at the disposal of the house elder, who may or may not turn over some part of them to the man who contributed them, to his wife or children.[19]

It would seem, however, that in practice the rigidity of these general rules was moderated by local custom.

The peasant household was a permanent feature of the organization of the peasants, not only in localities where communal tenure was prevalent, but also where land was held by individual peasant families.[20] In spite of the extreme importance of the question, practically nothing was done between the Emancipation and the reforms of Stolypin in 1906 to define the position of the members of the joint family in their relations to the house elder and to family property. The household was primarily a fiscal unit used for the purpose of assessments and taxation, and its members were bound by joint responsibility. The significance of this function may be seen from the fact that for failure to produce his share toward the payment of taxes the house elder could be dismissed, and another member of the family appointed to his place by a decision of the village as-

[19] *Sbornik Materyalov* (*Collection of Materials*) for the study of the land commune, edited by T. L. Barikov, A. V. Polovtsev, and P. A. Sokolovsky, published by the Imperial Free Economic Society and the Russian Geographical Society (St. Petersburg, 1880), I, 377, quoted in Meyendorff, *Krestyanski Dvor*, pp. 6–8. *See also* Kovalewsky, *op. cit.*, pp. 97–108.

[20] Meyendorff, *Krestyanski Dvor*, pp. 55–56.

sembly.[21] The Supreme Court of Russia (the Senate) singularly failed in its attempt to give the peasant household a standing as a *juridical person,* and to draw a line between the proprietary right of the house elder as an individual and as the head of the household. Baron Meyendorff rightly pointed out that the decisions of the Supreme Court dealing with this problem were contradictory and often meaningless.[22] As an example of the legal anarchy which prevailed in this field, Baron Meyendorff quoted the following instance: "The terminology of the law is so confused," he writes,[23] "that the fundamental question, who is the owner of a farmhouse freed from all fiscal obligations is practically insoluble." The law of succession was in a similarly chaotic condition. "The whole situation is so obscure," writes Baron Meyendorff,[24] "that it defies legal analysis."

What this legal anarchy meant can hardly be exaggerated. It meant that a peasant was by no means always entitled to the product of his labor. One must remember that the relations between the members of the household were not infrequently very strained, or even openly hostile. It could hardly have been otherwise under the conditions we have briefly described. Nevertheless the situation remained unaltered until the Ukase of November 9, 1906, which cut the Gordian knot of legal entanglements by declaring that the house elder in households which had left the commune was the sole owner of the family allotment land. No compensation was provided for the dispossessed junior members. Until this enactment, therefore, which became operative only a few years before the outbreak of the War, the bulk of the peasantry was living under a system of family communism governed by obscure and contradictory customs, and were largely at the mercy of the arbitrary rule of a house elder. The sacred right of private property, so passionately defended since the Bolshevik Revolution by Russian opponents of socialism, was, until 1906, very nearly an empty sound for the masses of the Russian people. We may recall in this connection the prophetic words of Count Witte in an address delivered in 1905. "Woe to the country," he said,[25] "whose people have not learnt to respect the principles of legality and the right of property; and where a system of collective ownership prevails that is regulated by obscure custom and arbitrary judgment. Such a country may become sooner or later the scene of unparalleled

[21] Meyendorff, *Krestyanski Dvor,* pp. 25–29.
[22] *Ibid.,* pp. 59–60.
[23] *Ibid.,* p. 52.
[24] *Ibid.,* p. 77.
[25] Quoted in Bilimovich, *op. cit.,* pp. 324–325.

calamities." And if in 1917 Russia submitted practically without resistance to the rule of the Soviets, and has been, ever since, the set stage for "the great socialist experiment," probably this has been due in no small degree to the traditional communist policy of the Imperial Government in matters of peasant ownership. Individual private ownership in Russia was, broadly speaking, a perquisite of the privileged classes, and it vanished with them.

Rural Overpopulation

It will be plain that the road which led the Russian peasant from slavery to freedom had been a thorny one. Even if we agree with Professor Kaufman that at the Emancipation a considerable portion of the former serfs received sufficient allotment land to meet their immediate needs, it nevertheless remains true that, with the passing of the years, the position of the peasants had been growing worse. One of the chief causes of their impoverishment was the rapid growth of a population which could not be absorbed either by agriculture or industry. The population in fifty provinces of European Russia in the 'sixties of the last century did not exceed 50,000,000. It rose to 86,000,000 in 1900, and to 103,000,000 by January 1, 1914.[26] Due to the slow process of urbanization only 10 or 15 per cent of the increase was absorbed by the towns.[27] The resulting growth of the rural population inevitably led to the reduction of the area per workman. No doubt there were also factors which to a certain extent mitigated the effect of this process. The yield of the peasant land increased from an average of 29 puds per deciatine in 1861–1870 to 43 puds in 1901–1910. This increase, however, was much less than the growth of the population.[28] There was also the migration of peasants from the more congested areas to Siberia and other parts of the Empire, where vast territories were still available for settlement.[29] Even more important was the expansion of the area of peasant land holdings by purchase and by the leasing of land from large estates and from the State. The question of peasant leases is one of the most controversial problems in Russian economic literature. The theory advanced by a number of Russian economists, that the

[26] Kaufman, op. cit., p. 44.
[27] N. Oganovsky, Ocherki po Ekonomicheskoi Geografii R.S.F.S.R. (Studies in the Economic Geography of the U.S.S.R.) (Moscow, 1923), p. 37, quoted in Rosenblum, op. cit., p. 21.
[28] Kaufman, op. cit., p. 48. These figures refer to the area actually under crops and do not include land lying fallow.
[29] See Bilimovich, op. cit., pp. 309–311, 322–324.

peasants were leasing land chiefly to obtain the amount of food-stuffs necessary for the bare maintenance of their families, and were willing to pay any price to escape actual starvation, or were making so-called "hunger leases," is a theory that has been largely destroyed by the recent investigations of Prokopovich.[30] In his opinion, which is supported by a scientific statistical analysis of a vast mass of data on peasant budgets, the leasing of peasants was governed not by conditions of starvation, but by the desire to obtain the most advantageous combination of the three essential factors in farming: labor, machinery and implements, and land. That is, it did not differ from the attitude of farmers all over the world.

Far more important was the expansion of peasant land holdings by the purchase of land, usually with the assistance of the State Peasant Bank. This bank was founded in 1882, but it was not until its reorganization in 1895 that its operations became a factor in the development of peasant holdings; and it was only after the reforms of 1906 that the transfer of land to the peasants assumed considerable dimensions, as will appear from the following figures. In 1883–1895 the Bank sold to the peasants 2,400,000 deciatines; in 1896–1905, 5,860,000 deciatines; and in 1906–1913, 8,460,000 deciatines.[31] There seems to be little doubt that the area of peasant holdings was steadily growing at the expense of other groups of landowners. In 1877 the peasants held 116,700,000 deciatines, or 31 per cent of the total area. On January 1, 1917, their holdings were estimated at 185,000,-000 deciatines, or 46.8 per cent of the total area. During the same period the area owned by the State and public bodies decreased from 166,300,000 deciatines, or 44.1 per cent, to 147,-200,000 deciatines, or 37.2 per cent, and that of private owners other than peasants from 94,000,000 deciatines, or 24.9 per cent, to 63,000,000 deciatines, or 15.9 per cent.[32] The process of concentration of land in the hands of the peasants was greatly accelerated after the reforms of 1906.

In spite of these mitigating factors—the increase in the average yield of crops, migration from the most congested districts, leases, and the expansion of the area of peasant land holdings—the shortage of land, or rural overpopulation, became by the end of the last and the beginning of the present centuries one of the most burning problems of Rus-

[30] Prokopovich, *Krestyanskoe Khozyaistvo*, pp. 45–73; *see also* Antsiferov and others, "Rural Economy," pp. 35–37.

[31] Bilimovich, *op. cit.*, pp. 307–309, 319–322.

[32] *Ibid.*, p. 306; Antsiferov and others, "Rural Economy," pp. 22–23.

sian economic and social policy. The term "rural overpopulation" and "shortage of land" have a peculiar Russian meaning. One could hardly speak of overpopulation in a country less densely populated than any other country in Europe, where no such complaints are heard. What is meant by Russian rural overpopulation is the inability of a large portion of the farmers, under existing conditions, to make a living from their farms and to use on them the labor of their families. The crop yield in Russia, in spite of the improvement we have noticed, was still far below that for farming in western Europe or the United States. The average net return per deciatine of peasant land in Russia, after a deduction for seeds, was only 23 puds, while it was 63 puds in France and Germany, 93 puds in Denmark, 112 in England, and 116 in Belgium.[33] The explanation of this difference lies, of course, not in the climate or the poor soil of Russia, but in the backwardness of agricultural methods. This backwardness, again, must be traced to the poverty and ignorance of the Russian people, the evils of communal tenure, the oppressive system of family ownership, the relatively slow growth of industry, which offered no sufficient outlet for excess population, the legal disabilities of the peasants, and inefficient and corrupt local administration. In other words the elimination of "rural overpopulation" and "shortage of land" was merely an aspect of the immense problem of rebuilding from its foundation the whole economic and social structure of the Russian State. We have seen[34] that, under the pressure of agrarian unrest in 1905–1906, the Government in the person of Stolypin embarked on a program of far-reaching agrarian reforms, which were put into effect, too ruthlessly perhaps, in the few years preceding the War.

Peasant Budgets

That reform was much overdue was made clear by the general depression in peasant farming and the deterioration of peasant standards of living which were already incredibly low. The problem of peasant budgets, like that of their leases, is one of the most controversial questions in Russian economic literature. The recently published volume of Prokopovich, to which we have already had several opportunities to refer, throws a great deal of new light on the subject. It is based on a number of budget investigations made in various parts of Russia and cover-

[33] Kaufman, *op. cit.*, p. 135. These figures refer to the whole arable area, including land lying fallow.
[34] *See above*, pp. 23–24.

ing the period between 1887 and 1915. F. A. Shcherbina, one of the pioneers in the field of statistical investigations of peasant budgets, advanced the theory that peasant expenditure was fairly uniform throughout the country, and that this indicated a uniform standard of living. He estimated that the average yearly expenditure of a peasant was 54.92 rubles (about $27).[35] Approximately the same figure was given by another student of the question, A. V. Chayanov, who put the annual average expenditure of a peasant at 50 rubles.[36] Prokopovich, however, denies the existence of any definite and uniform level of peasant expenditure, as asserted by Shcherbina and A. N. Chelintsev, and shows that it varies with the changes in the revenue of the farming establishment.[37]

Some idea of the distribution of expenditure may be given from the following illustration. The yearly expenditure of an "average" family[38] in the district of Vyatka, province of Vyatka, in 1900, was 202.4 rubles. It was distributed as follows: living quarters (repairs and construction), 11.4 per cent; clothing, 12.0 per cent; food, 65.8 per cent; tobacco, 4.8 per cent; medical help, .15 per cent; education and books, .07 per cent; church and clergy, 1.6 per cent; weddings and baptisms, 3.6 per cent; other expenditures, .6 per cent. For other localities where budget investigations were completed the figures were, of course, somewhat different. The expenditure of the "average" family varied from 200 to almost 500 rubles. But the distribution of expenditure among the various items was remarkably uniform. In every case the bulk of expenditure was represented by food (from 58 to 71 per cent), the larger portion of the residue being absorbed by clothing and lodgings. All other expenditure was insignificant, that on books and education, for instance, in the Vyatka district, amounting to about fourteen copecks (seven cents) a year.[39]

These figures speak for themselves. In the opinion of Prokopovich, the minimum annual income of a Russian peasant an income that would allow him to maintain his customary standard of living, was 40 rubles. In the black-soil belt this

[35] *Vlyanie Urozhaev na Khlebnya Tseni i Nekotorya Storoni Russkago Narodnago Khozyaistva (Influence of Harvests upon Grain Prices and Certain Aspects of Russia's National Economy)* (1897), II, 6-7, quoted in Prokopovich, *Krestyanskoe Khozyaistvo*, p. 81.

[36] A. V. Chayanov, *Voprosi Organizatsii Selskago Khozyaistva (Problems of Farming Organization)* (1912), p. 4, quoted in Prokopovich, *Krestyanskoe Khozyaistvo*, p. 85.

[37] Prokopovich, *Krestyanskoe Khozyaistvo*, p. 90.

[38] *Ibid.*, pp. 76-80.

[39] *Ibid.*, p. 104.

come could be obtained in a farming establishment with an
rea of not less than six deciatines, and outside the black-soil
rovinces, from a farm of no less than twenty deciatines. Fam-
es farming a smaller area had to depend on the outside earn-
gs of their members.[40] It is not surprising, therefore, that
utside earnings played an important part in peasant budgets.
n the black-soil belt they provided about 25 per cent of the
amily income, and in the less fertile provinces even as much as
0 or 50 per cent. The relative importance of this source of
evenue increased in inverse ratio to the area of land farmed
y the family.[41]

Such were some of the fundamental aspects of Russian peas-
nt farming at the beginning of the century. Let us now turn
om the figures and try to visualize for a moment what they
ctually meant to 85 per cent of the population of the Empire.

n Illustration

The following description is taken from the report of the Tula
ommittee on the Needs of Agriculture. It shows the conditions
nder which an average peasant family lived in the black-soil
rovinces.

The dwelling of a Tula peasant [says the report] is usually a cottage
18 by 21 feet, and about seven feet high. . . . Cottages having no
himneys are still very common, the smoke being let out through a
ole in the roof. In the Epifansky district they amount to 16.4 per
nt of all dwellings. Almost all cottages have thatched roofs which
ten leak, and in the winter the walls are generally covered with
ung to keep the place warm. A peasant family, sometimes a large
ne, lives in a space of some 2,400–3,000 cubic feet. They sleep in two
ers—on benches and in bunks, back of the stove. Earth floors are
e rule because in cold weather lambs, calves, pigs and even cows
e brought into the cottage. The terrible overcrowding makes the air
eavy and unhealthy. Dampness inside, the leaking roof, and the
ung outside soon destroy the buildings. A great many of them are in
state of decay, and need serious repairs or complete overhauling;
ut they are made to last by putting a support here, patching up a
ole there, and so on. In localities which have no forests the peasants
se straw for fuel, and in years of poor harvests even dung, thus de-
riving their fields of much needed manure. . . . Bath houses are prac-
ally non-existent. The peasants wash in their cottages . . . spreading
e dirt on their bodies with a little hot water. They almost never use
ap. . . . Skin diseases progress at a terrible rate. In the Epifansky

Ibid., p. 230; Professor Antsiferov, however, believes that a peasant family can
ke a living on a much smaller area. *See* Antsiferov and others, "Rural Economy,"
23.

Prokopovich, *Krestyanskoe Khozyaistvo,* p. 145; Kaufman, *op. cit.,* pp. 63–68.

district, for instance, 2.15 per cent of the population, or 21 in eve[r]
thousand, are registered as suffering from syphilis. . . . But it wou[ld]
seem that the actual number affected by this disease is still larger. . [.]
Generally speaking, in spite of the healthy out-of-door environme[nt]
the anti-sanitary conditions in the villages are such that the preventi[on]
of epidemics is almost impossible. An important factor is the wea[k]
ened physical condition of the peasants due to undernourishme[nt]
. . . Such foodstuffs as meat, meal, bacon, and vegetable oils appe[ar]
on the family table only on rare occasions, perhaps two or three tim[es]
a year. The normal fare consists of bread, kvass,[42] and often cabba[ge]
and onions, to which fresh vegetables may be added in the autum[n.]
And even then the peasants do not always eat as much as they wou[ld]
like to, not even in years of good harvests. . . . In a word, the pover[ty]
of the peasant establishment is astounding.[43]

Professor Kaufman remarks that this description is corre[ct]
not only for the province of Tula, but also for a large portio[n,]
if not for the majority, of the peasant farmers in the black-s[oil]
belt. And the inevitable result, for the peasant, had been phys[i]
cal degeneration.[44]

The Land and the Peasants

We have already seen that the "shortage of land" was real[ly]
an integral part of the much broader problem of Russia's po[v]
erty and backwardness, inefficiency, and mismanagement. Th[e]
peasant holding had considerably increased after the Emancip[a]
tion, and this process had been particularly rapid since th[e]
passing of the new land laws in 1906. The expansion of the are[a]
of peasant farming, however, brought little or no relief so lo[ng]
as it was not accompanied by the adoption of intensive metho[ds]
of husbandry. This is why the point was so often made that th[e]
land reform of Stolypin, with all its imperfections, was a[n]
immensely important step in the right direction. It was primari[ly]
designed to get rid of the bondage of the commune, the inte[r]
mixture of strips, and the confusion of family ownership. It n[o]
doubt encouraged the poorer section of the peasantry, tho[se]
incapable of earning a living on their plots, to dispose of the[ir]
land, to join the ranks of the urban proletariat, or to form [a]
class of agricultural laborers which till then had been practical[ly]
nonexistent in Russia. The process was certainly painful, b[ut]
it seemed unavoidable if the vicious circle was to be broke[n.]
These considerations, though almost self-evident, were e[n]

---

[42] A Russian drink.
[43] Quoted in Kaufman, *op. cit.*, pp. 55–56.
[44] Kaufman, *op. cit.*, pp. 56–62.

tirely beyond the grasp of the peasants themselves, and beyond that of a section of the intelligentsia, who persisted in seeing the crux of the land problem in the inadequacy of the area of the peasant holding and in the existence of large estates. The attitude of the peasants was unmistakable. They firmly believed that the reason for their poverty and sufferings was to be found in the inadequacy of their allotments, and that this could be easily remedied by a division among them of the estates held by the nobility. The countryside was being constantly swept by rumors that such a new redistribution was approaching.

The peasant is unable to understand [wrote the representatives of the Moscow zemstvo to the Committee on the Needs of Agriculture] why so little land was given to him at the Emancipation. In many cases he believes that his allotment is small not because of the provisions of the Emancipation Act, but because he received less than what he was entitled to. The peasant communes, therefore, often begin proceedings for the recovery of the land which they believe belongs to them. They attempt to alter the boundary lines of their holdings, and not infrequently engage surveyors at their own expense. The latter, however, seldom have an opportunity to complete their tasks because, if the surveys do not meet the expectations of the commune which has engaged them, their personal safety is much endangered.[45]

"We need more land"—this is the fundamental theme of the majority of statements made by the peasants to the Committees on the Needs of Agriculture appointed in 1901–1902 [writes Peshekhonov]. In the discussions of the committees the peasant members displayed remarkable unanimity in their approach to the problem of land shortage, and devoted to it most of their attention. Even stronger does this motive appear in the petitions and resolutions addressed to the committees by some of the village associations, and in the oral declarations of their representatives.[46]

There was no lack of warning as to what was the real attitude of the peasants.

Complaints of the shortage of land [writes Professor Kaufman], demands for more land, a deep conviction that they are entitled to the land held by the nobility—all this found clear and unanimous expression in thousands of petitions sent by the peasants to Government departments, in the instructions given to the peasant deputies, in the speeches of the latter in the First and Second Dumas. The same complaints and the same demands were heard at the Old Believers' congress which met in Moscow in 1906. Here, too, rose the clamor

Kaufman, op. cit., p. 86.
A. V. Peshekhonov, Zemelnya Nuzhdi Derevni (The Land Needs of the Village) cited in Kaufman, op. cit., p. 87.

187

for more land. And it was particularly significant in this case, because it could not be treated as the result of party propaganda. On the contrary, the attitude of the Congress was that of strict loyalty to the sovereign. Its members vested all their hopes in the Tsar, they were openly hostile to what they called "democracy," and they opposed the forcible solution of the agrarian problem. But in spite of all this they unanimously claimed more land, more land, more land.[47]

Whatever illusions on the subject might have existed in official circles were destroyed by the peasant demands in the First and Second Dumas. The electoral law then in force, a law eventually changed by Act of June 3, 1907,[48] was framed in a manner which would assure a large representation of the peasant population. This was done on the theory advanced by M. Lobko, then Controller General, and by Pobedonostsev, that the peasants were the only real supporters of autocracy. This view prevailed, and the electoral law was framed accordingly. The result, however, proved something of a shock to those who believed too deeply in the peasants' devotion to the throne. In the First and the Second Dumas the peasant deputies, irrespective of their party allegiance, supported the most radical proposals for the settlement of the land question, proposals openly aimed at the abolition of large property in land. Their demands found their counterpart in the wave of terrible agrarian disturbances which swept the country, caused immense losses to Russian agriculture, finally forced the Government to dissolve the First and Second Duma, and to alter the electoral law by enacting, in flagrant violation of the Fundamental Laws, the new electoral law of June 3, 1907.[49] At the same time the Government embarked, as we know, on a far-reaching program of agrarian reforms. These measures, as also the ruthless punitive expeditions organized by the Government of Stolypin succeeded for a time in subduing the revolutionary movement. But they naturally could not eliminate the desire of the peasant to possess themselves of the lands belonging to their more fortunate neighbors.

Baron Nolde commenting on the Reform of 1861, says that

in spite of the definite proclamation by law of the final character of the distribution of land between the peasants and the landlords, belief in new redistributions between peasants and landlords had

[47] Kaufman, *op. cit.*, p. 87.
[48] *See above*, pp. 95 sqq.
[49] Kovalewsky, *op. cit.*, pp. 32–32; also Count Witte, *Vospominanya*, I, 296–29
439–483; II, 312–314.

188

deeply imprinted itself in the imaginations of the masses. They could never forget that in 1861 the Government carried out, for their benefit, an expropriation of land on a large scale without regard to the existing proprietary rights. They could never understand why this measure should not be repeated when it became necessary to increase peasant allotments. The Government missed no opportunity to emphasize the final character of the distribution of 1861; but the masses refused to give up their old belief.[50]

It may be argued that Baron Nolde credits the Russian peasant with a keener power of logical reasoning than one is justified in attributing to a population mostly illiterate and living under the conditions we have described. But we feel fully in agreement with him when, summing up the provisions of the Emancipation Acts, he writes:

The situation thus created in the Russian rural districts, one that hedged in the peasants with insurmountable legal barriers, contributed powerfully to their psychological isolation. The vague but nevertheless tremendous sense of the necessity of a new re-distribution of land, a kind of latent socialism without a doctrine, constituted the foundation of this psychology.[51]

This "latent socialism without a doctrine" had always been in the background of Russia's history since the days of the Emancipation. It showed its real strength in 1905–1906, and then again in 1917, when the crumbling structure of the Empire could offer no more resistance to those long-suppressed desires of the masses.

The Peasant and the War

In contrast with the effects of the War upon labor, the economic condition of peasant farming suffered no immediate deterioration. The area sown by the peasants, excluding the provinces occupied by the enemy, increased during the three years of the War by some 13,000,000 deciatines,[52] and the requisition of horses and live stock worked far less harm than might have been expected.[53] It is also believed that as a result of new sources of revenue such as the savings due to prohibition, receipts derived from allowances to the families of mobilized men, and payments for the requisitioned live stock and

[50] Nolde, *L'ancien régime et la révolutions russes*, p. 77; also Witte, *Vospominanya*, 439.
[51] Nolde, *L'ancien régime et la révolution russes*, p. 79.
[52] See above, p. 35.
[53] See above, pp. 49–50.

the like, the average real income of a peasant family was increased by some 18 per cent.[54] On the other hand, the peasants suffered from the general shortage of manufactured goods, although less than the urban population. This, of course, was perfectly natural because, according to the investigations of peasant budgets, only about 40 per cent of peasant expenditure was in terms of money, the largest part consisting in the consumption of the produce of the farm.[55] With the decrease in the supply of manufactured goods the peasants were simply returning more and more to the conditions of a self-contained economy.

It would be obviously a mistake, however, to reckon the effects of the War in terms of merely economic losses or gains. Even if a slight improvement took place in the standard of living of the peasants—and one can never be too cautious in dealing with Russian war statistics—there still remain the stresses and readjustments resulting from the mobilization of millions of men. Russian war losses were exceedingly high, and the peasants had to bear the largest part of them, not to speak of the terrible hardships of those who were living in the area adjoining the front, and were compelled either to submit to enemy occupation with all its hazards or to join the ranks of the refugees.[56]

It is difficult to give an answer to the question as to how the peasants reacted to the declaration of war. The response to the mobilization order exceeded all hopes, cases of default being extremely rare.[57] This may indicate that the peasants accepted service in the army with that spirit of resignation and passive submission which seems to form so important a part of the Russian character. Probably the patriotic fever experienced at that time by all the belligerent countries also had something to do with it, although it is extremely doubtful if it played any important part in the attitude of Russian peasants, mostly illiterate, to whom France, England, Serbia, and Germany were equally empty sounds. Whatever might have been the reasons of the willingness of the peasants to join the army at the outbreak of the War, the feeling did not survive the disappointments and hardships of even the first few months of the struggle.

[54] See above, p. 50; also Demosthenov, op. cit., pp. 342–345.
[55] Prokopovich, Krestyanskoe Khozyaistvo, pp. 93–104.
[56] See below, pp. 197 sqq.
[57] Rodzianko, Gosudarstvennaya Duma i Fevralskaya 1917 Goda Revolutsya in Arkhiv Russkoi Revolutsii, VI, 17. Rodzianko maintains that 96 per cent of the men called out reported for duty. He does not disclose however the source of his information.

As early as the summer of 1915 Prince Shcherbatov, then Minister of the Interior, drew the attention of the Council of Ministers to the fact that "the calling out of new classes is becoming more and more difficult. The police are unable to deal with the large number of men who are trying to avoid military service. Men are hiding in the woods and in the fields." And he expressed the apprehension that if an attempt was made to call the second ban of the territorial army without the sanction of the Duma, the Government "would not get a single man."[58]

The general feeling of discontent and war weariness which were steadily gaining ground among all social groups found its way into the remotest corners of the country. Although the expenditure of the peasants on manufactured goods was exceedingly small, it extended to certain items such as tools, agricultural implements, sugar, etc., the scarcity and high price of which caused great irritation and inconvenience. For instance, the shortage of metal for farm use in the shape of horseshoes, nails, etc., presented real problems the solution of which within the peasant establishment could not always easily be found. The report of the State Police Department for October, 1916, gives the following picture of conditions.

The high cost of living is felt in the villages as keenly as in the towns; and here it is accompanied by rumors even more extravagant than those which circulate in the cities. The peasants give full credence to the stories that hides, grain, sugar, etc., are being exported to Germany, that Count Fredericks [Minister of the Imperial Household] has sold half of Russia to the Germans, and so on. All this creates, in the villages, a very disquieting atmosphere. . . . The attitude of rural Russia towards the War was negative from the very beginning because, more than the cities and towns, it felt the departure of mobilized men. Now it has lost all faith in the successful issue of the War. According to insurance agents, teachers, tradesmen and other representatives of the village intelligentsia, everybody is impatiently waiting for the end of this "damned war." The peasants are now eager to discuss political matters in which they had apparently lost all interest since 1906; and they declare that "Sukhomlinov [Minister of War] should be hanged," that "when ten or fifteen generals are on the gallows we shall begin to win." There is a marked increase in hostile feelings among the peasants not only against the Government, but also against all other social groups such as industrial workers, government officials, the clergy, etc.[59]

[8] Yakhontov, *op. cit.*, p. 38.
[9] *Politicheskoe Polozhenie v Rossii Nakanune Fevralskoi Revolutsii v Zhandarmskom Osvyashchenii* in *Krasni Arkhiv*, XVII, 19–20.

Less hard pressed by immediate economic needs than the urban proletariat and the middle class, the peasants remained faithful throughout the War to that attitude of fatalistic indifference which they had maintained, with the notable exception of the years 1905–1906, since the Emancipation. But the dynamic forces behind the "latent socialism without a doctrine" were slowly but steadily growing. And when the Revolution of March, 1917, suddenly freed the colossus of peasant Russia from the secular ties of legal entanglements and the administrative tutelage, and flashed before his eyes the long-coveted vision of "land and liberty," he rose to his feet, threw off his chains, stretched his tired limbs, and made an irresistible rush for the cherished object of his dreams—the land of his more prosperous neighbor.[60]

Chapter 9

The Nation in Arms

A Retrospective View of the Breakdown of the Army

No SURVEY of the social conditions of a country during a great modern war will be complete unless it contains an outline of the life and attitude of that all-important factor, the army. This is particularly true of a country like Russia, which called to the colors in the course of the struggle more than 15,000,000 men, or 37 per cent of her adult male population.[1] The mobilization of so vast a number of men not only dislocated to a great degree the economic life of the country, but also brought into being a most powerful and dangerous force, upon whose spirit and conduct largely depended the issue of the struggle and the future of the Empire. Added importance to an understanding of conditions in the army is lent by the part it played in bringing about the downfall of the monarchy and the establishment of a new social and political *régime*, which is likely to remain for years to come one of the most disturbing and puzzling factors in world politics.

In studying conditions in the Russian army the student is faced with certain peculiar difficulties. For obvious reasons the

[60] *See below,* pp. 232 *sqq.*
[1] *See above,* p. 34.

official and semiofficial statements regarding the army issued during the War were imbued with a spirit of optimism which had seldom much resemblance to the private opinions of their authors. But, even after the War was over, the spirit of national pride continued to be closely associated with the glorification of the country's military force. Notwithstanding the important steps toward international coöperation which were taken after the War, in spite of the League of Nations, the Pact of Paris, and the proposed "United States of Europe," the large majority of men and women in every country are still traditionally inclined to link their hopes for its security with its armed strength. The recognition of the inadequacy of one's army still gives one a disturbing feeling of insecurity and loss of prestige, with all the unpleasant consequences of an inferiority complex. The debates in the United States Senate on the Naval Treaty in the summer of 1930 and the attitude of important sections of public opinion in every European country seem to indicate that that moral disarmament, on which the limitation of physical armaments depends in the last resort, is still a question of the future.

The feeling for or even love of the army is naturally felt with particular strength by the professional soldiers who have devoted years of their life to its creation and organization, and for whom any moral inadequacy of their offspring would be something which they would find difficult to admit. In the large literature on the breakdown of the Russian army during the Great War strong emphasis is laid on the effects of the Revolution which is generally blamed for its annihilation. And it is undoubtedly true that the Revolution dealt the last blow and accelerated the process of disintegration. But it is also true that the ground for the revolt was more than ready, and that by the end of 1916, in spite of the immense improvement in the conditions of supply, munitions, and armaments, the army was terribly tired, and was thinking of practically nothing but peace at any price. This is exactly what many of the former Russian army leaders refuse to admit. But the fallacy of their contentions is demonstrated by a great number of contemporary documents, the sincerity and historical value of which cannot be impeached. They are supported by authoritative comments from competent observers, among whom the foremost place belongs to General Sir Alfred Knox. His book, based on a diary from which important excerpts are given, displays remarkable knowledge, power of observation, and soundness of judgment, and is probably the most illuminating publication on the Russian army in the War. The writings of the Russian generals, on the other hand, suffer from a bias inspired, no doubt, by the highest motives, the desire to rehabilitate the Imperial army in the eyes of the world. They, nevertheless, represent a decided falsification of history by their reversal of the actual order of events: the army did not break down because the Revolution took place, but the Revolution became possible and, perhaps, inevitable, because the army, like all other social groups and political institutions, had reached a degree of disintegration which made its further existence impossible. The refusal to recognize a well-established historical fact merely emphasizes that fundamental divorce between the outlook of the educated classes and actual conditions which constitutes one of the striking features of the Russian tragedy.

The Commander-in-Chief and Headquarters

In spite of all that has been said and written throughout the world of Russia's planning the War to achieve certain imperialistic aims, there seems to be little doubt today that the country was entirely unprepared for a war, and that the Russian steam roller, in which the western allies of Russia found so much comfort, was a creation of their own imagination. This unpreparedness which appeared from the very first days manifested itself not only in the appalling inadequacy of the supply of munitions and armaments, but also in the absence of a proper administration and the lack of well-trained officers especially of the higher rank. The very legislation which regulated the organization of the army in time of war was a hasty improvisation, enacted virtually on the eve of the mobilization.[2] It vested the Commander-in-Chief with practically unlimited powers and said next to nothing about the relations between the military and the civilian authorities which was one of the important causes undermining the position of the Government.

It must also be admitted that the choice of the man in whom these immense powers were vested, as well as of his immediate assistants, was extremely unfortunate. The Grand Duke Nicholas Nikolaevich was entirely unfitted to fulfil the high and responsible duties which confronted him as Commander-in-Chief. General Polivanov whom, it will be remembered, Sir Alfred Knox describes as "the ablest military organizer in Russia," explained that there had been no definite arrangement as to who was to lead the army in case of war. The appointment of the Grand Duke came more or less as a surprise to all, including

---

[2] See above, pp. 71 sqq.

himself. "He appeared to be a man entirely unequipped for the task," said General Polivanov,[3] "and, in accordance with his own statement, on the receipt of the Imperial order, he spent much of his time crying because he did not know how to approach his new duties." This unfitness of the Grand Duke could not be remedied by his experiences at Headquarters. Rodzianko describes his interview with the Commander-in-Chief in the spring of 1915, when he reported to him his impressions of the retreat from Galicia.

> This conversation [he writes] left an extremely painful impression. The Grand Duke did not possess sufficient enregy. . . . After my interview with the Grand Duke I had a long talk with his chief subordinates at Headquarters, Yanushkevich and Danilov. They both left an impression of mournful helplessness.[4]

It is nevertheless true that Nicholas Nikolaevich was very popular with the rank and file, and that his popularity was able to survive even the disastrous retreat of 1915. The mystery of his appeal to the soldiers must be sought in their extraordinary ignorance and credulity, in the Grand Duke's tall and handsome figure, and in his drastic methods with even his subordinates of the highest rank. The extravagant and probably exaggerated stories of the punishment suffered at his own hands by the generals who were unfortunate enough to incur the Commander-in-Chief's displeasure created around him a legend of primitive justice which endeared him to the common soldiers. For they themselves had only too often to endure similar treatment from their own superiors. In his unsparing brutality there was one element which in 1917 contributed to the triumph of Bolshevism. Baron Nolde is certainly generous in his estimate of the sources of the Grand Duke's popularity when he remarks that it may be ascribed to the "general enthusiasm of the early days of the War."[5]

The two immediate assistants of the Grand Duke, General Yanushkevich, chief of staff, and General George N. Danilov, quartermaster general, were also anything but happy choices.

> Yanushkevich has seen no service in the field [writes Sir Alfred Knox]. . . . His promotion to the chief of the general staff [which automatically gave him the position of the chief of staff of the army in time of war] . . . in the spring of 1914 excited general surprise. He

[3] Evidence of Polivanov in *Padenie Tsarskago Rezhima*, VII, 69.
[4] Rodzianko, *The Reign of Rasputin: an Empire's Collapse*, p. 130.
[5] Nolde, *L'ancien régime et la révolution russes*, p. 106.

gave the impression rather of a courtier than of a soldier. . . . Danilov, nicknamed "the Black" . . . was a stern silent man, a great disciplinarian and exacting chief. Throughout the war I was to hear many complaints from Russian officers of his "hide-bound" strategy, but no one ever suggested the name of an officer who could have done better.[6]

It does not seem, however, that the members of the Russian Government shared the opinion of the British general as to Danilov's extreme usefulness. They employed whatever influence they possessed to induce the Grand Duke to part with Yanushkevich and Danilov, whose experiments in strategy and social measures cost the country incalculable sufferings, and probably contributed in no small degree to the decision of the Emperor to take upon himself the command of the army, a decision fatal to the monarchy.[7] The correspondence of the Emperor with the Empress preserves an interesting instance of these efforts and of the way in which they were received by the Grand Duke.

I am quite aware [the Emperor wrote on June 16, 1915] that he [Danilov] is not liked, that he is even hated in the army, beginning with Ivanov [general commanding the southwestern front] and ending with the last officer. He has a terrible character, and is very harsh with his subordinates. N[icholas Nikolaevich] knows this and from time to time puts him in his place; but he considers it impossible to dismiss him after eleven months of hard work—so well does the man know his duties. Even Krivoshein [Minister of Agriculture] spoke to me on this subject—he thinks, for instance, that N. ought to make alterations among his staff, and choose other men in place of Yanushkevich and Danilov. I advised him to tell N. of it, which he did —from his own point of view, naturally. He told me later that N. obviously did not like his frankness.[8]

The loyalty of the Grand Duke to his immediate subordinates would commend itself more to the outside observer if he had displayed a little less ruthlessness in his dealings with commanding officers who did not belong to his immediate *entourage*. The necessity of getting rid of Yanushkevich and Danilov was urged upon him from all sides. It appeared that the Emperor was not opposed to the change. Rodzianko wrote to the Grand Duke begging him to appoint Alexeev in place of Yanushkevich.[9] All was in vain. Ties of personal friendship proved more

[6] Knox, *op. cit.*, p. 42.
[7] *Ibid.*, p. 332.
[8] *The Letters of the Tsar to the Tsaritsa*, p. 61.
[9] Rodzianko, *The Reign of Rasputin: an Empire's Collapse*, p. 148.

binding than considerations of public interest. Men whose unpopularity in both the army and the country was immense continued in office. The Grand Duke certainly displayed little of that genius for the selection of the right men for the right place which is one of the most important qualifications of a real leader.

The very interesting correspondence between Yanushkevich and Sukhomlinov, the Minister of War, to which we have already had opportunity to refer, throws a great deal of light on conditions in the army during the first year of the War, as well as on the mental attitude of its actual leader, the chief of staff. It shows convincingly that the charges directed against Headquarters by the Council of Ministers that they had entirely lost their heads and were in a state approaching panic, were not devoid of foundation. Yanushkevich was obviously not a man to withstand the strain of a modern war and to face the responsibility of his office. His letters are pathetic in their helplessness.

I imagine [he wrote to Sukhomlinov on December 7, 1914] that a day and hour will come when you and many others will tell me: "What were you doing there? Why did you not warn us of the horror of the situation? What were you relying upon? What did you do to justify the great and undeserved honors which were showered upon you?" And I am writing this not because I am looking for a legal excuse. No, I am responsible and no one else. I am writing this merely as a moral justification, so that the condemned man will still have the right to look in the face of everyone and say: "I am certainly guilty, but I did not deceive, I hid nothing, my conscience is clear."[10]

And in a letter written in March, 1915, we find the following characteristic statement: "It seems to me that in the stillness of the night I hear a voice which says: 'You have betrayed your country, you missed everything, you slept through it.'"[11] Such was the frame of mind of the man whom the Grand Duke insisted on retaining at the head of the army, and who was to lead it to victory!

"The Retreat of 1812"

The detailed investigation of the causes of the technical unpreparedness of the Russian army and the determination of the share of responsibility that should be borne by Headquarters are obviously beyond the scope of the present work. A few

[10] Perepiska V. A. Sukhomlinova (Correspondence of V. A. Sukhomlinov) in Krasni Arkhiv, II, 144.
[11] Ibid., in Krasni Arkhiv, III, 44.

illustrations of the conditions of supply will show their effect upon the morale of the troops and the country. Nor is it our purpose here to give a picture of the military side of the campaign. It is impossible, however, not to mention the fact that the advance in Galicia, which was pushed in the spring of 1915 in spite of the shortage of munitions of war, was a very hazardous undertaking, and one taken against the protest of some of the army leaders. General Ruzsky, for instance, resigned his command of the western front because he believed that the proposed operation would lead to disaster.[12] His apprehensions, as we know, proved only too well founded. The retreat of the Russian army, which began in the later part of the spring and lasted throughout the summer, brought with it a new and unexpected calamity in the shape of millions of refugees. The immense tide of them that moved eastward to an unknown destination was not merely spontaneous. It was a part of the deliberate policy of Headquarters where it had been decided to reënact the "great retreat of 1812," the Russian retreat that brought Napoleon to Moscow and to his ruin. The country abandoned to the enemy was to be turned into a desert. The obvious and criminal absurdity of this plan was beyond the grasp of Yanushkevich, and of the strategists of his school. The remarkable minutes of the Council of Ministers published by Yakhontov have preserved a very vivid picture of the effects of a policy so barbaric. We shall quote *in extenso* his summary of the discussion which took place on July 30, 1915.

Utter confusion prevails at Headquarters. They do not realize what they are doing and into what an abyss they are dragging Russia. The example of 1812 is no excuse for turning into a desert the territory abandoned to the enemy. The general conditions, the very scale of events, have nothing in common with what happened then. In 1812 separate armies were manoeuvering and the theatre of their operation was relatively small. To-day the front line stretches from the Baltic almost to the Black Sea, and comprises hundreds of miles. The devastation of a score of provinces and the expulsion of their population into the interior is equivalent to the condemnation of Russia to terrible sufferings. But common sense and the requirements of national interest meet with little favor at Headquarters. The arguments of civilians are silenced before "military necessity" whatever may be the horror covered by this term. The military defeat of Russia by the enemy is now completed by her internal ruin. In the stream of refugees three [four?] separate currents may be distinguished. First, the Jews, all of whom, in spite of the repeated protests of the Council of

[12] Yakhontov, *op. cit.*, p. 65.

Ministers, are brutally ejected from the area adjoining the front and accused of espionage, signalling, and other methods of aiding and abetting the enemy. Naturally they are deeply wounded in their feelings and bring revolutionary ideas to the localities where they finally settle down. The situation is made worse by the fact that the residents of those localities, already sorely tried by war-time privations, give the homeless and hungry Jews anything but a friendly reception. Second, the employees of State institutions and of various establishments working for the army who take with them dozens of truckloads of goods. While thousands tramp along the railroad lines, they are passed by trains loaded with couches from military clubs and various junk including cages with the pets of the bird-loving officers of the Army Supply Department. Third, there are the voluntary refugees, fleeing mostly from those atrocities and violences which, it is rumored, the Germans perpetrate. And then, fourth, there are the refugees who have been forcibly expelled by the military authorities in order to depopulate the territory about to be abandoned. This is the largest and most desperate group. Men and women are torn from their homes and are forced into the unknown. In their presence fire is set to their stocks of grain and not unfrequently to their cottages. It is easy to understand the psychology of these compulsory refugees. . . The immense stream of uprooted, desperate, suffering humanity rolls along the roads interfering with military traffic and completely disorganizing the rear of the army. They are accompanied by carts loaded with their belongings and by their domestic animals. It is obviously impossible to provide food and shelter for this multitude. Men and women die by the hundred from hunger, exposure, and disease. The death rate among the children has reached a terrible height. Unburied corpses are left along the roads. The decaying carcases of dead animals poison the atmosphere. And this flood of humanity spreads over all Russia, adds to war-time hardships, creates a shortage of foodstuffs, increases the cost of living, and accentuates the discontent which is nowhere lacking. . . . But Headquarters, it seems, is still clinging to Kutuzov's method of dragging the enemy into the interior and to the hope of stopping the German advance by turning the country into a desert.[13]

Such was the picture of the effects of the revival of the methods of 1812, as they appeared to the Council of Ministers. Information from other sources shows that it was in no way exaggerated.

A strikingly pathetic feature of the retreat [writes Sir Alfred Knox] was the mass of fugitives that blocked all the roads as the Russian troops retired. The whole of the Polish peasantry seemed to migrate from the districts east of the Vistula. The Russians said that they did not compel them to move unless their villages were likely to be the

13 Ibid., pp. 32-33.

scene of fighting. The requisition, however, had been ordered from all who remained of all cattle, horses, bacon, tea, and sugar, and it was impossible for the people to remain behind when deprived of their means of livelihood. Unfortunately the civil staff was always the first to leave, and it was left to the Corps Intendance to carry out the requisitions. This, having no proper staff for the purpose, carried out its task in a slipshod manner.[14]

A. R. Lednitsky, one of the leaders of the Polish national movement, gives a striking illustration of the monstrous logic with which the policy of destruction was carried out by Headquarters. Describing the forcible evacuation of the Polish provinces, he says:

One of the most appalling measures was an order which was cancelled only as a result of strong public opposition in Warsaw. It was directed that the gas works, water supply, and electric power station in Warsaw should be destroyed. And this in a city with a population which approaches a million. . . . Such was the decision of the Commander-in-Chief, the Grand Duke Nicholas Nikolaevich. It was later cancelled.

Lednitsky however points out that similar orders were carried out in a number of places.[15]

One can well imagine the feeling of horror and indignation with which the members of the Council of Ministers received the news of the atrocities perpetrated by Headquarters, and against which they were helpless to take a decisive action. It was forcefully voiced at the meeting of the Council of August 4, 1915, by Krivoshein, Minister of Agriculture.

Of all the grave consequences of the War [he said] this is the most unexpected, the most threatening, the most irreparable. And what is still worse—it is not due to a necessity or a spontaneous popular movement, but has been invented by the learned military experts as a deterrent to the enemy. A nice method of fighting the War. Maledictions, diseases, sufferings and destitution are spreading throughout the country. . . . I imagine that the Germans survey not without satisfaction the results of the revival of the 1812 retreat. . . . The details of the scheme are beyond my competence. They have been probably weighed at Headquarters. . . . It is my duty however, as a member of the Council of Ministers, to declare that the second great migration organized by Headquarters leads Russia to the abyss, to revolution, to perdition.[16]

[14] Knox, *op. cit.*, p. 322.
[15] Evidence of Lednitsky in *Padenie Tsarskago Rezhima*, VII, 245.
[16] Yakhontov, *op. cit.*, p. 37.

It is difficult to disagree with the indignant outburst of Krivoshein, and it is to the credit of the Council of Ministers that not a single voice was raised there to defend the folly of the military leaders. The whole policy of compulsory evacuation, it may be observed, was heavily tinted with that chauvinistic hatred of all non-Russian subjects of the Crown, especially of the Jews, which unfortunately is only too apt to develop among professional soldiers. Bark, Minister of Finance, very properly remarked that the Jews were submitted by Yanushkevich "to violences and indignities which would not be tolerated in any civilized country."[17]

The Emperor at the Head of the Army

The change in the High Command which took place at the end of August, 1915, brought to an end the rule of Yanushkevich. But whatever advantages may have been gained by his removal, they were more than counterbalanced by the growth of irresponsible influences in Petrograd, and the general disintegration of the bureaucratic system which followed the departure of the Tsar for the army. The Emperor himself was fitted still less than the Grand Duke to fulfil the duties of the Commander-in-Chief. "I believed," General Polivanov testified,[18] "that the Tsar should not assume the leadership of the army because he was familiar with merely the external side of the business. The organization of the army and strategical considerations were foreign to him. He had done little work in this field and was poorly informed." His leadership remained purely nominal, and the real work of the Commander-in-Chief was carried on by the new chief of staff, General Alexeev. Alexeev was a man who rose from the ranks, an indefatigable worker, and a good officer of the general staff, but lacking in those qualities which commend themselves to popular imagination and which are so important in a military leader. In the opinion of Sir Alfred Knox he "had few champions . . . and the assumption of command by the Emperor was generally condemned. . . . Alexeev's faults were that he tried to do everything himself, and that he lacked the necessary self-reliance to enable him to take decisions quickly."[19]

The change in the High Command did not evoke in the army the immediate results anticipated by its opponents. Rodzianko

---

[1] *Ibid.*, p. 48. A detailed treatment of the problem of the refugees and their relief will be found in Astrov, *op. cit.*, Chapter IX, and in Polner, *op. cit.*, Chapter IX.
[3] Evidence of Polivanov in *Padenie Tsarskago Rezhima*, VII, 68.
[9] Knox, *op. cit.*, pp. 331–332.

believed that by that time confidence in the Grand Duke had begun to waver.[20] The common soldiers probably shared the views of the Tsar as to its being his duty to take command of the army, and could see nothing wrong in his decision. For its political consequences were far beyond their understanding. Even the officers were less alarmed than might have been expected.

Most of the officers of the army [writes Knox] regretted the Grand Duke's dismissal, for they regarded him as an honest man who stood apart from court intrigue. They would be content to pay that dismissal as the price of the much-desired removal of Yanushkevich and Danilov, many of them thinking, with Bezobrazov [the general commanding the Guards], that the "Grand Duke was completely in the hands of those men."[21]

Although the assumption of command by the Emperor was regarded with misgivings, it seems safe to maintain that the army quietly submitted to the decision of the Tsar. Its disastrous effects were far more evident in the field of civil government and upon the general political situation.

The Unpreparedness of the Army

We have already seen that the choice of men at the head of the army was extremely unfortunate, and that they possessed neither the ability nor the qualifications which make real leaders. The whole military machine shaped by these inexperienced hands was lacking in vigor and coördination. Its weakness may be traced to pre-war conditions.

General Polivanov, who was in an excellent position to observe the methods of the Russian War Office, stated that

before the War the general attitude of the higher commanding officers, the former Emperor, and the former Minister of War [Sukhomlinov] towards military technical improvements was one of contempt. The belief was then supreme that the most important thing in the army was its spirit, its aggressiveness, and that the rest would follow of itself. When some suggestion was made of the necessity of a system, the necessity of some kind of technique, this was used against you; the answer was that those were the ideas of an old professor, that in life the important thing was spirit, the rapid advance of the army, the good morale of the troops; they would accomplish everything.[22]

[20] Rodzianko, *The Reign of Rasputin: an Empire's Collapse*, p. 148.
[21] Knox, *op. cit.*, p. 332; also Yakhontov, *op. cit.*, pp. 25, 26.
[22] Evidence of Polivanov in *Padenie Tsarskago Rezhima*, VII, 194–195.

The application of this theory to practice in 1914 naturally brought the greatest disappointment.

The whole machine was inferior to the German machine [writes Sir Alfred Knox discussing the defeat of the Russian army in East Prussia in the early autumn of 1914]. There was no proper coördination between corps commanders. The men were worried by orders and counterorders. . . . The morale of all ranks was much affected by the number of the enemy's heavy guns, by his H.E. shell, his machine-guns on motor cars and in trees, and his hand-grenades. On the other hand, many of the Russians fought with determination till the end. On the evening of the 30th Hindenburg reported: "The enemy is fighting with immense obstinacy!" . . . The Russians were just great big-hearted children who had thought out nothing and have stumbled half-asleep into a wasp's nest.[23]

Unfortunately the rank and file of the army had to pay with its blood for this "big-hearted children" policy of its military leaders.

It will be remembered that during the first eight months of the War the Duma and the liberal circles unconditionally supported the Government. This attitude, which was undoubtedly inevitable under the circumstances, had for its consequences the prolongation for a number of precious months of the *régime* of General Sukhomlinov's personal rule at the Ministry of War; and Sukhomlinov was, more than anybody else, responsible for the unpreparedness of the army. His correspondence with General Yanushkevich, to which we have already made several references, throws a great deal of interesting light on the working of the military machine and the personality of the two leading actors during the first year of the War. Yanushkevich, it appears from his letters, realized at an early date that the impossible conditions of the evacuation of the wounded and the lack of munitions were imperiling the issue of the campaign by completely undermining the spirit of the troops. As early as August, 1914, he referred to the latter situation as a "nightmare,"[24] and as time went on his demands grew more and more pressing and his own outlook, as we have seen, more desperate. Sukhomlinov, on the other hand, with that levity and ignorance which were characteristic of his administration, suggested, as a remedy, urgent measures for the sparing use of shells and munitions, and accused the army of extravagance. He was more concerned with the "subversive" activities of the unofficial or-

[23] Knox, *op. cit.*, p. 86.
[24] *Perepiska V. A. Sukhomlinova* in *Krasni Arkhiv*, I, 234.

ganizations and especially those of Guchkov, whose revelations of the shocking conditions in the supply of the army with munitions of war were, in the General's opinion, equivalent to high treason.[25]

The most amazing lack of coördination existed between the Ministry of War, Headquarters, and the Chief Artillery Department. The head of the latter, General Kuzmin-Karavaev, it appears from a letter written by Sukhomlinov in September, 1914, "has lost heart and keeps on repeating that 'we must make peace at once.' "[26]

I have just learned the following fact [Sukhomlinov wrote in May, 1915]. On September 9, 1914, I have assembled the owners of metal works and asked them to undertake the manufacture of shells. The "Russian Company for the Manufacturing of Shells and Munitions of War" offered its good services but on October 25, 1914, it received reply No. 56158 from the Artillery Department that "its offer could not be accepted because there was no need of shrapnel!"[27]

And these unbelievable and criminal entanglements of red tape were permitted to accumulate at a time when, as Yanushkevich himself put it, "an extra shell saved dozens of men wounded and killed, and kept other soldiers from surrendering to the enemy—such cases having already taken place."[28] Sukhomlinov himself, in spite of his denunciation of the methods of the Artillery Department was anything but free from blame. As an example of his own attitude we may quote his false representations to General Knox that the 1,400,000 recruits called in January, 1915, would be provided with rifles. As a matter of fact the order for these rifles was not yet even signed, and the rifles did not begin to arrive in any number until eighteen months later.[29] Sukhomlinov knew perfectly well that at the time he made his statement the available reserves of rifles were some 50,000–70,000.[30] It is hardly necessary, however, here to dwell at length on the activities of the former Minister of War which, as it is well known, led to his dismissal and trial for high treason. We have quoted a few instances as a mere illustration of the conditions which prevailed in the rear of the army, and on which its welfare and the very possibility of continuing the struggle depended. With the mobilization of industry in the summer of 1915 a considerable improvement in the condition of supply

[25] Ibid., in Krasni Arkhiv, I, 250.
[26] Ibid., in Krasni Arkhiv, I, 248.
[27] Ibid., in Krasni Arkhiv, III, 60.
[28] Ibid., in Krasni Arkhiv, III, 44.
[29] Knox, op. cit., p. 222.
[30] Perepiska V. A. Sukhomlinova in Krasni Arkhiv, II, 142.

ook place. By the end of 1916 the army had more munitions of war than it ever had before. But the immense losses of 1914–1915 when the army had to retreat without even being able to answer the fire of the enemy could not be made good, nor was it possible to efface the deep impression they left upon the morale of the troops.

There is one more important question of army organization to which we should like to draw the reader's attention, the question of the commanding officers. It seems that in this respect, too, Russia was most unfortunately situated. Sir Alfred Knox reports a conversation on the subject with Colonel Engelhard, of the Russian General Staff and a prominent member of the Military Committee of the Duma. "He [Engelhard] agreed with me," writes Knox,[31] "that there were many excellent officers in the Russian army up to the rank of company and squadron commander, but considered that the peace training of officers of higher rank has been conducted on false principles." These pessimistic remarks are corroborated by the whole history of the War on the Russian front.[32] Who are the Russian generals whose names will go down in history with those of Joffre, Foch, French, Haig, Hindenburg? The filling of important commands even in time of war was a matter of routine and seniority. The effect of this system is well described in an interesting memorandum submitted to the Emperor in August, 1915, by the members of the Military and Naval Committee of the Duma.

We have learned [says the memorandum] that the filling of responsible military commands, such as commanders of divisions and army corps, is carried out in accordance with seniority in rank in the order in which the names appear on a special list, and that exceptions are made in favor only of those who have sufficient backing. It is therefore neither gallantry, nor genius, nor knowledge, nor experience in military art as proved in action that determine promotions, but external considerations. Under these conditions really able men, gifted military leaders capable of leading us to victory seldom have reached the higher commands. They have usually been reserved for officers less able but senior in rank. It would seem that in military art success must largely depend on the right selection of the commanding officers, and that therefore the present order of promotion is fatal to the cause of victory.[33]

[31] Knox, *op. cit.*, p. 264.
[32] *See,* for instance, conversation of Alexeev with Guchkov on March 6, 1917, in *Krasni Arkhiv*, XXII, 63: "Take into consideration our extreme poverty in outstanding generals." Count Witte caustically remarks: "The majority of our officers of the general staff knows everything, except what they should really know: the art of waging war." *Vospominanya*, II, 229.
[33] *Monarkhya Pered Krusheniem*, pp. 272–273.

Military hierarchy, however, is something that defies any interference from the outside, and not infrequently shows more vitality and power of resistance than the very army which is its *raison d'être*. Nicholas II was certainly not the man to break the sacred tradition.

These preliminary remarks, it is hoped, will provide the background needed to explain the growth of disaffection and the desire for peace among the rank and file. The army was hopelessly mismanaged and as time went on began to realize it. The real causes of its demoralization, however, must be sought elsewhere.

The Rank and File

It is a mere truism to say that a modern army in time of war, an army recruited on the basis of compulsory military service and comprising millions of men, is a cross section of the adult male population and is intimately connected with the rest of the country by innumerable ties. The situation is different in time of peace, when military discipline is more strict and the ranks contain a large percentage of men who have served several years with the colors and had time to assimilate the peculiar military spirit which is always to be found in barracks. The officers and noncommissioned officers in a peace-time army are all professional soldiers who have been through the mill of military schools and years of service. Their authority and prestige are supreme and naturally influence the outlook of the men freshly arrived from the fields, factories, and offices. Under these conditions the army grows into a body which lives its own separate life, has its own tradition, its own interests, its own joys and sorrows, its own code of honor, and its own understanding of duty. The situation, however, is entirely changed in time of war. The relatively small number of professional soldiers is submerged in the multitude of mobilized men. The *cadre* of officers and noncommissioned officers is immensely increased by the calling of men from the reserve, of whom most have had but slight military training, much of which has been forgotten. Military schools begin to turn out junior officers by the thousand, reserve battalions get their men by the hundred thousand. The discipline naturally becomes slack. The military spirit of the peace-time army rapidly wears away and survives mostly at Headquarters and various bureaucratic military institutions where not a few of the professional soldiers have taken refuge or where they are detained by their superior knowledge and training. The army ceases to be an army in the narrow sense of the word: it is a nation in arms.

206

That this army has also a life of its own is undoubtedly true. But this new life is very different from that of the peace-time army. Its connections with the outside world are more numerous, more intimate. It shares in the feelings of the country at large, it finds it difficult to admit that their interests may be opposed. It certainly takes more than a uniform and a rifle to make a farmer, a workingman, or an office clerk, into a soldier; and in Russia both the rifle and the uniform were sometimes lacking. If we keep in mind these premises, which seem to us incontestable, the demoralization of the army, which we shall trace and which followed a course parallel to the breakdown of the other social groups we have discussed, will not come as a surprise.

The fundamental factor in determining the morale of the Russian army was the same thing we have met over and over again in the course of this study, the nation's low standards. Nothing else could be expected in a country where low standards were the outstanding feature of social, political, and economic life. The army was poorly organized; it was poorly armed and equipped; it suffered from the incompetence, ignorance, and stupidity of its leaders; and the raw material which composed it was also far below anything we find in any of the other Great Powers which took part in the struggle.

The raw material of the army still suffered from want of education and individuality [writes Sir Alfred Knox]. The proportion of literates among the reservists was said to be increasing. Of the 1903 contingent, only 39 per cent could read and write, but before the War the percentage was said to have risen to 50. It is believed that both these figures were grossly exaggerated, but in any case such smattering of education as the recruit possessed had not in any way expanded his mind or made him a civilized, thinking being.[34]

The personal observations of the present author, who made the campaign in the Russian army as a junior officer in a regiment of artillery and was for years in daily and friendly contact with the common soldiers, fully agree with the pessimistic conclusions of the British general. This does not mean that this daily intercourse was not enjoyable and even profitable. From the personal point of view the years spent with the troops present a most delectable and memorable experience, but in the course of it the immense and striking weaknesses of the Russian peasant-soldier had full opportunity to reveal themselves. It would be stupid and unjust to blame him for his lack of stamina, his low

---

[34] Knox, *op. cit.*, p. xxxi.

sense of duty, his inability to grasp anything outside the field of his immediate interests. All these were probably the inevitable results of the historical conditions under which he had lived since time immemorial. The progress of education since the Emancipation had been far too slow to bring any real results. The apathy and ignorance of the masses bore their evil fruit, and the historian who disregards or minimizes the effects of this fundamental factor is hardly doing service to the Russian people.

In 1914 the causes of the War had not yet been spread forth in innumerable volumes of controversial documents and unconvincing learned treatises. But even if they had been, it would have been difficult to persuade the Russian peasants that they were fighting for possession of Constantinople and the Straits, the very existence of which were entirely unknown to the overwhelming majority of them.

The Russian peasant population [writes Knox] is essentially pacific and the least imperialistic in the world. It never understood why it fought. It fought well on many occasions when the leading was moderate. It would have continued to fight well if it had had some measure of success, but it soon lost confidence in the Government and the leading. A higher type of human animal was required to persevere to victory through the monotony of disaster. . . . For a long war Russia was outclassed in every factor of success except in the number of her fighting men and in their mollusc-like quality of recovery after severe defeat.[35]

The cause that underlies the patriotic exaltation invariably evinced in every country entering a war is a controversial matter. The explanation recently suggested by Leon Trotsky perhaps deserves attention.

The people whose lives, day in and day out, pass in a monotony of hopelessness are many [writes the exiled Soviet leader]; they are the mainstay of modern society. The alarm of mobilization breaks into their lives like a promise; the familiar and long-hated is overthrown, and the new and unusual reigns in its place. Changes still more incredible are in store for them in the future. For better or worse? For the better, of course—what can seem worse to Popischil[36] than "normal" conditions?[37]

There is little doubt that this explanation contains a great deal of truth. Those who still remember their own feelings in the

---

[35] *Ibid.*, p. xxxiv.
[36] Popischil was a half-German, half-Czech bootmaker's apprentice in Vienna whom Trotsky observed taking part in a patriotic demonstration in front of the Austrian War Office.
[37] Leon Trotsky, *My Life* (New York, 1930), p. 233.

troubled days of July, 1914, may be able, perhaps, to find in their own personal reactions the element of thrill before the great adventure.

This feeling, the excitement before the adventure, is, however, of brief duration. The routine of military life in a modern war is still more depressing than any peace-time conditions. The excitement, at any rate, faded away as the result of the immense losses and terrible privations which prevailed on the Russian front.

The First Signs of Demoralization

That an army constituted of the type of men supplied by the Russian countryside and led by officers emerging from the Russian Staff College should be particularly susceptible to depression and demoralization would seem to be a foregone conclusion. This conclusion is moreover fully supported by the contemporary and authoritative evidence at our disposal. Sir Alfred Knox rightly pointed out that the soldiers were capable of fighting, and fighting well, as long as there was "some measure of success." This element, as we know, was entirely lacking. Some anticipation of the coming trouble may be found in a letter written by Yanushkevich as early as the middle of September, 1914.

In Pinsk [wrote the chief of staff] fifty-eight soldiers remained for two days without medical help and food, under the open sky next door to a military hospital which was not yet officially opened, and adjacent to another which was half empty. It has been established that one officer, one Moslem, four Old Believers, and ten men belonging to the Greek Orthodox Church who died in that hospital were all buried on the municipal refuse dump alongside the road.... One or two such incidents will be enough to start a blaze which it will be beyond my power to check.[38]

The coming weeks brought to the chief of staff much more serious preoccupations.

The thought is unbearable [he wrote on December 6, 1914] that the lack of shells and munitions will force us to surrender to William. ... The shortage of officers is also keenly felt. Some of the regiments have only from seven to ten left. ... Many men have no boots, and their legs are frostbitten. They have no sheepskin or warm underwear, and are catching colds. The result is that in regiments which have lost their officers mass surrenders to the enemy have been developing, sometime on the initiative of war-time officers. "Why

[38] Perepiska V. A. Sukhomlinova in Krasni Arkhiv, I, 251.

should we die from hunger and exposure, without boots? The artillery keeps silent, and we are shot down like partridges. One is better off in Germany. Let us go." Cossacks who succeeded in recapturing 500 prisoners were assaulted by them: "Who asked you to do this, you sons-of-dogs? We don't want to suffer again from hunger and cold." True, these are sad occurrences, but they are ominous.[39]

The general military situation in the meantime was getting worse.

The officers commanding the two fronts [wrote Yanushkevich on December 10, 1914] have sent me wires which make my hair stand on end. Munitions are melting away. The Germans are already publishing articles which say we are at the end because we do not answer their fire, and because our men when taken prisoner have testified that we are getting no reinforcements and our artillery is ordered not to fire. The conclusion? Germany's victory is near.[40]

And he added next day: "Our enforced inaction brings its fruit: Morale is on the decline. Nerves are breaking down under the strain of inaction. But nothing can be done as long as we have no munitions."[41] Describing the defeat of the Russian troops near Mlava, Yanushkevich wrote on February 5, 1915:

Our losses are immense. The territorials are simply offering to sell their rifles for seven rubles. Since our Russian knights are growing so fond of rubles and we have to carry on the struggle, only one method remains open: to offer them money for German rifles. Perhaps the lack of a sense of duty will be made good by mercenary considerations. A sign of the times.[42]

That this was not a passing mood of the chief of staff but his reasoned opinion will appear from the suggestion he submitted to the Council of Ministers in the summer of 1915. We shall discuss it a little later.

The causes of discontent among the soldiers were not limited, of course, to purely military difficulties. In April, 1915, Yanushkevich informed Sukhomlinov[43] that "the Commander-in-Chief was alarmed by evident feeling among the men, due to rumors which were reaching them from their villages to the effect that their 'womenfolk were having a good time with the prisoners of war.' Many are heavy-hearted at the thought, and others are furious." Another letter of Yanushkevich written soon after shows the progress of discontent among the troops:

[39] *Ibid.*, in *Krasni Arkhiv*, II, 143–144.
[40] *Ibid.*, in *Krasni Arkhiv*, II, 147.
[41] *Ibid.*, in *Krasni Arkhiv*, II, 155.
[42] *Ibid.*, in *Krasni Arkhiv*, III, 29.
[43] *Perepiska V. A. Sukhomlinova* in *Krasni Arkhiv*, III, 58.

It is vital that, without delay, we should get poison gas, because (1) our men are filled with a desire for revenge; and (2) it is often said that "they don't spare us, but we are sparing the Germans." Gossip has reached us that says the Artillery Department has refused an offer of the Obukhovsky Works and that they are running only half-time; and also that the Ruzsky and other factories are not employed to full capacity. This, of course, creates an atmosphere that is tense; and from the trenches we now hear no longer whispers, but outright clamor: "We have no munitions, no rifles, nothing to fight with! Treason!" The same accusations reach me by mail. Rumors of the slackness of work at the factories lends credit to the terrible and devilish charges of treason which the Germans have managed to start.[44]

The Second Half of 1915

That the picture of the position at the front outlined by the chief of staff was in no way exaggerated will be made clear by comparing his statements with the information at the disposal of the Council of Ministers. This has fortunately been preserved in the minutes drawn up by M. Yakhontov. It will be remembered that the relations between Headquarters and the Council of Ministers were anything but friendly, and that the ministers, indeed, believed that Yanushkevich was largely to blame for the terrible situation in which the army found itself in the summer of 1915. This makes the agreement of these two sources as to the morale of the army even more striking.

The meeting of the Council of Ministers held on July 16, 1915, opened with the following grave warning from the Minister of War: "I consider it my duty as a citizen and as a member of the Cabinet to declare to the Council of Ministers that the country is in danger." In support of this statement Polivanov told of the rapid retreat of the army, a retreat which had at times assumed the character of a disorderly flight, under the continuous pressure of an enemy immensely superior in artillery and munitions. No one knew when, where, and how the retreat would be stopped. The army was rapidly becoming demoralized. The number of desertions and voluntary surrenders to the enemy was increasing.

Headquarters [he said] is possessed by the deadly psychology of retreat, and is making preparations for further withdrawals into the country. Back, back, and back—this is the only order it sends out. No method, no plan can be discovered in its orders and actions, not a single courageous manoeuvre, not a single attempt to take advantage of the mistakes of our daring enemy.[45]

[44] Ibid., in Krasni Arkhiv, III, 72–73.
[45] Yakhontov, op. cit., pp. 15–16.

Further evidence of what the responsible leaders of the army thought of its morale will be found in the minutes of the meeting of the Council of July 24, 1915. Krivoshein, the Minister of Agriculture, informed the Council that he had received an urgent request from Headquarters demanding the immediate publication of a solemn proclamation by the Sovereign that soldiers who have suffered disablement and those who have given evidence of exceptional courage will receive allotments of land from 6 to 9 deciatines (16 to 24 acres). Such land is to be provided from the estates belonging to the State and the Peasant Bank, but especially from the confiscated estates of enemy nationals and German settlers. The idea underlying this suggestion is already familiar to us.

In this connection [said Krivoshein] I yesterday received from General Yanushkevich a most remarkable letter. He writes that "legendary heroes, champions of ideas, and altruists are very rare"; that "they represent no more than one per cent, and the rest of the army is made up of very matter-of-fact people"; that, of course, "it looks well to fight for Russia, but the masses are unable to understand this"; that "a Tambov peasant is willing to defend the province of Tambov, but a war for Poland is, in his opinion, foreign and useless"; that "therefore the soldiers are surrendering to the enemy *en masse*," etc. . . . From this General Yanushkevich draws the conclusion "that the Russian soldier must be given some personal interest in a victory over the enemy," that "he must be attracted by the additional allotment and deterred by the threat of confiscation in case of surrender," and so on, and so forth, in like vein, so flattering to the men fighting under the leadership of Headquarters. . . . The extraordinary naïveté or, to be exact, the unforgivable stupidity of this letter written by the chief of staff makes me shudder. . . . Every one is idle, every one is responsible for the continuous defeats we suffer from the Germans. Headquarters alone is free from blame. It alone is working. General Yanushkevich is full of self-admiration, he believes himself to be a genius persecuted by fate and human injustice. . . . How can General Yanushkevich continue to lead the army when he has no faith in his troops, in their love for their country, in the Russian people? Gentlemen, only imagine in whose hands is the fate of Russia, of the monarch, of the whole world.

Yakhontov states that the speech of Krivoshein provoked "general indignation."[46]

That the scheme of Yanushkevich was naïve and impracticable cannot be denied and it certainly does little credit to its author and the Grand Duke Nicholas Nikolaevich by whom, presumably, it was sanctioned. But that Headquarters decided

46 Yakhontov, *op. cit.*, pp. 23–26.

to launch so extravagant a plan is in itself a most notable fact and one that shows that information at its disposal as to the morale of the army must have been extremely grave. Indeed, the Minister of War told the Council six days later, on July 30, that "the army was continuously moving eastward, and the front line was changing almost hourly. Disorganization, surrenders to the enemy, desertion were assuming immense proportions. It appeared that Headquarters had completely lost its senses and its orders were given in fits of hysterics."[47] The general estimate of the situation given by Polivanov with its "surrenders to the enemy" and desertion "assuming immense proportions" did not fundamentally differ from the estimate of the chief of staff, although he naturally rejected his nonsensical scheme. Commenting on the military situation a few days later, Polivanov said that he relied upon "immeasurable distances, impassable roads, and the mercy of Saint Nicholas, patron of Holy Russia."[48] Such was the last hope of the Minister of War!

The responsible and well-informed members of the Duma were also greatly alarmed by the demoralization of the army. The memorandum of the Military and Naval Committee of the Duma, presented to the Emperor in August, 1915, emphasizes the necessity of immediate and far-reaching measures to improve the morale of the troops who were rapidly losing confidence in their leaders.[49]

About the same time, in the autumn of 1915, grave disturbances took place among the sailors of the Baltic fleet. In an official report submitted to the President of the Council of Ministers, Goremykin, by A. Khvostov, who was in charge of the investigation, the causes of the disturbances were given as follows: military reverses; animosity toward officers bearing German names; the prorogation of the Duma; the influence of liberal newspapers criticizing the policy of the Government for not combating German influence and the high cost of living; also the tactless behavior of some officers, and the poor food on certain warships. To these trivial grievances there was added general discontent with the Government and suspicions of German influence at the court. In spite of the seemingly superficial character of such discontents, from them there was undoubtedly kindled the revolt which burst into flame with such overwhelming force in 1917.[50]

[47] *Ibid.*, p. 30.
[48] *Ibid.*, p. 37.
[49] *Monarkhya Pered Krusheniem*, p. 273.
[50] *Volnenya vo Flote v 1915 Godu (Disturbances in the Fleet in 1915)* in *Krasni Arkhiv*, IX, 97–98.

The Eve of the Revolution

That discipline should have declined and discontent and weariness should have grown in the course of the War was probably unavoidable. In Russia what was beneath this was felt with special intensity, and the improvement in the conditions of supply in 1916 could do little to restore the morale of the army. The report of the Petrograd Police gives a vivid impression of the spirit of the troops in October, 1916. According to this document, the representatives of the Union of Zemstvos belonging to the Constitutional Democratic Party took an extremely pessimistic view of the conditions at the front and in the rear.

Particular interest in this respect [says the report] is due to the account of a commissioner of the Union who visited Riga and other places in connection with the organization of the supply of foodstuffs. He says that the atmosphere in the army is very tense, and the relations between the common soldiers and the officers are much strained, the result being that several unpleasant incidents leading even to bloodshed have taken place. The behavior of the soldiers, especially in the units located in the rear, is most provocative. They openly accuse military authorities of graft, cowardice, drunkenness, and even treason. One everywhere meets thousands of deserters perpetrating crimes and offering violence to the civilian population. These express their regret that "the Germans did not arrive," that "the Germans would restore order," and so on.

The same commissioner says that a number of armed conflicts between infantry men and the frontier guards and sailors took place in Reval and that on several occasions they developed into almost real battles. The officers who obtained positions in the rear thanks to favoritism and are in charge of transports, etc., are amazing, in the opinion of the commissioner, for their "lack of education, their insolence, and their absence of self-control." They spend their time in debauchery and in playing cards. The common soldiers despise their officers, especially the war-time officers, who from the point of view of military training and general education are frequently far beneath their subordinates. Even the higher officers in the battalions and military establishments of the rear are often lacking in experience, and are surrounded by scoundrels and grafters. The cases of exemption of private soldiers from service in the trenches on the payment of large sums are growing more and more frequent.

The wounded, whom the commissioner had frequent opportunities to meet, declare that the spirit of the army would be excellent if only the officers were of a better class. The things the wounded tell about the rear are simply unbelievable:—the extortion of bribes from them for transportation to the dressing stations, robbery of the wounded by orderlies, and so on. In the opinion of the commissioner, all that he has seen clearly indicates the disintegration of the army, and this forecasts the end of the War in the near future. The men are terribly angry because they get little or even no news from home, especially since the soldiers who have had leave have been returning with most extraordinary stories.

The employees of the zemstvos who deliver supplies are bombarded with questions: is it true that there are famines in Petrograd and Moscow? that the "merchants" are ejecting soldiers' wives and throwing them into the street? that the Germans have paid the ministers 1,000 million rubles to destroy as many common people as they possibly can? Even the German proclamations, with their fantastic inventions, begin to find numbers of credulous readers among our men. One may also see and hear outright propaganda, which usually takes the form of persuasions to desert. In the opinion of this commissioner, "every one who has approached the army cannot but carry away the belief that complete demoralization is in progress. The soldiers began to demand peace a long time ago, but never was this done so openly and with such force as now. The officers not infrequently even refuse to lead their units against the enemy, because they are afraid of being killed by their own men."[51]

Commenting on the information given above, the authors of the police report state that

although much of the stories of the commissioner seems incredible, they nevertheless are largely deserving of belief; for many doctors who have returned from the army have made communications similar in tone and general tenor: the complete disorganization of the immediate rear, the growth of discontent and general weariness of the War—such were the essential points of all these statements.

There seems to be no reason why we should doubt their truthfulness. The police had no object in representing the situation in unduly dark colors. We have also information from other sources, that points to the same general conclusions.

General Selivachev, commanding the Seventh Army, writes in his diary under the date of January 19, 1917:

The chaplain complains of the difficulty of his present position, since the men, who read many newspapers, are continually asking for explanations, and criticizing the Government, a sad departure but probably inevitable to-day, with the freedom of the press, the prorogation of the Duma, the Rasputin scandal, etc.[52]

On March 10, 1917, a few days after the abdication of the Tsar, Selivachev makes the following interesting comments:

[a] *Politicheskoe Polozhenie Rossii Nakanune Fevralskoi Revolutsii v Zhandarmskom Osvyashchenii* in *Krasni Arkhiv*, XVII, 18–19.
[2] *Iz Dnevnika Generala V. J. Selivacheva (From the Diary of General V. J. Selivachev)* in *Krasni Arkhiv*, IX, 105.

I am firmly convinced that the common soldier to-day wants only one thing—food and peace, because he is tired of war. No use trying to feed him—especially the kind of soldier we have now—on high-sounding phrases about "the land of our fathers," its glory and its might. He was not brought up in these ideas in his village; and the army, engaged as it is in fighting, has had no time to attend to his education. If our older men, brought up in this spirit, were disappointed at the beginning of the War because it was not over, as was expected, within three months, and we have witnessed a tenacious desire on their part to be transferred to the rear under every sort of pretext, then what can we say of the common soldier of to-day, brought up in the reserve battalions?[53]

This is, indeed, an eloquent confession!

At the beginning of January, 1917 [writes Rodzianko], General Krimov arrived from the front and asked to be given an opportunity of unofficially acquainting the members of the Duma with the disastrous conditions at the front and the spirit of the army. . . . His was a painful and grim confession. There could be no hope of victory, said Krimov, until the Government had changed its course, or given way to another which the army could trust. "The spirit of the army is such that the news of a *coup d'état* would be welcomed with joy. A revolution is imminent, and we at the front feel it to be so."[54]

In the army, as we know, there was much bitterness against the Empress who was openly accused of supporting the cause of Germany, a charge for which there was not a shadow of foundation. Nevertheless, on the eve of the Revolution it was generally accepted as true.

I have just had a visit from an officer arriving from the army [wrote Madame Rodzianko on February 12, 1917]. He says that the feelings against both of them [the Emperor and the Empress] are stronger than they have ever been before. It is openly said in the Riga sector that she supports all German spies whom, on her orders, the commanding officers let go free.[55]

It is highly characteristic that such nonsensical accusations were repeated by a woman of Madame Rodzianko's standing.

Another important factor in the demoralization of the army was the spread of extravagant and unjustified stories about the Allies. The traditional antipathy for Great Britain found expres-

---

[53] *Iz Dnevnika Generala V. J. Selivacheva (From the Diary of General V. J. Selivachev)* in *Krasni Arkhiv*, IX, 112.
[54] Rodzianko, *The Reign of Rasputin: an Empire's Collapse*, p. 244.
[55] *Krasni Arkhiv*, XIV, 246.

on in all sorts of inventions which one could hear everywhere. The Grand Duke Boris, for instance, indulged in malicious talk about the "bluff" that the Dardanelles expedition had been, and about Great Britain's keeping Russia from taking Bagdad. He also made statements to the effect that the next war would be between Russia and Great Britain. He was forced to withdraw his utterances and apologize.[56] The anti-British feelings of the Grand Duke were fully shared by the rank and file of the army. General Knox reports an interesting instance of the indignation provoked by the "inaction" of the Allies. "On one occasion," he writes,[57] "when we had had no post for a fortnight, I asked an officer who had got a paper what the Allies were doing in the western theatre. He laughed and said: 'Doing? They are lost in admiration for the Russian army and its marvellous valor.'" And one could hear over and over again the malicious phrase that the Allies were determined to fight "until the last drop of blood ... of the Russian soldier."

Subversive Propaganda

The question may arise to what extent the rapid growth of discontent among the soldiers and the progressive demoralization of the army were due to general causes, and to what extent they were the product of organized revolutionary propaganda. In our opinion the general causes were by far the more important. Revolutionary propaganda, after all, is never effective unless the ground is ready for it. On the other hand, there is no doubt that attempts were made by the revolutionary parties to take advantage of the favorable conditions created by the War, and to bring about the downfall of the Imperial *régime*. Casual reference to such propaganda was made in some of the documents we have quoted. An interesting example of such activities is offered by a "Letter from the Army" written in June, 1916, which contained a comprehensive and well-thought-out plan for revolutionary outbreak.[58] The disclosure of the plan greatly stirred the commanding officers. General Gurko, who was temporarily performing the duties of chief of staff, outlined a whole program of counter-propaganda through the education of the soldiers. General Ruzsky, however, who commanded the north front, deprecated the idea on the ground that the officers were entirely incapable of undertaking such a task. In his opinion the

Knox, *op. cit.*, pp. 429–431.
Ibid., pp. 318–319; *see also*, pp. 352–353.
Revolutsionnaya Propaganda v Armii v 1916–1917 (Revolutionary Propaganda in Army in 1916–1917) in *Krasni Arkhiv*, XVII, 36–50.

217

attempt would do more harm than good. The matter was take up in January, 1917, but never had time to materialize. I seems safe to maintain, in spite of the meager documentation a our disposal, that revolutionary propaganda before the Revolu tion had gained no firm hold in the army. Its demoralization wa due to more profound and elemental causes.

It may be said that the picture of the deterioration of the arm even before the Revolution, as given in this chapter, is an undul dark one. And it is undoubtedly possible, by making a differer choice of evidence, to present the matter in a more favorabl light. We believe, nevertheless, that the picture given here repre sents the actual conditions. Our evidence in the majority c cases has been taken from sources contemporary with the even we have described. A considerable part of it—the correspond ence of Yanushkevich with Sukhomlinov, the minutes of th Council of Ministers, the memorandum of the members of th Duma, the reports of the police—was not intended for publica tion. Practically all the authorities quoted were in an exceptio ally good position to obtain reliable information and were usin it under full responsibility for the consequences of their action Further evidence, of course, may help greatly by adding deta to the picture we have given, and by lighting up certain impo tant features. It seems doubtful, however, if anything woul change its general outlines.

Soldiers' Letters

We have refrained from using one sort of evidence whic naturally suggests itself, letters written by officers and me serving with the colors. The military censorship was very activ in examining such correspondence, and it appears that detaile reports of the contents of many letters were drawn up, an some of them are still preserved in the Russian archives. B these reports have not been published. They are therefore be yond our reach. And it is by no means certain that they woul add much to our knowledge of the morale of the army. W know that the proportion of literates among the reservists i 1914 was quoted by Knox as 50 per cent, and that he felt th: such a percentage was a gross exaggeration. He was undoub edly right. It will be also remembered that numbers of enliste men who appeared on the official lists as able to read and wri had had one or two years at school at the age of eight or te but had never seen a book or newspaper since. Their literac therefore, was purely nominal. The letters they sent home we usually written for them by their more enlightened fellow so

218

diers, and still more frequently by noncommissioned offi..
and junior officers. Under these conditions any free criticism.
of the conduct of the War, commanding officers and the Government could hardly be expected, especially as it was a fact of
common knowledge that letters went through a double censorship, first that of the regimental officer, and then that of the
official censor. No wonder, therefore, Knox could be informed
in February, 1916, that "in all units 80 per cent of the letters
were said to show a good spirit, and in some units 100 per
cent."[59] The nature of this official optimism was an open secret.
Knox, with his excellent common sense, was not slow in dis-
covering it.

> Stogov, the new chief of staff of the Eighth Army [he writes] ...
> is excellent company. ... I told him of the enthusiastic patriotism
> of the extracts from the officers' and soldiers' letters that Dukhonin
> had read me, and he laughed and said that they were written either
> by the censor himself, or by some ambitious non-commissioned
> officer who wanted promotion. I think so too, for the letters had not
> natural tone. Why, for instance, should a man write to his sister
> to say that he was "still whole [alive], but ready at any moment to
> die for his Emperor and country"? What a devil of a time some
> Russians waste in putting their heads in the sand and in trying to
> induce their Allies to follow their example![60]

If we agree with General Knox, we shall accept the logical
inference, that the evidence used in this chapter is really more
reliable than any "first-hand" information we could derive from
thousands of letters written with the special purpose of deceiving the censor.[61]

The Army and the Nation

The results here set forth—the demoralization of the army
by the end of 1916—will come as a natural conclusion if we
keep in mind the general trend of the development of the country during the war years. The army was, to repeat, merely a
cross section of the entire male population. Its ties with the rest
of the country were close, numerous, and indissoluble. That

Knox, op. cit., p. 389.
Ibid., p. 464.
A selection of letters from the army was recently published in a Soviet periodical.
Indicates that the feeling of discontent we have observed among the troops found
expression in the messages they sent home. While corroborating our conclusions,
evidence thus presented is too slight to offer sufficient ground for generalizations.
Golos Iz Okopov (Voice from the Trenches), Soldiers' Letters 1915-1916, in
Krasnaya Letopis, No. 25, pp. 112–118.

feeling of general war weariness, of discontent with the Government, the realization of the inevitability of a change, which gradually grew in practically every class and social group, was bound to make a deep imprint upon the morale of the troops. Even more than the civilian population did the soldiers suffer from the inadequacy of organization, the absence of supplies and munitions, the unintelligence and ignorance of the military leaders. Their losses in killed, wounded, and prisoners had been immense. Their zest for adventure or their patriotism of the first days was no longer in them. The army, together with the country at large, was living in the expectation of the coming catastrophe. And when the Empire fell, in March, 1917, it found no defenders among His Majesty's troops. The final breakdown of the army in 1917[62] was merely the certain end of a process of disintegration that already was far advanced long before the Revolution. It is true that the Revolution struck the last blow at the army; but it is also true that the demoralization of the army was one of the important factors in bringing about the Revolution.

[62] See below, pp. 238–243.

From the Downfall of the Empire
to Bolshevism

> *Prise en elle-même, l'oeuvre du gouvernement*
> *transitoire ne compte pas dans l'évolution poli-*
> *tique de l'État russe. On en conservera la mém-*
> *oire comme on conserve celle des années de*
> *jeunesse, pleines de désordre, de conceptions*
> *idéalistes et de sentiments généreux, jamais*
> *réalisés. Les deux phénomènes historiques qui*
> *se placent au début et à la fin du régime inter-*
> *médiaire sont autrement importants que ces*
> *rêves nébuleux et ces tentatives aussi stériles que*
> *désordonnées.*
>
> *Nolde, L'ancien régime et la révolution russes,*
> *p. 147.*

he Downfall of the Empire

ᴛE EVENTS of February–March, 1917, which led to the abdi-
tion of the Emperor and the creation of the Provisional
overnment, while generally anticipated, took a form which
 one had foreseen. It will be remembered that the imminence
 the catastrophe was almost openly discussed everywhere.
t the end of 1916 and early in 1917 the possibility of a revolu-
nary change in the *régime* had been canvassed behind closed
ors by a small group of men representing the Progressive
oc, the Unions of Zemstvos and of Towns, and the war
dustries committees. Simultaneously a discussion of the same
estion was undertaken by another group which included
me of the military leaders and was inspired by General
rimov. Both groups arrived quite independently at the same
nclusion: the Emperor must abdicate in favor of his son,
th the Grand Duke Michael Alexandrovich, the Emperor's
other, as regent.[1] They also prepared a tentative list of the

vidence of Miliukov in *Padenie Tsarskago Rezhima*, VI, 350; Miliukov, *Istorya*
ʐroi Russkoi Revolutsii*, I, Part I, 36.

future ministers and many of their nominees were actuall
called to take office in March, 1917.

In spite of these preparations, the Revolution came as a sur
prise to both the liberal and the revolutionary leaders of Russia
It was at first a popular movement which started in Petrogra
probably as a result of a shortage of foodstuffs, the importanc
of which rumors had much exaggerated. It began on Februar
23 as a strike of some 70,000 or 80,000 men employed in th
metal industries. At first it gave no reason for any great anxiet
and few realized at the time that the fate of the Imperial *régim*
was at stake. Soon, however, it grew in volume and was joine
by the troops of the Petrograd garrison. The first desertio
among the troops occurred on February 27 when the Volhynsk
regiment of the foot guards refused to obey orders and joine
the revolutionary populace. It was soon followed by other mil
tary units. From that moment the fate of the monarchy wa
sealed.

The defense of the existing *régime* was in the hands of
Cabinet headed by the senile Prince Golitsin, with the mental
unbalanced Protopopov in the responsible office of Minister
the Interior. General Khabalov, the military governor of Petr
grad, proved entirely incapable of dealing with the emergenc
The Emperor was at his Headquarters, in Mogilev, and it wa
several days before he was brought to realize that the disturl
ances in the capital were more than a passing outburst. N
wonder therefore that the popular movement in Petrograd m
with practically no resistance.

The Duma, which assembled on February 27 only to lear
that it had been prorogued, was confronted with a situation
extreme seriousness, and appointed a Provisional Committee
take command of the situation. Its leadership, however, re
mained largely nominal, events pursuing their own course ind
pendently of the confused and often contradictory counse
issued from the Taurida Palace. The Taurida Palace itself wa
soon invaded by a revolutionary mob of soldiers and workmer
which put an end to all attempts to transact business in an o
derly manner. With the new and unruly elements which can
to the surface apparently from nowhere, Russian liberals, wi
their balanced minds and good intentions, had little in commo
On March 1, the eve of the abdication, Rodzianko, heading t
Provisional Committee of the Duma, telephoned directly
General Ruzsky, commanding the north front. "I am hangi
by a mere thread," he told him,[2] "the control of events is slippi

[2] *Fevralskaya Revolutsya 1917 Goda (The Revolution of February 1917)*, in *Kra.
Arkhiv*, XXI, 59.

om my hands. . . . I am afraid, the worst is still awaiting us."
s a matter of fact, he had never had any control of events.

Revolutionary circles were taken by surprise just as much as
ie liberals. Their organizations at the time, it will be remem-
ered, were practically nonexistent.[3] The majority of their lead-
's were abroad or in local prisons, or in Siberia. Those still at
)erty apparently failed to play any important part in the
ovement. It was, indeed, said by one of their own writers that
he Revolution found them sleeping, like the foolish virgins."[4]
hey soon realized, however, that their day had come; and they
rganized in the Taurida Palace the Soviet of Soldiers' and
/orkmen's Deputies which played so important a part in the
ter period of the Revolution.

The spontaneous nature of the movement of February 23–
larch 2 is generally recognized. Professor Miliukov, a leading
gure in the Duma and later for a time Minister of Foreign
ffairs in the Provisional Government, admitted that the move-
ient was "entirely chaotic. . . . It was clear that it had nothing
• do with the prorogation of the Duma. The two events merely
appened to coincide."[5] General Klimovich, a former director
f the State Police, also expressed the opinion that "the Revo-
ition was a spontaneous movement . . . it was not the fruit of
irty propaganda."[6] "The whole of Russia appeared to me like
stormy ocean," said Protopopov,[7] "and where were the social
:oups that were satisfied? There were none. Where were the
)cial groups one could trust, that one could depend upon?
here were none."

The movement which led to the abdication of the Emperor
id the establishment of the Provisional Government was purely
·cal and was limited to the capital. The arrests of the members
f the Imperial Cabinet and the seizure of public buildings were
irried out by the rebellious troops and by the populace of
etrograd; but the success of the Revolution obviously depended
1 the support, inarticulate at first, that it received throughout
e country. The movement itself had no organization, no lead-
s and, at the beginning, it would seem, even no definite pur-
)se. Like a snowball rolling down the slope of a steep hill it
·ew in size and gathered strength on its way. It would hardly
: correct to say that the Imperial *régime* had been overthrown:
merely collapsed because it had nothing to rely upon. The
:ws of the abdication of the Tsar was received everywhere

'ee above, pp. 159 sqq.
)uoted in Nolde, *L'ancien régime et la révolution russes*, p. 124.
:vidence of Miliukov in *Padenie Tsarskago Rezhima*, VI, 352.
:vidence of Klimovich in *Padenie Tsarskago Rezhima*, I, 98.
:vidence of Protopopov in *Padenie Tsarskago Rezhima*, I, 149.

either with satisfaction, even with enthusiasm, or with fears fo the future and a recognition of its inevitability. The Revolutio was the outcome of the work of the disintegrating forces set i motion by the War. The end of the monarchy came with a ease which few would have ventured to predict. This even however important in itself, was merely the beginning of a infinitely more fundamental and far-reaching readjustment.

We will not attempt to tell again, with details, the familia story of the political revolution. It will suffice to recall the fac that Nicholas II, out of affection for his son, refused to abdicat in favor of the Tsarevitch Alexis, as he was urged to do by th emissaries of the Duma, Guchkov and Shulgin, and nominate his brother, the Grand Duke Michael Alexandrovich, as h successor. But by the time Guchkov and Shulgin had returne to Petrograd, the situation had already changed, and antidy nastic feelings had greatly increased in intensity. At a confer ence called by the Provisional Committee of the Duma o March 3, the necessity of preserving the monarchical form c government, with the Grand Duke on the throne, found n supporters except Miliukov and Guchkov. The Grand Duk accordingly declined to accept the Crown, and put the futur organization of the Russian State in the hands of a Constituer Assembly to be elected by popular vote. In the meantime th work of government was to be carried on by a Provision. Government which was to be appointed by the Provision. Committee of the Duma.[8]

This was, indeed, an unforeseen development. Instead of mere change of sovereign and the establishment of a *régime* constitutional monarchy with a boy-emperor under the regenc of a benevolent and effaced Grand Duke, the liberal leade: unexpectedly found themselves vested with what amounted i theory to dictatorial powers, and had to face the prospect c elections to a Constituent Assembly in an illiterate country i the midst of a war. The Constituent Assembly was, to say th least, an unknown quantity, and those coming elections lent the Provisional Government, resting on the uncertain legal fou dation of a revolutionary *coup d'état*, a character of the ten porary which was fraught with danger.

The Provisional Government

The Provisional Government, especially the Provisional Go ernment of the first period, was flesh of the flesh of the Russia

[8] Gronsky, *op. cit.*, pp. 43–55; Nolde, *L'ancien régime et la révolution russes*, 110–145; Miliukov, *Istorya Vtoroi Russkoi Revolutsii*, I, Part I, 40–52.

liberals. It was headed by Prince Lvov, president of the Union of Zemstvos and one of the most popular men in liberal circles. Prince Lvov's long and untarnished record of public work, his close association with the institutions of local government, his eminent services to the country during both the war with Japan and the present War, gave him an exceptional position and practically pointed to him as to the logical leader of the new Government. The men who joined his administration were chosen from the more prominent figures of the former opposition. With a few minor exceptions they seemed particularly well qualified for the task they had undertaken. Professor Miliukov, for instance, the new Minister of Foreign Affairs, was not only an eminent scholar and historian, known throughout the world, but also one of the Duma's foremost spokesmen on foreign affairs and a trusted friend of the Entente. A. J. Guchkov, the new Minister of War and the Navy, was a leader of the war industries committees and one of the Duma's experts on military questions. A. J. Shingarev, Minister of Agriculture, was the rapporteur of the budget committee of the Duma whose erudite expositions of the country's financial problems were always listened to with the greatest respect. The socialist elements were represented in the first Provisional Government by A. F. Kerensky, Minister of Justice, an eloquent young lawyer without much practical experience, temperamental and self-confident, but not really extreme in his views or unmanageable. All things considered, the first Provisional Government embodied a realization of the dreams of the Russian liberals when they pressed the Tsar for a government enjoying the confidence of the nation.

It is obviously idle to speculate on what the fate of Russia would have been if Prince Lvov and his colleagues had been called to power by the Tsar, but not as any result of a revolutionary *coup d'état*. Enough that under revolutionary conditions their administration brought nothing but disappointment. We shall not endeavor here to describe the political struggles of the Provisional Government, struggles that made necessary six important changes in its constitution in the course of eight months, and the resignation of Prince Lvov, who was succeeded by Kerensky. It is true that none of the members of the Provisional Government proved to be men of large caliber. Prince Lvov was completely lacking in the determination and aggressiveness of a national leader in an emergency. The gentleness of his nature and disposition, coupled with an inborn inability to make rapid and clear-cut decisions, markedly disqualified him for any position at the head of a revolutionary government. Indeed, in the light of his postrevolutionary activities, his immense popularity in the prerevolutionary period must seem something of a miracle. Kerensky succeeded him in July, and was an even less fortunate choice than his predecessor. The peculiar position he occupied in the Provisional Government as the only link between that body and the Soviet of Soldiers' and Workmen's Deputies resulted in giving him an entirely false and grossly exaggerated idea of his own importance. He sincerely believed himself to be the chosen leader of the nation, and proceeded to carry out a program of reëstablishing the morale of the army by a campaign of speech-making. Indeed, he was fully confident that his mere presence was sufficient to imbue the troops with an invincible will for victory. This preposterous idea was naturally doomed to disappointment.[9] A poignant and essentially correct characterization of Kerensky is given by Leon Trotsky.

Lenin called Kerensky a "petit braggart" [he writes]. Even now there is little one can add to that. Kerensky was and still is an adventitious figure, a ruling favorite of the historical moment. Every mighty wave of revolution, as it draws on the virgin masses not yet trained to discrimination, inevitably raises on its crest such heroes for a day, heroes who are instantly blinded by their own effulgence. . . . His best speeches were merely a sumptuous pounding of water in a mortar. In 1917, the water boiled and sent up steam, and the clouds of steam provided a halo.[10]

The Divorce between the Educated Classes and the Masses

It would be a mistake, however, to attach too much importance to the personalities of the men who happened to be at the helm. Professor Miliukov, writing in 1920, wisely remarks that "we must revise [in the restrictive sense] our ideas as to how far the will of the individual can control such mass phenomena as national revolutions."[11] The real source of the difficulties of the Provisional Government lay much deeper than mere personalities and must be sought in the divorce between the educated classes and the masses.[12] After the tumultuous days of

[9] It is interesting that among the admirers of Kerensky was the former Emperor. With that remarkable lack of sound political judgment which cost him his crown, Nicholas II entered in his diary on July 8, 1917: "At the present time he [Kerensky] is positively the right man in the right place; the more power he has the better it will be." *Dnevnik Nikolaya Romanova (Diary of Nicholas Romanov)* in *Krasni Arkhiv*, XXI, 91.

[10] Trotsky, *My Life*, p. 289.

[11] Miliukov, *Istorya Vtoroi Russkoi Revolutsii*, I, Part I, 5–6.

[12] *See above*, pp. 28 sqq.

February–March the rebellious troops and the workingmen of Petrograd had been prevailed upon, not without difficulty, to return to their barracks and their factories but they refused to resign themselves to their prerevolutionary, passive attitude and to allow any well-meaning liberals and moderate socialists to arrange the future according to their particular ideas. The Petrograd Soviet, supported by other local Soviets which rapidly sprang up all over the country, was a constant and most active reminder of the new factor in Russian politics. The Petrograd Soviet itself was steadily moving toward the Left. The relatively moderate composition it had had in the first days of the Revolution, with its mere handful of Bolsheviks, had been gradually replaced by elements much more radical. Against this rising tide of the social revolution in its most extreme forms the Provisional Government waged a losing batttle.

Professor Miliukov and his colleagues in the Government on the one hand, on the other, the masses of the Russian peasants and workmen, only now awakening from their secular sleep and seeking redress from the grievances that had accumulated in the course of centuries, did not speak the same language. Since the beginning of the War the liberals had staunchly advocated the cause of the Entente and fought the Imperial Government on the ground that it was putting in jeopardy the cause of victory. They refused to admit that this was not the attitude of the masses. The spontaneous movement of the people of Petrograd, exasperated by the privations of a war the purpose and necessity of which they had never understood, a movement which was primarily a protest against war, was officially interpreted as the desire of the masses to establish a *régime* which would bring the country to victory. With the supreme contempt for facts of a professor turned politician, Miliukov expounded the theory that the Revolution was primarily a protest against the slackness of the Imperial Government in conducting the War and the prospect of a separate peace with Germany—"one of the most naïve self-deceptions of a period which produced so many illusions."[13] And this at a time when the garrison of Petrograd, "the glory and pride of the Revolution," refused to leave for the trenches, and the disorganization of the army, with its thousands of desertions, was proceeding at full speed! The liberal intellectuals and moderate socialists who succeeded in high places to the bureaucrats of the Imperial *régime* were thinking, like their predecessors, in terms of Russia's international obligations, her position among the Great Powers, her national honor.

[13] Baron B. E. Nolde, *Dalekoe i Blizkoe (Old and New)* (Paris, 1930), p. 149.

They were irresistibly attracted by the long-coveted prize of Russian diplomacy—the Dardanelles—which was at last within their reach. Partly as a matter of expediency and partly on grounds of social justice, they were willing to make real concessions on the land problem, to transfer to the peasants the large estates, the land for which they had so long and so passionately been hungering. But this transfer was to be carried out legally. The question was to be decided by the Constituent Assembly. And in the meantime no interference with the right of private property was to be tolerated.

The peasant—in his cottage, in the trenches, in the workshop —approached the problem from a very different point of view. To him the international obligations of Russia, her position among the Great Powers, her national honor, were equally meaningless. The Dardanelles was merely a foreign word conveying nothing. The Constituent Assembly was just another strange and suspicious innovation. And while Professor Miliukov extolled the necessity of bringing the War to a victorious end, and Prince Lvov and Kerensky pictured the millennium which the Constituent Assembly was to bring about, the long-suffering, ill-treated, illiterate peasant stubbornly thought of that particular estate of a few hundred acres near his native village the division of which among his fellow villagers had always appeared to him to be the one solution of all his problems, and an act of social justice long overdue. "The sole preoccupation of our soldiers," wrote General Selivachev in his diary, on March 13, 1917,[14] "is whether they will receive additional allotments from the estates belonging to private owners, the appanages, and the monasteries; this is their chief desire." And then came the terrible thought that the redistribution of land might take place before they had time to get home, and that their share in the landlord's estate would be taken by others. What was the fate of the Great War, the loss of international prestige, the abandonment of Constantinople, when compared with this fearful possibility?

The conflict between the attitude of the masses and that of the educated classes, with the exception of the extreme radical wing, was fundamental, insoluble, fatal. It was as impossible for the educated classes to renounce the ideas and principles in which they had been brought up and accept the peasant's point of view, as it was for the latter to understand that there were things which might be more important than the increase of his allotment.

[14] Selivachev, *op. cit.*, in *Krasni Arkhiv*, IX, 117.

There was no room for compromise between the two points of view, and the conflict had to be fought out to its bitter end. In this struggle victory was naturally on the side of the masses.

The members of the Provisional Government were, of course, not unaware of the general drift of events. Prince Lvov, for instance, while maintaining an extremely optimistic attitude in his official pronouncements, frankly admitted to General Kuropatkin in a private conversation that circumstances had carried them much farther than they intended to go. "We are tossed about," he said, "like *débris* on a stormy sea."[15]

The parties of the extreme Left, whose ranks were strengthened by the return of exiles from Siberia and *émigrés* from abroad, were in a much more favorable position. There was nothing in their political outlook to keep them from adopting the only slogans which the masses could understand and rally to: immediate peace for the soldiers, land for the peasants, abolition of private ownership of the means of production for the workers,—and then the overthrow of the whole social hierarchy and the confiscation of all private wealth. In a country like Russia, where the well-to-do and educated groups represented an infinitely small minority, where the bulk of the population lived in extreme poverty, and the potential forces of social discontent were immense, no other policy had any chance of success. In 1917 the Bolsheviks had just as little control over the masses as the other parties. But they rightly understood the underlying factors of the situation, and their watchwords corresponded with the inevitable course and development of the Revolution.

Professor Miliukov, who displays infinitely better judgment as a historian than as a statesman, rightly points out that the masses of the people were not, as is sometimes maintained, passive witnesses of the revolutionary storm. "The masses," he writes,[16] "accepted that part of the Revolution which corresponded with their desires; but they opposed a wall of stubborn passive resistance as soon as they began to suspect that events were taking a turn unfavorable to their interests." This is, indeed, one of the lessons of the Russian Revolution.

Economic Decay

The eight months of the rule of the Provisional Government were characterized by a steady decline in every department of

[15] *Iz Dnevnika A. N. Kuropatkina (From the Diary of A. N. Kuropatkin)* in *Krasni Arkhiv,* XX, 66. Entry under the date of April 25, 1917.
[16] Miliukov, *Istorya Vtoroi Russkoi Revolutsii,* I, Part I, 6.

the national economic life. The process of the elimination of the *bourgeois* State, and the substitution for it of the then still untried communist rule found its external expression in the struggle between the Provisional Government and the Soviet of Soldiers' and Workmen's Deputies on the one hand, and the movement of both alike toward the Left, on the other. The Petrograd Soviet came into being simultaneously with the Provisional Government. It was a self-appointed body modeled on the Soviet of 1905. An idea of the conditions which prevailed in it at the start may be gathered from the following description by an eyewitness.

It was, in the beginning, a confused and mixed assembly [writes M. Labry] towards which the people turned nevertheless as to something that really represented them. It became the meeting place of soldiers who had escaped from their barracks, of workmen on strike, of domestic servants, of cab-drivers. . . . It was the refuge, the port, the pound. One went there to palaver, to drink, to smoke, even to sleep. It truly was the house of the people.[17]

Soon, however, the Soviet grew into a kind of popular parliament.

In spite of its extremely loose organization it had a firm hold over that section of the populace which carried out the *coup d'état* of February–March, the workers and the garrison of Petrograd whose interests it represented. Even in its early days, the Petrograd Soviet, while still quite a conservative assembly as compared with the same body in the autumn of 1917, was nevertheless infinitely more bold and radical than the Provisional Government. Supported as it was by the revolutionary soldiery and workmen of the capital, it proceeded at once to carry out, partly through pressure upon the Provisional Government, and partly by "revolutionary" methods, a policy of radical social reforms, especially in the field of labor legislation and organization. We are already familiar with the growth of organized labor in 1917 and the methods by which it fought not only for the defense of its professional interests but also for the nationalization of industry and the establishment of the dictatorship of the proletariat.[18] We may now turn our attention to the effects of this policy and the Revolution in general upon the economic condition of the country.

As may well be expected they were nothing short of disastrous. The output of practically every industry suffered a drastic

[17] Raoul Labry, *L'industrie russe et la révolution* (Paris, 1919), p. 12.
[18] *See above*, pp. 167 *sqq.*

230

reduction. At the Putilov Works, for instance, a comparison of the production in June, 1916, and June, 1917, will stand out in the following figures. Mild steel decreased from 240,185 puds to 69,104; cast steel, from 357,676 to 118,325; pig iron, from 70,301 to 45,279. In one of the biggest iron foundries of the Donets Basin the output of pig iron fell from 460,000 puds in June, 1916, to 280,000 in June, 1917.[19] Of a total number of 65 blast furnaces in the south, only between 34 and 44 were working, and not even all of these were producing at full capacity. Of 102 Martin furnaces, only 55 were in use in October, 1917. The rail-rolling mills reduced their output by 45 per cent.[20]

In the coal mining industry the situation was somewhat different. For the first four months of 1917 the mines of the Donets Basin showed an increase of 70,000 puds over the same period in 1916. No sharp decline appeared until May; and the decrease for the first eight months of 1917, as compared with 1916, was only 15,000,000 puds, the respective figures being 1,052,000,000 and 1,066,400,000. Production, however, remained considerably below pre-war figures (in 1917, by 73,000,000 puds). The relatively high output of the coal mines was purchased at a heavy price: the number of miners increased substantially while the output per miner steadily fell. From the average monthly figure of 710 puds in January, 1916, it dropped to the notably low level of 410 in August, 1917.[21] The same decrease in the output per workman occurred in the metal industry; and in each case it was accompanied by a drastic increase in wages. M. Labry quotes figures which indicate that at the Putilov Works the outlay in wages for the production of one pud of steel increased 14.5 times from June, 1916, to June, 1917 (from 14 copecks to 2.24 rubles).[22]

Even more ominous was the decline in the quantity of coal transported by rail. Here, too, a downward movement manifested itself, beginning with May, 1917. In January, 1916, some 112,000,000 puds were loaded in the Donets Basin. In August, 1917, the corresponding figure is only 80,000,000 puds. The reason for the decline lay in the shortage of rolling stock and the rapid disorganization of the railroads.[23]

It seems hardly necessary to multiply these examples. The

[19] Zagorsky, *op. cit.*, p. 191.
[20] Zagorsky, *op. cit.*, p. 192.
[21] *Ibid.*, pp. 205–206.
[22] Labry, *op. cit.*, p. 107.
[23] Zagorsky, *op. cit.*, p. 207; Labry, *op. cit.*, pp. 120–124.

fall in industrial production was merely one of the forerunners of the approaching nationalization of industry. Labor demands, it will be remembered, were no longer directed to the defense of their professional interests but were aimed at the elimination of the class of capitalistic employers. The Provisional Government at its best was capable of giving lip service to the employers, but could offer them no real protection. The position of owners, directors, managers, and engineers became impossible. In the summer of 1917 the Provisional Government received a number of requests from the foreign owners of industrial concerns to take over the management of their works. The leading British and French manufacturers in Russia informed the Government that under existing conditions they could be no longer responsible for the management of their enterprises. They suggested the adoption of the British system of control of industry which the Provisional Government, more than ever under the influence of the extreme elements, could not possibly accept.[24]

The breakdown of industry was naturally accompanied by other manifestations of an acute economic crisis which are so familiar a feature of the history of post-war Europe, by inflation,[25] depreciation of currency,[26] and a rise in the cost of living. It does not seem necessary to dwell here on these aspects of the situation. The index number of prices for 1917, it will be remembered, was computed as 673 (1913 = 100) an increase of 470 over the 1916 figure. Although extreme caution is urged in accepting this figure, there is no doubt that the rise in prices in 1917 proceeded by leaps and bounds.[27]

The Rural Community

The reaction of the rural community to the overthrow of the monarchy was slower and less manifest at the beginning than that of the city proletariat. We have seen that the peasants, as such, took no immediate part in the events of February–March, although their passive acceptance of the change was, no doubt, a fundamental factor that made the *coup d'état* possible. No less important was their attitude toward the burning problems of the day, especially toward the War. It did, indeed, seem for a

---

[24] Miliukov, *Istorya Vtoroi Russkoi Revolutsii*, I, Part I, 195–196.

[25] *See above*, pp. 41–42.

[26] The depreciation of the ruble on foreign markets in the course of 1917 was catastrophic. The par exchange of a pound sterling was £1 = 9.46 rubles. The average London quotation for the second half of 1916 was £1 = 15.53 rubles; in October, 1917, it was £1 = 34.00 rubles. *See* Bernatzky, *op. cit.*, Appendices II, III, and IV.

[27] *See above*, pp. 117–120, 149–155.

ime as if the issue of the great international struggle, and with
t the immediate fate of the whole civilized world, was in the
ands of the illiterate Russian peasant. It is no easy matter to
determine what took place in his mind. Fortunately the very
interesting reports received by the Provisional Committee of
the Duma covering the first three months of the Revolution
contain some first-hand information on his attitude. It must be
remembered that they were prepared at a time when the enthusiasm of the first days of the Revolution was still very much
alive. They should not be suspected therefore of giving an unduly gloomy picture of rural conditions.

It is highly characteristic of the general situation that the
question of the feelings of the peasants about the War are discussed at the very end of the official summary of the reports.[28]

It is almost symbolic [it says] that the problem of the War has
been relegated to the very end of this survey. One could well expect
that the War would be the most pressing and all-absorbing interest.
In fact, however, it has been pushed into the background. In the capital, in the large cities, one at least discussed and still continues to discuss war and to pass resolutions about it, but the far-away provinces
are so absorbed by the work of re-organization that war is often
completely forgotten.[29]

These eloquent lines were written in the first half of 1917, soon
after the United States entered the War, when the entire world
was watching with suspended breath and immense anxiety the
issue of the titanic struggle which followed the declaration by
Germany of the submarine campaign. The entire world—yes,
but not that immense majority of the people of Allied Russia
who had "completely forgotten" that there was a war. And at
this very time Professor Miliukov, the recognized leader of the
Russian liberals, chanted in Petrograd the eulogy of the Russian
people for overthrowing the Imperial *régime* as the only method
of bringing the War to a victorious end!

The all-absorbing interest of the peasants was naturally the
land question. In the opinion of the authors of the report, all
other questions were of secondary importance when compared
with it. For the peasants it was the real problem. Their fixed
and universal conviction was that the land must be transferred
to the people. Partly because of this conviction, a relatively
small number of outbreaks had been reported so far. Instead a

* *Mart-Mai 1917 Goda (March–May 1917)*, with an Introduction by Y. Yakovlev,
in *Krasni Arkhiv*, Vol. XV. The report here quoted is a summary of the reports
received by the Provisional Committee of the Duma from twenty-eight provinces.
It was prepared in 1917 by P. Romanov.
  Ibid., p. 56.

way had been found which would peacefully eliminate all priva
owners, both small and great. The peasants demanded wages f
agricultural labor which were so high that the employer coul
not pay them; they refused to lease land from the large estate
on non-peasant landowners they assessed special levies for th
use of prisoners of war, the proceeds of which were to go t
the volost[30] committee. And if the owner so assessed refuse
to pay, the prisoners of war were withdrawn from his estate an
put gratis at the disposal of the families of mobilized men. Som
times the committee simply forbade the villagers to accept en
ployment on the estates. "We won't give them any laborer
Then they will all starve like cockroaches." The struggle again
private owners was waged not by individual peasants: it w
the chief business of the volost committees. The peasant owne
of individual farms, the owners of moderate-sized estates, an
the large landowners, were subject to the same heavy, and som
times irreparable, blows at the hands of the volost committee
The hostility toward private owners was also in evidence in th
case of the peasants who availed themselves of the new arrang
ments provided by the reforms of Stolypin.[31] Almost ever
peasant conference passed resolutions demanding the abolitic
of private ownership of land. Land must belong to the peop
as a whole. They demanded the increase of allotments up t
areas large enough to provide employment for the whole lab
of the family, and this must be done locally, without having t
remove people to other places, and settle them there. The tran
ferred land must be free not only of all charges, but even o
mortgages. Sometimes the demands were even more extrem
and included such items as freedom from taxation and the retu
to the peasants of payments made, redemption obligations, an
the interest they had paid for advances from the peasant bank
The report rightly remarks that the peasants were living n
in any atmosphere of realities but in one of party slogans.[32]

Even more enlightening, perhaps, is the account given t
the report of the insurmountable difficulties which met a belate
attempt to pull down the secular wall of illiteracy, ignoranc
and prejudice that had separated the peasantry from the re
of the world.

One of the greatest obstacles to the sound and healthy develo
ment of the new *régime* [says the report] is the ignorance of t
people, which is so overwhelming that everyone who comes face
face with it from the standpoint of an educated man feels his ener.

[30] *Volost*—a rural administrative unit comprising several villages.
[31] *See above*, pp. 23–24.
[32] *Mart-Mai 1917 Goda*, in *Krasni Arkhiv*, XV, 45–49.

elt away, and loses all confidence in the possibility of consolidating
e conquests of our new era. To-day, with the departure to the army
f the younger men, the rural community is illiterate almost to a
an. The schools to which went the "literate" men left behind in
e villages taught them merely to read, not to understand what they
ad. And now this impotence, this impossibility of making use of
e printed word, creates a terrible situation, one that cannot be met.
he unanimous cry from the country is: Books, books! But the
evolution has taken the book market by surprise. There was
ctually not a single book containing an answer to the questions
hich are the only ones of interest to-day. It could hardly have been
herwise, because all these questions were taboo with the Imperial
overnment. The old revolutionary literature of 1905 was unearthed
om the archives and the attics, and distributed to the impatient
ultitudes. New pamphlets were hastily written and sent to the
rovinces. . . . But such books as did get to the villages were written
any language you could imagine . . . except the one used by the
mmon people. And the greater the effort to accomplish the task
nscientiously and with the assistance of first-rate men, the worse
ere the results. Instead of bread the peasants were given a stone.
ne needed someone to translate the incomprehensible jargon into
e parlance of the masses. . . . Nothing creates such a barrier
tween two men as the absence of a common language. It eventually
ayed an important part in the growth of feeling hostile to the
ucated classes. As to the story that must be told of the influence
f the newspapers, it is an even more unhappy one. The greater the
asant's ignorance of the printed word, the more importance he
tached to it; and he firmly believed that everything printed was
ue. And now he found in one newspaper one "truth," and in an-
her the very opposite. He pondered, tried to understand "freely
d without outside influence," and his head went round. Or one
d of the village read one paper, the other, another. And hence
ore confusion. Nevertheless, that cry for books, and more books,
ver for a moment ceased.[33]

We may sum up this rather long excerpt by quoting the re-
ark of a peasant representative from far-away Siberia: "We
el," he writes,[34] "that we have escaped from a dark cave into
e bright daylight. And here we stand, not knowing where to
 or what to do."

It would be a mistake, however, to imagine that the demands
r books really meant a general and uniform craving for edu-
ation. On this subject, too, we find some interesting information
 the report.

The attitude of the peasants towards the schools differs a great
al [says our report]. Some of them ask for an extension of the

Mart-Mai 1917 Goda, in *Krasni Arkhiv,* XV, 52–54.
Ibid., p. 55.

curricula of the elementary schools which would make it possib'
for students to enter secondary schools. On the other hand, th
peasants of the province of Smolensk, Tula, and of a number o
other provinces declare: "We don't want these school teachers, the
are too costly. The ex-service men will soon get home from th
army and they will teach the children free of charge." An illiterat
peasant, who never went to school himself, is extremely relucta
to contribute for the maintenance of the schools. He wants fre
schools, free books, and free teachers.[35]

If we remember what the peasant budget was, we shall hardl
blame him for his lack of enthusiasm for the advancement o
education.

The ideas of class struggle which made such rapid progres
in the cities and among industrial workers were not slow i
reaching farms and villages. The owners of large estates wer
not the only ones against whom was directed the rising tide o
social recriminations and hatred which had accumulated in th
course of centuries. With them the small group of village inte
ligentsia, the school teachers, zemstvo experts, the clergy, an
the like, also came under suspicion, and rapidly lost their ir
fluence with the masses.

Again quoting from the Duma's report, the peasants

are decidedly unwilling to elect educated people to their institution
The attitude gaining ground among them says virtually: "There
no room for the intelligentsia among us. We shall look ourselve
after our own affairs." Not infrequently, however, the volost com
mittee has not a single man who possesses education enough t
prepare the minutes; the former clerks have been dismissed a
embezzlers. It is true that school teachers are occasionally electe
chairmen of the volost committees; but such are exclusively me
who follow the peasants' wishes, owe their success to this polic
and exercise no restraining influence. . . . School teachers, especiall
women teachers, . . . have nothing in common with the peasan
and enjoy no authority. Even those representatives of the intell
gentsia in whom the peasants have always seen a friendly intere
and whom, in the early days of the Revolution, they themselve
unanimously elected chairmen of their committees, are now bein
removed.[36]

The helplessness of the peasantry suddenly confronted wit
a situation for which they were entirely unprepared is vividl
depicted.

The volost committees are often incapable of dealing with th
questions they have to discuss; they don't know how to approach th

[35] *Ibid.*, p. 56.
[36] *Mart-Mai 1917 Goda* in *Krasni Arkhiv*, XV, 42.

oblems. The absence of educated men, who have been intentionally
cluded, and even of men able to read and write, is strongly felt.
very resolution published in a newspaper is treated as if it were
e law. . . . Even the committees which subscribe to the *Official
azette* (*Pravitelstvenni Vestnik*) cannot see the difference between
project for a law and the law itself. And they usually accept as
ie most binding law" those paragraphs from a newspaper article
party resolution which embody the expression of the long-
ppressed wishes of the peasantry, irrespective of the prevailing
nditions and the interest of the other social group.
One must take into account the psychology of a man who has
st escaped from the tutelage of a highly centralized State. This
plains the pilgrimage to Petrograd in the first months of the
evolution. But the same difficulties which the peasant encountered
der the old *régime* in his attempts to see the Tsar he encounters
w when he tries to discover what the law is. There have been
ses when a peasant deputy on his return from Petrograd, where
had found himself listening to a turmoil of party discussions, has
swered the questions of his fellow-villagers as to what he had
irned: "I have forgotten! I have forgotten everything that I heard.
iave heard so many things that I cannot remember a single one."
. And he has been locked up because he only squandered com-
unity funds and brought home nothing.[37]

That under these conditions the idea of a Constituent Assem-
y met with little success will hardly come as a surprise.

In the majority of cases [says the report] nobody thinks about the
onstituent Assembly or has any idea what it really means. In
rtain localities nothing whatever has been heard of it, especially
iong the women. Men, as a rule, tell them nothing, and the larger
rtion of the population is, therefore, entirely ignorant as to what
expected from it. The peasants have no opinions on the Constituent
ssembly. This is a fact. And it must be reckoned with. An intensive
mpaign for the enlightening of the masses must be undertaken at
ice. It must be carried on not through pamphlets which the peas-
ts, almost all of them illiterate, do not understand, but by personal
terviews. For even meetings are of little use. A peasant is capable
grasping an argument only if he speaks himself and asks ques-
ins, but not when he is listening to a speech which is not addressed
him personally. It is essential to speed up this work, because one
ars even to-day the cautiously whispered question whether one
ould vote for the Tsar or the university undergraduates.[38]

Can you believe [the report continues] that a peasant woman will
ally leave her cottage and children and go to town to cast her vote?
ow can the principle of a direct and secret ballot be put into actual
actice among people of whom half or, with the mobilization of
e male population, even as many as 90 per cent, are illiterate?[39]

bid., p. 43.
bid., p. 37.
bid., p. 37.

237

The answer to this tragic question will be found in the fate of the Constituent Assembly, which met an undignified and unlamented death at the hands of the Bolsheviks.

The aggressive nature of the peasant movement became more evident as time went on. At the beginning it usually took the form of a "peaceful" elimination of private owners. With the establishment of a system of land committees in May, 1917, and especially in July, with the vesting in these committees of wide powers to deal with land problems, the attitude of the peasants became bolder.[40] They gradually realized that the moment for the fulfilment of their age-long dream had at last arrived. When the downfall of the Empire had been followed by the collapse of the whole machinery of local administration, nothing was left between the desire of the peasants for the land of their wealthier neighbors and its realization, but a few vague legal notions which never meant much to the peasant mind and the still vaguer promises of an obviously impotent liberal government. Such restraints were hardly sufficient to stop the mighty surge of popular feelings. Freed from their fetters, the peasants moved irresistibly toward that goal which had been so long denied to them; and by the autumn of 1917 Russia found herself in the grasp of a violent agrarian revolution.

The Army

The Revolution of February–March, 1917, dealt the last blow to the army, the demoralization of which, as we have seen, was already well advanced in 1915 and 1916. The troops of the Petrograd garrison had had an important part in bringing about the downfall of the Imperial *régime* and sent their representatives to the Petrograd Soviet of Soldiers' and Workmen's Deputies. One of the first measures of this body was to issue an order which completely upset the recognized principles of military discipline. The essential provision of this order established in every military unit committees of men and officers the functions of which were not clearly defined. We shall not here go into the details of the bitter controversy which arose around this order. The really important fact was that as early as March, 1917, the system of committees was introduced into the army; and military hierarchy, which seems to be one of the essential conditions

[40] Antsiferov and others, "Rural Economy," pp. 261 *sqq.;* also *Agrarnoe Dvizhenie v 1917 Godu (The Agrarian Movement in 1917)* in *Krasni Arkhiv*, XIV, 182–22; also Martinov, *Agrarnoe Dvizhenie Nakanune Oktyabreskoi Revolutsii (The Agrarian Movement on the Eve of the October Revolution)* in *Krasnaya Letopis*, XXV, *sqq.*

he organization of a military force, was shaken to its very
 undations.[41] The army was now thrown open to political
ropaganda, which was made not only legitimate but even
ecessary by the fact that the soldiers were to vote in the elec-
ons to the Constituent Assembly. "There was everywhere a
assion for speech, the right to which has been so long denied,"
rites General Knox describing the conditions in March, 1917,[42]
and a moment of silence seemed to everyone a moment lost."

It is undoubtedly true that the sweeping tide of revolutionary
ratory was an important factor in bringing to the fore the pro-
ound discontent which had accumulated in the army in the
ourse of 1914–1916. We nevertheless agree with the Soviet
riter, M. Yakovlev, when he says that the attempts to explain
e breakdown of the army by the "defeatist" propaganda alone
re obviously futile. In the opinion of Yakovlev, the real "de-
eatist" propaganda among the 15,000,000 soldiers came from
n immense fatigue, from uninterrupted military reverses, the
sufficiency of supplies, the War's lack of purpose, as seen by
e peasant-soldier, and his growing hostility to his leaders.[43]
o this list we may add that all-absorbing interest in the ap-
roaching redistribution of land which was the only consequence
f the Revolution with which the peasant-soldier was really
oncerned.

The command of the army found itself in the same predica-
ent, in the same inescapable situation, as the Provisional Gov-
rnment and the whole of the educated classes. Shortly before
he Revolution, at the conference of Chantilly in November,
916, and at the conference of Petrograd on February 16, 1917,
he Russian High Command had given the Allies a definite guar-
nty to take part in a joint offensive against the Central Powers.
n a letter written on March 12, ten days after the abdication
f the Emperor, to Guchkov, then Minister of War, General
lexeev, the Commander-in-Chief, was forced to admit that
ussia was no longer in a position to meet such an obligation,
t least for some time to come.[44] The tragedy of the High
ommand and the army officers lay in the losing struggle they
ere pledged to wage, as against the steadily growing determi-
ation of the peasants to bring the War to an end.

The full effect of the Revolution upon the army did not ap-

Razlozhenie Armii v 1917 Godu (The Breakdown of the Army in 1917), collection
f documents with an Introduction by Y. A. Yakovlev (Moscow-Leningrad, 1925),
ocument No. 42, pp. 58–59.
Knox, *op. cit.*, p. 575.
Razlozhenie Armii v 1917 Godu, p. iv.
Ibid., document No. 25, pp. 28–30.

pear at once. Some of the commanding officers reported t
Headquarters that the army's fighting spirit and discipline wer
not adversely affected by the abdication of the Tsar. Genera
Danilov, commanding the Second Army, and a few others wer
even so far as to maintain that the troops under their comman
were in better fighting condition than ever.[45] One may we
question the sincerity of this official optimism. Any expressio
of doubt as to the beneficial effects of the new *régime* was treate
in those days as disloyalty to the Revolution, and the change
in command were sweeping. There is little question that th
grandiloquent promises to defend Russia and the Revolutio
against the enemy embodied in the resolutions passed by inn
merable army units were not always taken at their face value.

For three days the regiments of the reserve have been calling c
me to express their willingness to fight to the bitter end [wrote c
March 29, 1917, General Dragomirov in "strict confidence" 1
General Ruzsky]; they promised to obey my every order and d
for the country. Nevertheless it is difficult to make them obey orde
that send them to the trenches. One gets no more volunteers for t
simplest military operation, even for a mere reconnaissance, ar
no one can be induced to move from our trenches in the directi
of the enemy. The fighting spirit has dwindled away. Not only hav
the soldiers no desire to advance, but their will even to defer
themselves has been so terribly shaken that it is a real menace 1
the issue of the War. All the thoughts of the common soldiers tu
towards home. Their only desire is to leave the trenches.[46]

The patriotic declarations of the first days soon gave plac
to demands for peace without annexations and contributions, 1
refusals to fight for the benefit of British and French capitalis
and to promises to defend the existing front, which were no
accompanied by refusals to participate in any attempt to brea
the enemy's line. This, of course, was nothing but a slightly di
guised demand for immediate peace. The ball which had starte
rolling could no longer be stopped.

The introduction of a system of committees which exercise
control over the officers put them into an impossible positio

There was a general illogical mistrust of the command [writes Ge
eral Knox], and the credulity of the men was fantastic. A non-cor
missioned officer . . . told me that he had himself counted 14,0
head of cattle that were driven to the front by order of the o
Government in order that they might fall into the hands of t
Germans when Vilna was evacuated in September 1915.[47]

[45] *Ibid.*, document No. 24, p. 25.
[46] *Razlozhenie Armii v 1917 Godu*, document No. 27, p. 31.
[47] Knox, *op. cit.*, p. 595.

There was no villainy and no crime of which the officers were not suspected and found guilty. They were made the immediate scapegoats for all the hardships and sufferings of the War which they themselves had so largely shared. The impossibility for the majority of the officers' corps to back the demand of their men for immediate peace and their desperate attempts to restore discipline singled them out as supporters of the old *régime* and exposed them to the worst indignities and insults. The dismissal of officers by their men, their arrests, not infrequently their murders, were matters of daily occurrence. The same hatred of the educated classes which we have observed among the peasants manifested itself in the army.

The officers are real martyrs [wrote M. Mankov, a member of the Duma, on May 10]. An officer of the Volchansk regiment, menaced with violence by his men who refused to obey his order to take their turn in the trenches, has committed suicide. The real motive of all refusals by the men to obey orders is the fear of death.[48]

Refusals of whole regiments, divisions, and even army corps, to be moved to the front; desertions *en masse;* fraternizings with the Germans—such were the conditions which prevailed in the army at the end of the spring of 1917.

I returned to Petrograd from a visit to the Northern front on April 28 [writes General Knox]. I gave you [the British Ambassador in Petrograd] my opinion of the deplorable state of things at the front. Units have been turned into political debating societies; the infantry refuses to allow the guns to shoot at the enemy; parleying in betrayal of the Allies and of the best interests of Russia takes place daily with the enemy who laughs at the credulity of the Russian peasant-soldier. Many senior officers complained that the Government, to which every army has a right to look for support, has left all the burden of dealing with agitation to the army. In Petrograd things are growing worse daily. The tens of thousands of able-bodied men in uniform who saunter about the streets without a thought of going to the front or working to prepare themselves for war, when every able-bodied man and most of the women in England and France are straining every nerve to beat the common enemy, will be a disgrace for all time for the Russian people and its Government.[49]

These feelings were fully shared by the majority of Russian officers, and this ruled out the very possibility of an understanding between them and the men they were supposed to lead.

On the other hand, the recriminations of the superior officers against the Government, referred to by Knox, while undoubt-

[48] *Razlozhenie Armii v 1917 Godu,* document No. 41, p. 57.
[49] Knox, *op. cit.,* p. 613.

edly well justified by the conditions under which they had to perform their duties, appear in a different light when we take a retrospective view of the situation. As a matter of fact, it is difficult to imagine what measures the Provisional Government could take to prevent the immense landslide started by the Revolution from reaching the bottom of the abyss. In addition to the effects of revolutionary propaganda, it had to face insurmountable difficulties to provide the army with supplies in the midst of complete economic disorganization and the acute transport crisis.[50] Extraordinary measures were tried by the Provisional Government. Some of them may appear as sound and, indeed, necessary, for instance the restoration of capital punishment, which was abolished in the early days of the Revolution; the creation of new military courts; the use of armed force against the military units which refused to perform their duty. Others, such as the creation of national troops—Polish, Ukrainian, Lithuanian, and Moslem battalions—of "shock" troops and volunteer units bound by special oaths,[51] were of a more doubtful value. Still others, such as the formation of women's battalions, were merely grotesque. All alike, however, proved equally useless and futile and had no more effect than a single barrel of oil poured upon the mountainous waves of the revolutionary storm. Kerensky even tried to carry out the promise given by the Russian High Command to the Allies and in June, 1917, launched an offensive against the enemy. He believed that victory would restore the spirit of the army. In spite of his innumerable speeches, the enthusiasm with which he was received by the troops, and even the largest accumulation of artillery and munitions the Russian front had ever seen, the offensive proved a complete failure. The same men who solemnly promised to defend revolutionary Russia to the last drop of their blood either absolutely refused to advance, or merely passed through the first line of the enemy trenches, which had been leveled to the ground by the fire of the artillery, and then turned back and returned to their old lines. There was no human power which could change the fundamental fact: to use the expression of General Knox, "the War had gone into the background everywhere."[52] This was just as true of the army as it was true of the peasants. And Knox was again right when he said that "it was no use appealing to higher feelings which should have existed, but did not."[53]

[50] *Razlozhenie Armii v 1917 Godu*, pp. 10–24.
[51] *Ibid.*, document No. 54b, pp. 69–70.
[52] Knox, *op. cit.*, p. 586.
[53] *Ibid.*, p. 597.

It is hardly necessary here to mention the Kornilov episode which had no practical bearing upon the general trend of events. Kornilov, a gallant general with a brilliant war record and Commander-in-Chief in August–September, 1917, endeavored to save the Provisional Government against its own will by restoring discipline in the army and establishing a *régime* approaching that of a military dictatorship. It would seem that Kerensky, who for a time lent his support to the scheme, deserted Kornilov at the last moment, and the General was arrested by the very men he was trying to save. It was just one more ephemeral attempt to restore order that was doomed in advance.[54] In the meantime the army was rapidly degenerating into an unruly mob which became the terror of the districts adjoining the front.[55] It was accurately described in October, 1917, as "an immense, desperate and weary crowd of poorly clad and poorly fed men united by their common desire for peace and their disillusionment."[56] And we find its *post mortem* in the official report of December 28, 1917, which estimated the fighting capacity of a group of military units forming the Special Army (*Osobaya Armya*) as "equal to zero."[57] This was undoubtedly true of the Russian army as a whole.

The Growth of Bolshevism

It will be remembered that the Bolsheviks had no immediate part in bringing about the downfall of the Empire. In February, 1917, their organization among the working people was negligible; practically all of their prominent leaders were either in Siberia or abroad. Lenin was still in Switzerland engaged mostly in literary work, and Trotsky had Union Square in New York for the chief field of his activities. Even after the downfall of the Empire, in the Soviet of Soldiers' and Workmen's Deputies —that vanguard of the revolutionary forces—the Bolsheviks were represented at the beginning by a mere handful of men who exercised very little influence. Until the arrival of Lenin *via* Germany on April 4, 1917, the Bolshevik chieftains in Petrograd were entirely unconscious of the events which were to make them the masters of Russia within eight short months.

Not one of those leaders of the party who were in Russia [writes Leon Trotsky] had any intention of making the dictatorship of the proletariat—the social revolution—the immediate object of his policy. A party conference which met on the eve of Lenin's arrival

[54] Vernadsky, *op. cit.*, pp. 242–245.
[55] *Razlozhenie Armii v 1917 Godu*, pp. 119–154.
[56] *Ibid.*, document No. 149, pp. 143–144.
[57] *Ibid.*, document No. 183, p. 175.

and counted among its members about thirty Bolsheviks showed that none of them even imagined anything beyond democracy. ... Stalin was in favor of supporting the Provisional Government of Guchkov and Miliukov and of merging the Bolsheviks with the Mensheviks![58]

Even with the arrival of Lenin, followed a month later by Trotsky, the prospects of the Bolsheviks seemed anything but bright. The extreme doctrines of Lenin, his demands for an open declaration in favor of communism and class war were given a cool reception by the Social-Democrats. One of them, Stankevich, has recorded in his *Memoirs* the general reaction of the conference of the party: "A man who talks such nonsense is not dangerous. It is a good thing that he is here. At least we know now what he is like."[59]

Undoubtedly, with the arrival of Lenin and Trotsky the revolutionary movement found its real leaders. The organization of the party was enlarged and improved. In the first two weeks after the Revolution, according to Shlyapnikov, one of the Soviet leaders, the burden of all the party work, as well as that of participation in the deliberations of the Soviet, was carried by only three men.[60] But even six months later, it was a party still inefficient and loose in the extreme. Speaking of the situation at the end of October, after the successful *coup d'état* which brought the Soviets to power, Trotsky says: "Three weeks ago we had gained a majority in the Petrograd Soviet. We were hardly more than a banner—with no printing works, no funds, no branches."[61]

The forces which worked for the Bolshevik cause were not, as it is sometimes imagined, their superior skill in rallying the masses by creating a powerful secret organization. It consisted merely in the fact that the Bolsheviks were the only political party which had openly proclaimed as their program the sole ideas which the immense majority of the country could understand and was longing for: the immediate end of the War, the land for the peasants, "the taking back of what had been taken away," that is, the right to take immediate possession of all private wealth. And the fulfilment of this program was promised through the dictatorship of the proletariat, embodied in the sacramental sentence "All power to the Soviets," accompanied

[58] Trotsky, *op. cit.*, pp. 329–330.
[59] Stankevich, *Vospominanya (Memoirs)*, p. 110, quoted in Miliukov, *Istorya Vtoroi Russkoi Revolutsii*, I, Part I, 89.
[60] Quoted in Nolde, *L'ancien régime et la révolution russes*, p. 162.
[61] Trotsky, *op. cit.*, p. 326.

by a merciless class struggle. In this program the "latent social-ism without a doctrine" of the masses at last found its expression. And what did the Russian liberals and moderate socialists oppose to this program: the myth of the Constituent Assembly and "war to a victorious end"! What chance of success did a program of that kind have in a country which had reached the degree of demoralization we find in Russia in 1917?

The great service of Lenin to the Bolshevik cause consists in his recognition of the importance of the peasant revolution in a country constituted as Russia is. While the more orthodox Marxists shrank from the idea of an agrarian revolution, Lenin boldly accepted it as a stepping-stone to the social revolution, and the course of events in 1917 proved that he was right.

In the life of the country and in the life of the individual, those were extraordinary days [writes Trotsky]. In social passions, as well as in personal powers, tension reached its highest point. The masses were creating an epoch, and their leaders felt their steps merging with those of history. On the decisions made and the orders given in those days depended the fate of the nation for an entire historical era. And yet those decisions were made with very little discussion. I can hardly say that they were even properly weighed and considered; they were almost improvised on the moment. But they were none the worse for that. The pressure of events was so terrific, and the work to be done so clear before us, that the most important decisions came naturally, as a matter of course, and were received in the same spirit. The path had been predetermined; all that was required was to indicate the work. No arguments were necessary, and very few appeals. Without hesitation or doubt, the masses picked up what was suggested to them by the nature of the situation. Under the strain of events, their "leaders" did no more than formulate what answered the requirements of the people and the demands of history.[62]

If the analysis offered by this volume truly reflects the course of events in Russia during the War it seems impossible not to agree with Trotsky. The overthrow of the Provisional Government and the establishment of the Soviet rule was merely the completion of the process which started with the outbreak of the War, shattering, as it did, the fragile structure of Imperial Russia. The next stage was reached in February–March, 1917, when the long rule of the Tsars was brought to an end and the forces of discontent and social hatred, so long suppressed, were suddenly set free. The result of this new process was the establishment of a *régime* adhering to principles such as those pro-

[62] Trotsky, *op. cit.*, p. 334.

claimed by Lenin. With complete contempt for the rather flattering theory of a sinister and powerful Soviet conspiracy, Trotsky frankly admits that "it was impossible to tell in advance whether we were to stay in power or be overthrown." And he also confesses that the work of the Soviet Government in the first months was nothing else but "an immense legislative improvisation," an exposition of the party program "in the language of power" rather than a constructive policy of political and social reforms[63] But it flattered the masses, encouraged them to follow a line of conduct on which they had already set their mind; and it was only a government supporting such a policy that could maintain itself in the midst of the revolutionary upheaval. Under the conditions which prevailed in Russia in the second half of 1917, it would seem hardly correct to picture the Bolsheviks as mere usurpers.[64]

Conclusion

If we look back on the period of Russia's history covered by this volume and attempt to appraise the forces which brought about the fall of the Tsars and paved the way for Bolshevism, all Russia in 1914–1917 will appear as an uneasy sea gradually lashed to fury by the winds of the approaching revolutionary storm. The source of the catastrophe which overcame the Empire may, undoubtedly, be traced far back in the history of the Russian people. As long as the country was not asked to make the supreme and heroic effort imposed upon it by the War, it managed to trail, and not without a certain degree of success, behind the other European countries along the road of economic development and progress. But the Great War put the whole framework of the Empire to a severe test. The obsoleteness and the imperfections of its political, social, and economic structure could no longer be concealed and ignored. Following the example of England, France, and Germany, who, reacting from the blows they were receiving, made superhuman efforts to meet the emergency, Russia, or rather her educated classes, tried to organize their country for the War; but their attempts were sporadic, uncoördinated, and almost pathetic in their help-

[63] *Ibid.*, pp. 342–343.
[64] Nolde, *L'ancien régime et la révolution russes*, p. 146; Labry, *op. cit.*, p. 16. This statement should not be interpreted as an apology for the Soviet rule and its policy since 1917. The fact that the analysis of Lenin and Trotsky met the situation in 1917 does not necessarily indicate its infallibility. The dramatic changes in Trotsky's own fortunes seem to suggest that even so expert a craftsman in the mysterious art of Marx and Lenin may find himself considerably at variance with the "revolutionary situation." The discussion of this question, however, lies outside the scope of the present volume.

lessness. A ship without a captain and manned by an unskilled and undisciplined crew, Russia drifted along an uncharted course.

Few are the instances in the history of the human race when the impotence and inadequacy of a political *régime* revealed themselves with such striking force. None of the elements of the Russian State proved equal to the burden which was thrown upon them. The Emperor was a weak and obstinate man, a mere tool in the hands of an unbalanced woman guided by vulgar adventurers. The bureaucracy was senile, unadaptable, and helpless in an emergency. It soon lost whatever virtues it might have possessed before the War. The Duma was sadly lacking in authority and leadership. The educated classes, in spite of their honest desire to champion the cause of the people, were crippled by the opposition of the bureaucracy and their aloofness from the masses. There was no organized labor, no real self-government on a broad democratic basis, no real tradition of public service. The economic and educational standards of the masses were appallingly low. And beneath the thin layer of refined European culture one could feel the subdued, heavy breathing of the millions of peasants, inarticulate, ignored, and often forgotten in their snow-clad cottages in the immensity of the Russian plains. The menacing murmur which rose at times from the countryside reminded those in power that everything was not well. But the machinery of the bureaucratic State is slow, and the "peasant question" presented so many interesting problems that had to be threshed out before a decision could be reached!

The War—the losses in men, territory, and wealth, the economic hardships, the flagrant impotence of the ruling clique when faced with crisis, the degeneration of autocracy itself—all brought to the top the powers of discontent and social antagonism which had been gathering beneath the ominously quiet and peaceful surface. Who will be bold enough to determine which was the factor that played the leading part in bringing about the Revolution? Was it the folly of the Emperor and the Empress? the decay of the Government? military losses? the secular grievances of the peasants? the starving conditions of the cities? the weariness with the war? We cannot answer these questions, just as there is no way of determining, when the storm bursts, which of the many streams pouring into a river is responsible for the breaking of the dam and the flooding of the country below, or which handful of snow started the avalanche that buries in its deadly path the villages and pastures of the hard-working mountaineers. One thing, however, is clear. When the swollen river breaks the dam or the avalanche begins its descent into the valley, there is no human power which can stop it until the elementary forces of nature over which men have no control have exhausted their destructive energies. The same may be said of the Russian Revolution. Here the landslide which started in March, 1917, did not reach the bottom of the valley until the establishment of the Soviet rule.

253